Good Little Thomas Hardy

Good Little Thomas Hardy

C. H. Salter

First published 1981 by
THE MACMILLAN PRESS LTD
London and Basingstoke
Companies and representatives
throughout the world

ISBN 0-333-29387-8

Typeset by
CAMBRIAN TYPESETTERS
and printed in Hong Kong

To H.H.O.C., K.P.A.D., A.R.L.M. and L.G.T.

Contents

	Preface	ix
1	Modernity	1
2	The Social Critic	27
3	Ideas	53
4	Invention	99
5	The Good	141
	Short Titles	162
	Notes	167
	Appendix: The Dynasts	194
	Index	198

Preface

Hardy is now widely read, in schools and universities and by the general public, and is seen on films and television. Apart from his merits, the reasons for this may be the brevity of his novels compared with other Victorians, his intelligibility without knowledge of the period, and our nostalgia. Signs and perhaps additional causes of this interest are the numerous editions of his works and of books about him, informative, critical, and hack. By informative I mean particularly the notes in the New Wessex edition of the novels, 1974–5; the collection of the prefaces and essays in a single volume of *Personal Writings;* the edition of the *Literary Notes I* and "1867 Notebook"; Professor Purdy's *Bibliographical Study*: and Mr Pinion's *Hardy Companion*. But these have been accompanied by excessive claims for Hardy as a Victorian man of ideas and social critic, and elaborate accounts of his art, some of which simply ignore his inferior work. In what follows I have tried to restore to the reader his freedom to respond to Hardy in what, to Hardy, can be the only right way – simply. This has resulted in a largely negative and destructive approach, even in my final, more positive, chapter: I hope I have shown my kindness for my subject *obiter*, and that some of my evidence may be useful to those reaching different conclusions. My title is, of course, taken from James's letter to R. L. Stevenson (19 March 1892).

I would like to thank Irene Elsey for typing my illegible manuscript on top of all her other work.

1 Modernity

The actual dramatic dates of the main actions of most of Hardy's novels and short stories are long anterior to the dates of publication, and often vague. *Under the Greenwood Tree* is "intended to be a fairly true picture . . . of fifty to sixty years ago"; *The Return* happens "between 1840 and 1850"; *The Trumpet Major* about 1805; *The Mayor* about 1850; *The Woodlanders* both about 1858 and about 1865. Of the *Wessex Tales* "The Three Strangers" is "fifty years ago"; "A Tradition of Eighteen Hundred and Four" explicit in the title; "The Melancholy Hussar" "ninety years ago"; "The Withered Arm" 1825; "Fellow-Townsmen" "five-and-thirty years ago"; and "The Distracted Preacher" "founded on certain smuggling exploits that occurred between 1825 and 1830"; of "Interlopers at the Knap" we only know they interloped "some few years ago". In *Life's Little Ironies*, there is modernity in "An Imaginative Woman" in denying that Trewe is *symboliste* or *décadent*; in references in 'For Conscience' Sake" to an "utilitarian theory of moral sense" and to "the century's decadence"; in "On the Western Circuit" in calling Raye an "end-of-the-age young man"; but the main action of "The Fiddler of the Reels" is contemporaneous with the Great Exhibition; and all the actions in "A Few Crusted Characters" begin fifty years before the date of publication: Lackland left the village thirty five years before he returned, and "it is now a dozen or fifteen years" since he returned. The date of "A Changed Man" is 1849 or 1854, the Dorchester cholera epidemics, and that of "The Waiting Supper" "fifty years ago". "The Grave by the Handpost", "Enter a Dragoon" and "A Committee-Man of 'the Terror' " date to the Napoleonic Wars, "Master John Horseleigh, Knight" to the sixteenth century, and "The Duke's Reappearance" to Monmouth's rebellion. All the *Noble Dames* stories relate to the remote past.[1]

Nothing requires the main action of *Jude* to be later than 1874 (Hardy said 1870), or of *Tess* to be much later than 1862 (though Hardy said it "embodies the views of life prevalent at the end of the nineteenth century") or of *Far from the Madding Crowd* to be later than 1834.[2]

This leaves, as contemporary novels, only the inferior *Desperate Remedies, A Pair of Blue Eyes, The Hand of Ethelberta, A Laodicean, Two on a Tower* and *The Well-Beloved. Desperate Remedies* is explicitly dated in Chapter 1 up to 1863, and the specific time indications in the chapter headings carry the end down to 1865. A letter in *A Pair of Blue Eyes* is dated "1864" in the first edition. *Ethelberta* speaks of "the artistic gymnastics prevalent in some quarters at the present day"; *A Tower* "seems to have utilised two events of 1881"; *The Well-Beloved* spans the period 1850—1890; and *A Laodicean*, Hardy's worst novel, is the only one triumphantly announced on its title-page as "A Story of To-day"![3]

Hardy stresses the pastness of the past about which he is writing and goes back even further than the main action whenever he can. The time of *The Return* is "when Budmouth still had some Georgian gaiety". Egdon recovers the "original unity" of the separate heaths. Through Tullidge and Simon Burden *The Trumpet-Major* reaches back to Valenciennes and Minden, 1793 and 1759. "It was a period when romance had not so greatly faded out of military life." "How entirely have they all passed and gone." In *The Mayor*, the obsolete wife-sale is included by making the novel start nineteen years before the main action and the obsolete skimmington by having Mrs Cuxsom comment that the last one "must have been ten years ago": it is in fact "the England of those days" Hardy is describing: "Time and progress have obliterated . . . many or most of the old-fashioned features here enumerated." The action of *The Woodlanders* begins "on a bygone winter's day". In *Far from the Madding Crowd* the obliteration is what Weatherbury is threatened with and thanks to Oak doesn't happen, but it is still the ancientness of this way of life that Hardy exhibits: "in Weatherbury three or four score years were included in the present".[4]

Nevertheless Hardy does of course claim to be modern and

indeed to be in advance of his time: to have "spread over art the latest illumination of the time" in *The Dynasts*; "the modern expression of a modern outlook"; to anticipate Ibsen in *The Woodlanders* and Proust in *The Well-Beloved*; to have written in *Ethelberta* a novel thirty or thirty-five years before its time; to have expressed "philosophies and feelings as yet not well established": and to have created characters (Clym, Jude and Sue) who failed because they were before their time. "The rural world was not ripe for" Clym. Jude says " 'It takes two or three generations to do what I tried to do in one' "; " 'Perhaps the world is not illuminated enough for such experiments as ours' "; and " 'Our ideas were fifty years too soon.' " Sue says " 'We are a little beforehand, that's all. In fifty, a hundred years the descendants of these two [who get married] will act and feel worse than we.' "[5]

It seems worthwhile therefore to begin the discussion of Hardy's "modernity" by examining his own use of the term. Much that he called modern was not, and often he used the term vaguely. Thus in the Preface to *Far from the Madding Crowd* he says he "projected" a "series of novels" about "a modern Wessex of railways, the penny post, mowing and reaping machines, union workhouses, lucifer matches, labourers who could read and write, and National school children": the railways were built between 1836 and 1848, the penny post available from 1840, the unions from 1834, lucifers from 1831, and National schools from 1811. In *The Return* we are told the reddleman's "place is filled by modern inventions" but these are only the railways, since the introduction of which 'Wessex farmers have managed to do without them": these inventions are not modern. Again, in *Tess*, the railway is the modernity: "modern life stretched out its steam feeler". Again in *Jude*, it is because of the railways – because Sue regards the railway station as the centre of life – that Jude calls her modern, though she denies it. Just as Sue prefers to meet Jude in a railway station rather than a cathedral, so Paula asks whether one should be more proud of one's father building a railway or one's ancestor a castle. Paula's telegraph "also signified ... the modern fever and fret" but telegraphs were available to the pub-

lic from about 1850. Parson Torkingham and Lady Constantine
had no "awkward modern ideas on land-ownership or church
formulas": if anything more specific than disapproval of the absentee landlord is meant it could be Chalmers's *Political
Economy* (1832) or William Thomson's *Enquiry into the
Principles of the Distribution of Wealth* (1824): the church formulas are presumably those of 1833. Avice I's "modern
feelings" in 1850 are simply dislike of "prenuptial union".
Sometimes "modern" means merely not medieval: in the Great
Barn at Weatherbury "for once mediaevalism and modernism
had a common standpoint" – it is still used as a barn: the
"modern peculiarity" of Shaston, as distinct from its character
as a medieval religious community, is to serve fairs and markets.
Not-medieval includes not-religious and it is in that sense that
Paula, however Arnoldian she becomes later, is considered
"modern" originally by Somerset: she had merely refused to be
baptised. French Impressionism is not meant when Hardy writes
of "the livid shades of modern French painters – the phrase
exactly fits a painter such as Georges Michel (1763–1843).[6]

The term is often used vaguely. We cannot guess either who
the "modern ethical schools" are, before which, says *A
Laodicean*, men were characterised by "mechanical admixture
of black and white qualities without coalescence," or what
Avice III's "intensely modern sympathies" are, or when the
"modern patterns" of waggon ousted Melbury's, or how Grace
"combined modern nerves with primitive feelings" – she is
sexually aroused by Fitzpiers but also has a "Daphnean [i.e.
timeless] instinct" to run away from him. Tess is vague in reflecting that " 'All is vanity' . . . was a most inadequate thought
for modern days. . . . All was, alas, worse than vanity – injustice, punishment, exaction, death": again, injustice, etc. are
timeless. It is vague when Jude's provisional acceptance of a job
is called "his form of the modern vice of unrest. . . . He did not
. . . see that mediaevalism was . . . dead . . . [did not see] the
. . . animosity of contemporary logic and vision towards so
much of what he held in reverence. . . ."[7]

In *The Return* the vagueness is a vague sadness found in the
landscape and in Clym's face. Egdon must be modern since it is

unsmiling, and "smiling champains" are not "harmonious" with "the present": "Egdon appealed to a more recently learned emotion", yet it is also timeless: "everything . . . had been from prehistoric times . . . unaltered." The same kind of point is made in *Tess* about the same kind of landscape, the surroundings of the Cross-in-Hand: "so far removed from the charm which is sought in landscape by artists and view-lovers as to reach a new kind of beauty, a negative beauty of tragic tone." Sensibility to this kind of beauty was not new in Hardy's day, it is found in Wordsworth and Romantic art, in the eighteenth-century treatises on the Sublime of which Burke's is the best known, and, intermittently, in eighteenth-century poetry. As to Clym's face, we are told it conveyed the idea of experience rather than age: "the age of a modern man is to be measured by the intensity of his history". Clym's face "showed that thought is a disease of the flesh" and was "the typical countenance of the future": an unconcerned face lacks "modern perceptiveness".[8]

Since *The Return* has been seen as genuinely modern, "a reconciliation of two major Victorian concepts – the Darwinian world of mechanical science and natural law, and Arnold's world of culture and poetry" (although I shall discuss Darwin and Arnold later), I must now point out the vagueness of everything connected with Clym, the owner of the face. Clym claims that his "system of education . . . is as new as it is true" but we never discover what it is. " 'Do you think I have turned teacher too soon?' " he asks, when Eustacia is pricked for a witch – a point made in the *Spectator* in 1711. Or his aim is "to teach them [the Cantles etc.] to breast the misery they are born to" – a timeless situation which there are various ways of dealing with. Clym "was in many points abreast with the central town thinkers of his day. . . . In Paris . . . he had become acquainted with ethical systems popular at the time": this *may* refer to the not very modern S. Simon and Comte, but it may not – they are not otherwise present in the novel. He believes men need "knowledge of a sort which brings wisdom rather than affluence", and this *may* be a reference to Carlyle and Ruskin, but again it may not.[9]

If Hardy had really wanted to be modern, to reflect social change and the impact of the ideas of Darwin, Mill, Arnold and Schopenhauer, he had the perfect opportunity in *The Well-Beloved*, written between *Tess* and *Jude*, with their "ache of modernism" and "modern unrest", at the end of his novel-writing life, with parts devoted more clearly and specifically to three generations — 1850, 1870, 1890 — than in any other of his novels, and with sophisticated receptions in London and sophisticated characters such as Lady Channelcliff, Mrs Pine-Avon, Somers and Pierston himself. Yet there is no discussion of ideas, only the vague statement that Mrs Pine-Avon "held ... sound rather than current opinions on the plastic arts". The only effect of time is the ageing of individuals, particularly Pierston himself and Marcia Bencourt "the image and super-scription of Age — an old woman, pale and shrivelled, her fore-head ploughed, her cheek hollow, her hair white as snow". In fact the novel is a continual turning away from London to the Isle of Slingers, and it is only change on this "hoary peninsula" that is described: "the general change ... was small. ... Men drank, smoked, and spat in the inns with only a little more adulteration in their refreshments and a trifle less dialect in their speech than of yore."[10]

"The misery they are born to", in Clym's phrase, is an example of Hardy's pessimism: the opposite is joy, or "the Hellenic idea", and has been connected with Arnold, Mill and Comte. In *Tess*, the "inherent will to enjoy" (it is shown to be inherent in all the characters except Angel's brothers and Mercy Chant) is defeated by the "circumstantial will against enjoy-ment". In *The Return* "the view of life as a thing to be put up with" has replaced the "zest for existence" of "early civiliza-tions", which is also called "the Hellenic idea". The pessimism is congenital to Hardy, is frequently stated, as here, antecedently to any suffering by a character, or it emerges as the result of narrative contrivance. It is not the product of modern causes. Hardy admitted that the rural labourer's lot had improved in his lifetime, he presents so many unattractive features of the Wessex way of life that he could only have mixed feelings about its passing, he is not troubled as Carlyle and Arnold are by shooting Niagara and Hyde Park riots, and the first World War was still to come. Tess, before anything has happened to her, believes we live on "a blighted star". In *The Woodlanders* we are already in "this sorry world" in the Preface. Angel's harshness to Tess is at once generalised to "the universal harshness . . . the harshness of the position towards the temperament, of the means towards the aims, of to-day towards yesterday, of hereafter towards to-day". "Nobody did come, because nobody does" – not because Jude wasn't at school.[11]

Extreme forms of this pessimism are the wish not to have been born, the wish to die, and considered, attempted or actual suicide. The frequency of the death wishes and suicides amounts to more than people's normal habit of saying, perhaps many times in their lives, that they wish they were dead. Bathsheba, Eustacia, Lady Constantine, Henchard, Abel Whittle and Tess *consider* suicide: Bathsheba on discovery of Fanny Robin's baby, Eustacia after the quarrel with Clym, Lady Constantine because of her pregnancy, Henchard particularly because of the prospect of losing Elizabeth-Jane and more generally because of "life's contrarious inconsistencies", Tess twice, by drowning and hanging, upon loss of Angel's love; Abel Whittle because of the prospect of going to Blackmoor Vale without his trousers. Retty, Jude and Boldwood *try to commit* suicide. Jude's mother, Little Father Time, Manston and Felice's South Carolina suitor actually do so. Boldwood, Clym, Swithin, Elizabeth-Jane, Retty, Tess (at least twice), Little Father Time, Avice I and Pierston wish they were dead. Eustacia, Tess at least twice, Jude at least thrice (once including Sue in the wish), and Little Father Time at least twice, either wish they hadn't been born or think they ought not to have been: it even occurs comically, when Anne Garland, at her mother's marriage to Miller Loveday, "had a distressing sense that she ought not to be born". Statements that life is not worth living are often authorial. Life is "the plight of being alive". About Jude Hardy says, before the story starts, that "he was the sort of man who was born to ache a good deal before the fall of the curtain on his unnecessary life should signify that all was well with him again". When Tess learned that "in some circumstances there was one thing better than to lead a good life, and that was to be saved from leading any life whatever" and when Jude quotes the doctor as seeing "the beginning of the coming universal wish not to live", Hardy means that Tess had learned the truth and what was coming was right. We are also told that Tess's brothers and sisters "had never been asked if they wished for life", and that the boy Jude "did not want to be a man".[12]

Fear of the future is a, perhaps mild, form of the wish to die or not to have been born. It is this which Tess voices by "expressing in her own native phrases — assisted by her Sixth Standard training — feelings which might almost have been called those of the age — the ache of modernism". It is characterisic of Hardy to say "almost" when he is being fanciful, but one must take the remark seriously. In fact there is nothing modern about Tess's fear of the future, which she expresses by comparing trees to to-morrows which say "I'm coming! Beware of me!" Tess is afraid that discovery of her loss of virginity will alienate Angel, and, more generally, her experiences — Alec, social stigma, the deaths of Prince and Sorrow — have made her afraid that the future will be like the past. That Tess's consciousness is not modern is emphasised here by reference to her having reached the Sixth Standard, and immediately afterwards by saying that Angel "reflected that what are called advanced ideas are really in great part but the latest fashion in definition — a more accurate expression, by words in *logy* and *ism*, of sensations which men and women have vaguely grasped for centuries". Only the words "in great part" save this statement from nonsense, but even so one must object to, say, phrenology or naturalism being called the expression of sensations. Hardy himself uses words in *ism* improperly — modernism for modernity, conventionalism for convention, mediaevalism for the middle ages, realism for reality — and this may increase in some readers' eyes his intellectual content.[13]

Finally some occasions where the modernity is trivial or disliked by Hardy may be mentioned. Eustacia has "modern ideas" about furniture, but the only specificity in the passage is of the "time-honoured furnishing" which the "modern" Clym doesn't want displaced. Eustacia is like Lucetta, whose taste in furniture was exactly as advanced as Jude's ideas about life, not to be satisfied in Casterbridge "till fifty years more of civilisation have passed over the town". Such false modernity is to be distinguished from the useful modernity of a Farfrae, or even, since it saves Grace's life, a Fitzpiers. It is natural to assume Hardy's sympathy with the reviewer of Elfride's novel who hoped to escape "wearisome details in modern social scenery" – the kind of details Hardy himself sometimes tried to give but never succeeded. When Troy is called "a farmer of a spirited and very modern school", the modernity is again bad – he neglects the farm. Fitzpiers's "keenly appreciative, modern, unpractical mind" is pejorative: Hardy, talking authorially in the same way that Angel reflects, says that Fitzpiers seemed "to be a dreamy ist of some sort, or too deeply steeped in some false kind of ism".[14]

Here – although elsewhere in *The Woodlanders* Hardy allows Fitzpiers to be an efficient doctor – modern and unpractical go together. Hardy is all for the practical, and his anti-intellectualism, and in particular his use of the words "idea" and "ideal" to mean unreal, make it all the more unlikely that he himself would be influenced by modern ideas. Fitzpiers reads a book by "a German metaphysician, for . . . [he] much preferred the ideal world to the real, and the discovery of principles to their application": the end of the sentence is like Fielding's Square's attitude to Aristotle which "he carried so far as to regard all virtue as matter of theory only". Fitzpiers shows the influence of the German metaphysician when he says "I am in love with something in my own head, and no thing-in-itself outside at all." Angel is all right as long as he trusts his feelings and not logic, reason or his judgement. His "hard logical deposit" prevented his forgiving Tess, but he "instinctively manifested a fondness for her . . . when reason slept": in declaring himself "his heart had outrun his judgment". The wisdom he learns in Brazil is simply not to generalise at all, not to "be influenced by general principles to the disregard of the particular instance". In Angel, till then, ideal is connected with fanciful and opposed to real: for such a man "corporeal absence" may "create an ideal presence that conveniently drops the defects of the real": "he loved

her . . . perhaps ideally and fancifully". To Tess's dreams and
fancies we are more sympathetic, but they are part of the same
contrast with reality. On her wedding-day she "moved about in
a mental cloud of many-coloured idealities, which eclipsed all
sinister contingencies" but the sinister is the reality. "A spiritual
forgetfulness [of her past] coexisted [in her] with an intellectual remembrance." This is important because the central
movement of *Tess* is her discovery of reality, of a short way by
experience, in a world in which appearances are difficult to
penetrate. Tess's way is to reach it through various false hypotheses, such as that " the past was past" or that she need not
fear a man who was not in love with her, or had nothing to fear
but humanity. But at the end "both [she and Angel] seemed to
implore something to shelter them from reality".[15]

The same language comments adversely on Jude's love of
both his women as on Angel's of Tess. "His idea of [Arabella]
was the thing of most consequence, not Arabella herself, he
sometimes said." Sue "was almost an ideality to him still". And
whereas in *Tess* the reality of Tess's sufferings is contrasted with
the ideality of Angel's mind, in *Jude* it is Jude who not only has
that momentary "true illumination" that "the stoneyard was a
centre of effort as worthy", but for whom at the end "the theo-
logians, the apologists and their kin the metaphysicians, the
high-handed statesmen and others . . . [have] been spoiled . . .
by the grind of stern reality". Little Father Time is born with
the same fault that Angel corrects in Brazil: he "seemed to have
begun with the generals of life and never to have concerned
himself with the particulars". Hardy's way of thinking is shown
even in a passage where the contrast is slightly different, and the
speaker (Eustacia about Clym) is unsympathetic: "He's an en-
thusiast about ideas, and careless about outward things.' "[16]

This anti-intellectualism is confirmed by the simple and unintellectual nature of the concepts by means of which Hardy explains events. "Circumstances" are more often blamed than the
Immanent Will. It is, we have seen, circumstances, the "circumstantial will", which defeat the characters in *Tess*. Although
stated as the "fancy of some people" the sentiment in *A Pair of
Blue Eyes* that "circumstance only tries to prevent what intelli-

gence attempts" is an early version of the same statement and is authorial. In the same novel, referring to the growth of intimacy between Smith and Knight, "circumstance as usual did it all". It is "circumstances" that Oak deplores his "powerlessness to counteract" when Bathsheba sees the baby in Fanny Robin's coffin. The "impishness of circumstance" is blamed for the anticipation of St Cleeve's work on the variable stars. Fitzpiers "she could forget: her circumstances she had always with her", Grace reflects: and earlier, "Not herself but the pressure of events had dissipated the dreams of their early youth." Most emphatically, at the break with Sue, where Hardy comments that they had "travelled in opposite directions" and "events had enlarged" Jude's views of life, and after Sue has said " 'It is no use fighting against God!' " Jude replies " 'It is only against man and senseless circumstance.' " Hardy's satires are "Satires of Circumstance".[17]

When a more abstract explanation is offered, it is often fate, luck, providence, caprice or coincidence. The frequent *use* of coincidence in Hardy is familiar: " On the earth, so conceived," comments Dorothy Van Ghent, "coincidence and accident constitute order, the prime terrestrial order, for they too are "the given", impenetrable by human *ratio*, accountable only as mystery." Coincidences may be so explained, or they may be explained as the work of the Will: the point here is that they are not themselves explanations, they are "accountable only as mystery". And sometimes no further explanation seems possible, as when Paula calls it "a happy coincidence" that Mrs Camperton asked the elder Somerset to design the costumes for the performance of *Love's Labour's Lost*, without knowing that he was George's father, without knowing of any connection between George and Paula, and without knowing George. Hardy, when what he is doing is creating a number of meetings between Oak and Bathsheba to lead to Oak's proposal, calls it "one of those whimsical coincidences . . . [of] Nature" that he happens on one of these occasions to recognise her. The way Hardy is forced to comment on his own use of coincidence creates doubt whether he usually saw anything more in it than narrative convenience. Some of the extraordinary coincidences in *Desperate*

Remedies are discussed at length by Owen and Cytherea Graye.
Cytherea concludes "like an elderly divine" that they are the
effects of Providence. In *The Mayor* again, where the tragedy
depends on a coincidental order of events – Elizabeth-Jane in
love with Farfrae, Farfrae forbidden to address her, Henchard
accepts her as his daughter, finds she isn't, Farfrae thinks of
leaving Casterbridge, is asked to be Mayor, Henchard drives
Elizabeth-Jane away, finds out about her "endeavours for improvement" – Hardy feels the need to comment: "The
mockery was, that he should have no sooner taught a girl to
claim the shelter of his paternity than he discovered her to have
no kinship with him." Through Lucetta, he points out that the
first meeting between Lucetta and Elizabeth-Jane, which he
needs in order to produce the situation of Elizabeth-Jane's wit-
nessing the courting of Lucetta by both her father and her ex-
suitor, "was . . . an accident". In *The Return* he speaks
authorially of "the gloomy corner into which accident as much
as indiscretion had brought"Eustacia.[18]

Cytherea explains coincidences as the effects of Providence.
It hardly needs to be said that Hardy does not believe in Providence. Characters therefore who explain things in terms of Providence are offering non-explanations. They frequently do.
" 'It's Providence,' " says Farfrae, invited to stay and work for
Henchard. It isn't. " 'See now how it's ourselves that are ruled
by the Powers above us,' " he says on being invited to become
Mayor, an act which leads to his wife's death. " 'That performance of theirs killed her but kept me alive. . . . It seems that
even I be in Somebody's hand,' " reflects Henchard, reserved
for worse suffering. Throwing Fitzpiers off the horse would
have been "a crime, but for the mercy of Providence in providing leaves for his fall": it didn't. " 'O Edred, there has been an
Eye watching over us,' " says Grace: it was only Tim Tangs's.
Poorgrass is absurd, within his own range of hypocritical reli-
giosity, when he says of his orthographical weakness " 'Providence ordered it should be no worse.' " Or Hardy attacks the
idea authorially: "Providence is nothing if not coquettish":
Eustacia doesn't meet Clym when she wants to, but does meet
him after she's given up the idea, so they do get married and

disaster follows. "Where was Tess's guardian angel? Where was the providence of her simple faith?" "If she were only sure . . . how confidently she would leave them to Providence . . . ! But in default of that, it behoved her to do something; to be their Providence." Having missed Sue by going to see the composer at Kennetbridge, Jude at first thinks this was "Providence to keep him away from temptation" but concludes by ridiculing "the idea that God sent people on fools' errands". The wise Elizabeth-Jane alone speaks of "tempting Providence": like calling it "coquettish", this expression implies that Providence, if it exists, is not necessarily benign.[19]

In discussing coincidence, Providence and fate in Hardy, I am not here concerned with the extent to which he in fact allows characters free will. I think the problem there is to reconcile the different things he says. I am only concerned to show that, to the extent he explains things other than as the effects of character, the explanations are not intellectual or modern but simple. His characters do frequently blame fate, but Hardy does not always blame them for doing so, and does not always make it clear whether it is himself or a character who is blaming fate. Even when he says that "instead of blaming herself for the issue she [Eustacia] laid the fault upon the shoulders of some indistinct, colossal Prince of the World", it was after all not Eustacia's fault that Mrs Yeobright called while Wildeve was there. Grace is only joking when she says " 'There's destiny in it. . . . I was doomed to join in your picnic.' " Fitzpiers is only using an argument to bind her when he says " 'See how powerless is the human will against predestination. . . . We have met.' " Sue, one might suppose, is simply wrong when she says " 'And now Fate has given us this stab in the back.' " And yet Jude, who three pages later blames man and circumstance, replies here with a quotation from Aeschylus: "Things are as they are, and will be brought to their destined end.' " It is Grace's thought, to make it easy for herself, that "fate, it seemed would have it this way" — that she should not marry Winterborne; Tess's, that "she was doomed to come" to Flintcomb-Ash and that "the fates seemed to decide" she was not to be a schoolteacher. But it is Hardy who asks "why she [Tess] was doomed to be seen and courted

. . . by the wrong man", Hardy who says that "the finger of fate
. . . turned [Grace] into a wife". He never clearly distinguishes
himself from "the fatalistic convictions common to field-folk".
On the one hand, he likes to present the Wessex way of life, for
all its poverty, inefficiency and superstition, as in touch with
basic realities. " 'Boundless love: I shouldn't have supposed it in
the universe' " is the realistic sentiment of Joseph Poorgrass.
" 'You've no faults. . . . And he's none. So it must be something
outside ye both' " says Marian to Tess about Angel — surely
only a slight simplification of Hardy's view. Even Leaf gets the
essential point about the girls singing in church; it " 'will make
it louder' ".[20] Truth is simple. On the other hand, almost every
time a character utters the folk formulation of fatalism, " 'twas
to be", he is wrong.[21] Only Tess, using the significantly different expression "What must come will come" in reference to
her arrest and execution, is right, and that is tragic recognition
and acceptance, not of fate, but of the consequences of the law
and the action of the novel.[22]

To explain things, then, in terms of coincidence, Providence
or fate, is not to say much about them. Hardy also uses as explanation far more frequently than any modern or intellectual
concept, the terms "nature" and "civilisation" or "society".
What does he mean by these terms? To establish what he means
by society one must discuss his social criticism in detail, which I
do in Chapter 2. My conclusion is that Hardy's real social concerns — poverty, marriage, religion and education — are seen as
timeless rather than modern issues. Unless they are somehow
subdivided or given particular content, nature and society or
civilisation comprise the simplest and oldest way of accounting
for everything. Nature is the physical constitution of the world,
including man, the nature of Milton's Nativity Ode, with "her
foul deformities", the nature who is Edmund's goddess and
about which Lear enquires "Is there any cause in nature that
makes these hard hearts?" Unless one looks as Milton did to a
divine order, civilisation or society are everything else.

It is in this sense that Hardy uses the terms:

As for the outside, Nature, in the ample time that had been

given her, had so mingled her filings and effacements with the marks of human wear and tear upon the house . . .

— his description of Oxwell Hall. Unchanging Egdon was nature: "Civilisation was its enemy." When Susan Henchard looked at her child she was pretty, otherwise apathetic and hopeless: "The first phase was the work of Nature, the second probably of civilisation." When Grace "threw off the veneer of artificiality she had acquired at the fashionable schools", we hear of her "lapse back to Nature unadorned". When Giles for once behaves naturally and kisses her, it is a "social sin" because she is legally married to the adulterous Fitzpiers. Revd Swancourt claims that, in the same way that country labourers "learnt the signs of nature" he had "learnt the language of her illegitimate sister — artificiality". That Hardy does use the word "nature" in the old or timeless sense he makes very clear on one occasion, when he says that "as Nature was hardly invented at this date [1805] Bob's Matilda could not say much about the glamour of the hills, or the shimmering of the foliage, or the wealth of glory in the distant sea": this is the Romantic Nature.[23]

The difficulties Hardy gets into over nature in *Tess* have been discussed by Ian Gregor and B. J. Paris. He "uses nature as a moral norm and at the same time regards nature as amoral". He "juggles with the word nature in a way damaging to his artistic purpose. . . . In exploring and assessing Tess's situation, Hardy continually uses a double standard." It would be possible to defend Hardy against inconsistency in *Tess* by saying that he never uses nature as a moral norm. Its plan is not "holy", it is "shameless" and "cruel", Car's friends *err* in supposing that its parts "harmoniously and joyously interpenetrated one another", Mrs Durbeyfield *errs* in characterising Tess's seduction as " 'nater . . . and what do please God' ", Angel *errs* in seeing Tess, to whose culture history contributed, as "a fresh and virginal daughter of Nature" — and so on. The idea that nature is, sometimes, a moral norm in *Tess* is derived from those passages in which it is opposed to civilisation or society. This is precisely the point I am making, that together they comprise everything. "She had been made to break an accepted social law, but no law known to the environment [i.e. nature] in which she fancied herself such an anomaly." She "was ashamed of herself for her gloom of the night, based on nothing more tangible than a sense of condemnation under an arbitrary law of society which had no foundation in Nature". In one such opposition in reference to the death of Tess's baby, both terms are seen to be causes of suffering: "Now that her moral sorrows [i.e. those imposed by society] were passing away, a fresh one arose on the natural side of her which knew no social law."[24]

In fact, the movement in *Tess*, her tragic learning too late, is from the idea that only man, only society, is against her, to the idea that nature — Flintcomb-Ash — is too. But the opposition between nature and civilisation is mentioned in other novels, and is explicit in *The Mayor* and particularly important in his most mature work, *Jude*.

> Out of all this tampering with social law came that flower of Nature, Elizabeth. Part of his [Henchard's] wish to wash his hands of life arose from his perception of . . . Nature's jaunty readiness to support unorthodox social principles.

> "I [Sue] said it was Nature's intention, Nature's law and *raison d'être* that we should be joyful in what instincts she afforded us — instincts which civilisation had taken upon itself to thwart."

How important the two terms and their synonyms are in *Tess* and *Jude* may be seen by assembling some instances of their use together or separately, and, when separate, generally each implying the other. In *Tess*:

> An immeasurable social chasm was to divide [Tess] . . . from that previous self . . .

> A convulsive snatching at social salvation might have impelled her to [marry Alec].

> Most of the misery had been generated by her conventional aspect [being unmarried], and not by her innate sensations.

The recuperative power which pervaded organic nature was surely not denied to maidenhood alone.

[Angel] began to evince . . . indifference to social forms and observances.

They [the other dairymaids] writhed feverishly under . . . an emotion thrust on them by cruel Nature's law. . . . The full recognition of the futility of their infatuation, from a social point of view; . . . its lack of everything to justify its existence in the eye of civilisation (while lacking nothing in the eye of Nature) . . . imparted to them a dignity . . .

". . . your husband in nature . . ." [Angel calls Alec this, Angel being her husband in Society.]

He [Angel] was . . . bitterly disposed towards social ordinances [i.e. he is married to Tess].

"It [for Izz to go away with Angel, who is married to Tess] will be wrong-doing in the eyes of civilisation."

. . . the beloved man whose conventional standard of judgement had caused her all these latter sorrows.

". . . the whole unconventional [i.e. natural] business of our time at Trantridge."

"I [Alec] was on the way to, at least, social salvation till I saw you" [Parsons are respectable].

And in *Jude*:

Nature's logic was too horrid for him to care for. That mercy towards one set of creatures [the birds] was cruelty towards another [Man] sickened his sense of harmony.

"O why should nature's law be mutual butchery!" [Sue on her pigeons bought by the poulterer.]

There seemed to him . . . something wrong in a social ritual which made necessary a cancelling of well-formed schemes . . . because of a momentary surprise by a new and transitory instinct [sex].

[Jude] was licensed by the laws of his country to love Arabella and none other unto his life's end. . . . He feared that his whole scheme had degenerated to, even though it might not have originated in, a social unrest which had no foundation in the nobler instincts; which was purely an artificial product of civilisation.

". . . You are quite a product of civilisation," said Jude . . . "Indeed I am not, Jude. I like reading and all that, but I crave to get back to the life of my infancy and its freedom."

" . . . The social moulds civilisation fits us into have no . . . relation to our actual shapes . . ." [Sue speaking].

"It is none of the natural tragedies of love that's love's usual tragedy in civilised life, but a tragedy artificially manufactured for people who in a natural state would find relief in parting" [Sue speaking].

. . . He was as unfit . . . by nature, as he had been by social position [to be ordained: Jude's reflection after kissing Sue].

"Cruelty is the law pervading all nature and society" [Phillotson speaking].

"There is something wrong in our social formulas" [Jude speaking].

" . . . It is a law of nature" [that people have children, says Sue].

"It was in his nature to do it" [Little Father Time's, to hang the children, says Jude].

To indulge one's instinctive and uncontrolled sense of justice and right was not . . . permitted with impunity in an old civilisation like ours [Phillotson, writing to Sue].[25]

Since no one, I think, has done for *Jude* what Gregor and Paris did for *Tess*, I will point out some of the difficulties of the use of these categories in *Jude*. One must not of course forget that some of the above statements are by characters. Hardy does not think that the sense of justice and right is instinctive, and in fact he makes Phillotson cut this remark out of his final draft. But its inclusion is significant of Hardy's way of thinking as well as Phillotson's. Hardy does not think — although the remark is similar to the opposition in *Tess* between the "will to enjoy" and the "circumstantial will against enjoyment", that cruelty is the law pervading all nature and society. But it *is* Hardy who thinks Jude was licensed by his society to love only Arabella until he dies, and this is not true as is shown by the ease with which both couples obtain their divorces when they ask for them, and it is the same thing, namely marriage, that Sue calls "love's usual tragedy in civilised life" so that here too it is Hardy speaking. One wonders what "the natural tragedies of love" are. One would expect them to be those knowingly catalogued by Shakespeare's Lysander and Hermia to prove that "the course of true love never did run smooth" — but all *their* instances are of failure to end in marriage. And in saying that the social unrest connected with Jude's plan to study at Christminster was an artificial product of civilisation Hardy forgets that the alternative, the stoneyard, was not the product of nature.

Places where the words "nature" and "civilisation" are improperly used are signs that the categories are too large and simple. In fact where they are opposed, civilisation is either used more pejoratively, or is used pejoratively and nature not. Civilisation is synonymous with artificiality and convention. The only civilisation not so treated is folk culture. This culture is an essential part of what we value in Hardy and is well-known and does not need to be described. It includes the moral qualities of the peasant, the dialect, the sense of the past, the "folk ways" and the music. It is not of course presented as faultless, and its first presentation, in *Under the Greenwood Tree*, is largely comic and patronising. Normally only the author is allowed to stray into the world of upper-class art, architecture, literature and history: there are no Ladislaws, Brookes or Lydgates. Hardy sometimes suggests that Wessex does have its own Coliseum, Mediterranean, Cerealia, and Gregorian melodies; its Fausts and Sauls and Bellerophons and Scheherazades; and things which can only be described by words like diapason, catenary, or maphrotight. This is a two-edged weapon and a complex question. The comparison of Wessex characters to persons famous in history or legend only involves a single point of contact. The comparison is often dismissive of the external cultural element, as when "Prouts's brown" is substituted for Vandyke brown. When the Wessex character makes the comparison he often gets it wrong – Oliver Grumble, Monmouth rebelling against the Romans[26]

In *The Woodlanders* "so-called culture" which Winterborne lacks, is contrasted with "honesty, goodness, manliness, tenderness, devotion" which he has, and "nothing had ever brought home to her with such force as this death how little acquirements and culture weighed beside sterling personal character". These are Grace's reflections although put rather authorially and Grace of course is placed between Winterborne and Fitzpiers. Fitzpiers is in all Hardy the most cultured person in the normal sense of the term. We must go carefully with such characters, as to them applies Hardy's demand for "a social system based on individual spontaneity" rather than "a curbed and uniform one under which all temperaments are bound to shape themselves to a single pattern of living". We are meant to sympathise with Fitzpiers and not Grace when she, like Faustus, burns his books – his philosophies, old plays, and French romances. Nevertheless, Fitzpiers's culture is sarcastically described: "In the course of a year his mind was accustomed to pass in a grand solar sweep through the zodiac of the intellectual heaven." And the subjects are given: alchemy, poesy [why not poetry?], astrology and astronomy [astrology to make astronomy absurd], German literature and metaphysics. If it be objected that Hardy is trying in Fitzpiers only to represent "so-called culture" the fact remains that he doesn't represent any realer culture anywhere else. Hardy's use of autobiography is too various for us to move in the other direction and quote his own reading of German literature and metaphysics as evidence of the intention to present Fitzpiers sympathetically here. The absence of content in Hardy's concept of culture makes difficulties for him when he attempts to connect it with the attraction Fitzpiers has for Grace: "the possibilities of a refined and cultivated inner life of subtle psychological intercourse had their charm". Perhaps this was her inexperienced guess. And yet after the honeymoon Fitzpiers reflects: "in their travels together she had ranged so unerringly at his level in ideas, tastes and habits." Somehow it is difficult to feel that Fitzpiers's culture was so bogus that he didn't know that Grace didn't realise it was bogus. The change in Grace seen in Giles's impression of her after her marriage – "a creature of more ideas . . . dignity . . . assurance" – is not clearly attributed to Fitzpiers's influence, but rather to the fact that "she was a woman who had been married". The difficulty is, I think, connected with what is the undoubted success of *The Woodlanders*, the development, from the idea of woodlands, of the ideas of enclosure and inwardness and their opposites, outsideness and externality. Little Hintock is "innermost" in contrast with "the outer world". Winterborne's "want of so-called culture" is linked with "his exterior roughness", and contrasted with his inner, moral qualities such as honesty and devotion, and he himself reflects that "external phenomena" – clothes, stance – are what women judge men by. There are plenty of other places in Hardy where appearance is contrasted with reality, but elsewhere appearance is clothes, or commercial credibility, or, in *Tess*, the general deceptiveness of appearance. For culture to be included, as it is only in *The Woodlanders*, in a structure of inside and outside it must be all one or all the other or, if both, we must be clear about which is which. Because Grace is the heroine the cultivated life she hopes for is called "inner", but there is simply not enough content to the concept of culture and not enough clarity in the writing for us to know whether she gets it, or for us to say that Hardy takes the further, Laurentian, step of denying that the "cerebral" in itself can provide an important bond between people. It is to be noted that *The Woodlanders* is also the only novel in which the idea of refinement is connected with the idea of culture, both by Grace and by Fitzpiers who calls her "refined and educated". Elsewhere in *The Woodlanders* and the other novels refinement and delicacy are either false or they are simple Wessex qualities, shown by Sgt Stanner in leaving out a questionable verse in mixed company, or by Henchard in his way of showing Elizabeth-Jane out of the office. And the good – Elizabeth-Jane, Giles and Tess – are "unsophisticated": Fitzpiers, Felice, and "in many things" Sue, are "sophisticated"[27]

We have seen Sue characterise her tragedy as artificial, simply the product of civilised life. She doesn't even claim that it's modern, and it isn't. Hardy himself quotes, as Farquhar had done, from Milton's *Doctrine and Discipline of Divorce*. The power of Hardy's tragedies is due to their simplicity. They are more like Synge's, and they are not modern like Ibsen's, or like the tragic possibilities in Shaw. They are simple, and their only weakness is the extent to which they are reached by narrative contrivance. Henchard's tragedy is a recurrence to the medieval type, in which the tragedy consists simply in the fall, which is described in four consecutive sentences either physically or with physical metaphors:

> On that day – almost at that minute – he passed the ridge of prosperity and honour and began to descend rapidly on the other side. It was strange how soon he sank in esteem. Socially he had received a startling fillip downwards; and having already lost commercial buoyancy from rash transactions, the velocity of his descent in both aspects became accelerated every hour. He now gazed more at the pavements and less at the housefronts when he walked about: more at the feet and leggings of men. . . .

The only intellectual complication in Hardy's view of tragedy is that he sometimes seeks to show that his simple tragedies actually obey Aristotle's rules, just as his Wessex has a Coliseum and Cerealia. I think this is the reason why Marty's words — "You was a good man, and did good things!" — form the conclusion of *The Woodlanders*. Hardy expressed the hope that "Aristotelian qualities might be found" in *Jude*. More elaborately, Tess is in Aristotle's words, "in some sense a bit superior", "misfortune is brought upon [her] not by vice or depravity, but by some *hamartia*", she undergoes Anagnorisis or "the change from ignorance to knowledge", and, since tragedy is "the imitation of people acting" she, like Winterborne, "does good things". To Henchard, I incline to think Hardy intended to deny even the Aristotelian elements of responsibility \ and recognition. Since he was drunk when he sold his wife he was not certainly morally responsible though he was legally, and it is as a "crime" (not a sin) that he afterwards refers to it: he refers to it only vaguely along with other things as possibly his fault: "All had gone from him . . . either by his fault or his misfortune." And Hardy explicitly says: "Though under a long reign of self-control he had become Mayor and churchwarden and what not there was still the same unruly volcanic stuff beneath the rind of Michael Henchard." Any "change from ignorance to knowledge" only occurred immediately after the wife-sale on becoming sober, and about that Hardy comments: "He experienced the superadded bitterness of seeing his very recantation nullified." I believe that Henchard's inability to learn is restated in his Will at the end, which is ironical: he really wants all the things he says he doesn't.[28]

But whether or no, Hardy's use of the word tragic to mean simply misfortune or death does support the idea that his concept of tragedy was simple. He is sometimes quoting Wessex. Thus Egdon thinks about Clym that "if he were making a fortune and a name, so much the better for him: if he were making a tragical figure in the world, so much the better for the narrative". Robert Creedle "was still in a tragic mood" because the Melburys had come too early to the party. Behind the light use of the word there is still the same simple reference when the consciousness is not Wessex's. " 'The case . . . is rather one for satirical laughter then for tragedy' " says Angel, when Tess has just threatened suicide. Jude refers to the hanging of the children as "the tragedy". Miller Loveday loved Mrs Garland but "not tragically": not enough to commit suicide if she refused him. Bob, Anne, and his father wonder whether Matilda's disappearance "had a tragic intent" and later abandon "the theory of a tragical end" — suicide again. "Tragedy" was the "end" of Fitzpiers's and Felice's affair: her murder. "Creedle, with his ropes and grapnels and air of impending tragedy" is simply prepared to dredge up a corpse. Or tragic means simply serious, as when Tess looked "pale and tragical" because "thoughts were . . . grave" at the beginning of "The Rally", or when, at the Kennetbridge fair, before any possible inkling of any misfortune, Sue thinks it " 'a terribly tragic thing to bring beings into the world' ", or when the setting of the Cross-in-Hand has "a negative beauty of tragic tone". It is in this sense that tragedy is distinguished from comedy, which is simply funny, not serious: Farfrae "seemed to feel exactly as she felt about life and its surroundings — that they were a tragical rather than a comical thing": "What was comedy to them was tragedy to her" — the story of Jack Dollop, to the other dairymaids and to Tess.[29]

Finally, this view of Hardy agrees with two aspects, his impressionism and tentativeness, to which, since they have been noticed by Hardy himself and his critics, only a brief reference is necessary. In the *Life* he speaks of the "tentative character of his theories" and says "I have troubled myself very little about theories . . . I am content with tentativeness from day to day." The *Poems of the Past and Present* were offered as "unadjusted impressions . . . diverse readings of its [life's] phenomena". The General Preface to the Wessex edition of 1912, denying "a consistent philosophy" and "a coherent scientific theory of the universe", calls his works "mere impressions". The *Life* says "the mission of poetry is to record impressions, not convictions" and the Prefaces to *Tess* and *Jude* say that is what they do. Hardy's tentativeness is most explicit, naturally, in his most "philosophical" work, such as the poem "Nature's Questioning" or Sue's "vague and quaint imaginings" about "man's development" and "the First Cause"; but it is a fundamental characteristic of all his work. It is seen in the way he describes the appearance of people, and only conjectures their character, in the way that he says, particularly throughout *Tess*, that this or that "seemed" to be the case, or was "almost" or "as if" so. Angel "rightly or wrongly" preferred sermons in stones, Tess "rightly or wrongly" believed in his "sense of duty", Elizabeth-Jane was "rightly or wrongly" not effusive about life, Melbury "wisely or unwisely . . . resolved to fight his daughter's battle". "We may *wonder* whether . . . these anachronisms [Tess meeting Alec before Angel] will be corrected." Even the landscape, Salisbury Plain, expresses "reserve, taciturnity, and hesitation". Tentativeness and impressionism are of course connected, and are by Hardy: "In getting at the truth, we get only at the true nature of the impression that an object produces, the true thing in itself being still, as Kant shows, beyond our knowledge." But Hardy meant this, as perhaps Kant did, as a metaphysical fact, and not, as the British Empiricists do, as a mere epistemological problem for the empiricist to overcome. In Hardy, not knowing is connected with another admitted characteristic, his sense of isolation, in poems such as "Old Furniture" and "The Impercipient": "I known not how it may be with others . . . But well I know how it is with me"; "Why joys they've found I cannot find." Hardy's sense that we can only wonder and not know made him exceptionally sensitive to ordinary human ignorance. Some examples from a single novel, *The Woodlanders*, will suggest how frequent this is. Giles does not know his own power of suspending emotion, the conditions of his holding, or that Grace was determined to be less fastidious. Grace does not know her father deliberately preserved the brown spot on the ceiling or that Giles is ill. Melbury does not know that Grace is miserable, does not know why Felice changed her mind, or that he himself comes of an ancient family. Grace and Fitzpiers do not know that he will be unfaithful to her. Marty does not know that her revelation about her hair-piece will matter to a gentleman of fashion.[30]

This chapter has considered some factors hard to reconcile either with Hardy's claim to be modern in his day or with the idea that Victorian thinkers seriously influenced him. He chooses to write about a fairly remote past wherever possible, stressing its pastness, and writes better about it than about more recent times. He uses the word modern vaguely and applies it to much that is not really modern or only trivially so, and sometimes as a term of reproach. He expresses a pessimism not produced by modern causes, but timeless and congenital. By modern he sometimes means unpractical, and he is always for the practical and real against the intellectual or unreal. The concepts by which he generally explains event — circumstances, fate, change, providence — are unintellectual and do not really explain. Most often explanation is in terms of a too simple contrast between nature and civilisation: the latter is on the whole a hostile concept equated with artificiality. The ordinary interests of educated people are not presented sympathetically but only folk culture. Hardy's idea of tragedy is simple and medieval. He insists without irony on his and his characters' ignorance, and claims only to offer tentative impressions: surely someone with views about life in his own day, or someone to whom some particular ideological influence was important, would be more positive.

2 The Social Critic

Most criticism of Hardy is philosophical or artistic: On his "philosophy" (Braybrooke), "psychology" (Thurley), "pessimism" (Barzin), "art and thought" (Webster, Pinion), "background" (Rutland), "vision of man" (Southerington), and "universe" (Brennecke); on the influences of Schopenhauer (Garwood), Comte (Hyman), Darwin (Peckham, Stevenson), Arnold (de Laura) and Mill (Hyde); on his "art" (Lionel Johnson), "technique" (Beach), "poetic structure" (Brooks), the "form" or "forms" of the novels (Gregor, Kramer), his "aesthetic" (Zabel), and, on particular novels, the "style" of *The Mayor* (Heilman), the "language", " colour and movement" in *Tess* (Lodge, Tanner), symbolism in *Jude* (Holland). Or criticism is biographical (Evelyn Hardy, Blunden, Gittings). In some of these, and in other works (Grimsditch, Firor, Cecil) there is social reference but mainly to help the modern urban reader understand the rural subject-matter: "In clay-built cramped cottages men struggled year after year against wind and weather to support a wife and family on 7s. a week."[1] Some have explicitly denied that Hardy felt much concern about the "social condition" of the peasant, or was a "social reformer".[2]

But Hardy does advertise his social concern: hopes for "a closer interaction of the social machinery", thinks "there is something wrong in our social formulas'," enslaves Sue to "the social code".[3] If Hardy's actual social criticism were extensive, important, valid and contemporary, then the largely verbal argument so far, proceeding by examination of his use of words, such as modern, ideal, fate, nature and society, would be much less cogent. Even if Hardy's social criticism were important but not contemporary, it would alter the picture. He might, for example, be like George Eliot, who, in order that her readers might understand the problems of her own day, chose a dramatic date for her novels which was usually one generation, and in our instance two generations, earlier. The subject *is* discussed by Kettle, Brown, Maxwell, Merryn Williams, Raymond Williams and Lerner; Maxwell and Lerner focusing on *The Mayor*. Maxwell takes issue with Brown's statement that Henchard is representative of the fate of his agricultural community. It seems to me that Maxwell's arguments are really a criticism of Hardy rather than Brown. The contrast between old and new is cardinal in *The Mayor*, and, in his accounting methods, his entertainment, his approval of the seed drill and his scientific ability to nearly restore the growed wheat, Farfrae does represent the new, and the structure requires that Henchard should in every way be contrasted with him. But Hardy is unable to choose a dramatic date late enough for wheat prices not to be greatly affected by the home harvest, because he wants a wife-sale and a skimmington, so the failure of Henchard and success of Farfrae is due to a difference in their abilities to play the market in the same way, and not between innocent agrarian economy and new market ethics: not, that is, socially representative, but one of the many personal differences between them.

Brown regards the "agricultural tragedy" as "the substance of Hardy's narrative art", but in fact he always qualifies the emphasis he places on "the agricultural theme": here, by the word "narrative", elsewhere by preferring the agricultural to the "philosophical context" and by making the "fabular" a second pole of Hardy's art beside the sociological.[4]

Raymond Williams, influenced by Marxism, sees Hardy's Wessex as already a changing society, changing in accordance with historical process. For Lerner "what Williams finds is often really there" but "his emphasis is wrong . . . and there is far more truth in the more familiar reading of Hardy, which sees him as recording the advent of change in a world hitherto hardly touched by historical movements . . . a single cultural upheaval". Lerner rightly points out that on the one hand there is more social reference in *The Mayor* than Maxwell allows for, but, on the other, that Henchard is not ruined by economic forces. He mentions Hardy's letter to Rider Haggard (*Life*, 312) and "The Dorsetshire Labourer", and concludes that as between old and new, "it is difficult to say clearly which side Hardy is on" — he is a sociologist rather than an economist and an archaeologist rather than a historian. "His greatness lies . . . in his full rendering of the life of Gemeinschaft."

A sociologist who does not take sides is fine as an academic, but as a novelist he is without social concern. Moreover, if some of Lerner's particular judgements are not accepted, the rendering becomes less full. For him, Elizabeth-Jane's marriage is sociological: "the normal way for women to rise in that society was by marriage" and marriage to Farfrae was "a happy ending . . . society having given her a fit reward". But she marries to become respectable, to escape the slur of illegitimacy, and it is not a particularly happy or social ending: she shows "nervous pleasure rather than gaiety" at her wedding, and after it her complexion becomes "somewhat richer . . . an incipient matronly dignity settling on her face": time, not society. Nor is she, as Lerner says, for the old, rejecting the seed-drill: characteristically she is neutral as between Farfrae and Henchard and says only " 'How things change!' " In his unwillingness to make a hole in a guinea Farfrae represents not "a new world" (Lerner) but the comic Aberdonian, as he does when referring to "Willie Dunbleeze and Maitland Macfreeze". To reduce Whittle's wages instead of debagging him is not "to introduce into the agricultural world of Wessex the spirit of the industrial revolution, the depersonalising of labour relations": it is two different people's ways of dealing with the problem. And while Mixen Lane is of course sociological in that it is a picture of society's unfortunates, the vagueness of the picture lessens the fullness of the rendering: "distress, . . . debt, and trouble of every kind. . . . Vice ran freely in and out . . .; recklessness dwelt under the roof . . .; shame in some bow windows; theft . . . even slaughter . . . disease" — abstractions recalling Gray's *Eton* Ode: the only specific element is the lifeholders, who had already figured in *Desperate Remedies* and were to reappear in *The Woodlanders* and *Tess.* Lerner claims that the stories told in the novels are signs of tensions in the society, but gives no examples: the stories told at the end of *The Woodlanders* are of married couples quarrelling, parting and coming together again — continuity, not tension.[5]

Rather than a sociological "single cultural upheaval" we are

aware of something gradual and natural: the long, slow continuous action of time, something more powerful because of its
length than the individual life-span. Angel has advanced some
way in twenty-five years, but is still "the slave to custom"; Jude
and Sue went too far too soon, but another fifty or a hundred
years will do it. The slowness of change at Weatherbury is
shown by the fact that "nothing less than century set a mark on
its face or tone". Some of the centuries are briefly introduced,
for instance (in *Tess*, to contradict the notion that Tess is a
"daughter of Nature") the medieval, Jacobean, Georgian,
Victorian and modern ages; or (in *Jude*) the effect of the Dissolu-
tion of the monasteries on Shaston. Casterbridge's "venerable
seedlip" and Marty's stone age barking tool, like geological time,
the "pounded champains of the past", remind us of the great
length of past time. Hardy's preference for the period just before
he was born, the lack of detailed reference to earlier periods, and
his limited interest in social questions, are the sources of any
impression of a single cultural upheaval. If that was what he intended to record, he should have done so emphatically, concen-
tratedly, and unmistakably.[6]

Since poverty, wealth and marketing are unavoidable subjects
in a market town, conclusions about *The Mayor* are not necessarily valid for the other novels. But even in *The Mayor* the contrasts are felt to be not so much social as poetic or imaginative.
I discuss the contrast between poverty and wealth later in this
chapter. The other contrasts are between the characters of
Henchard and Farfrae and between the old and the new.
Farfrae's method of accounting is as old as Minos – simply
book-keeping – and only new in comparison with people like
Henchard: Hardy is vague about how he will restore the growed
wheat: the main social effect of the seed-drill, that it will cause
unemployment, is not mentioned.

A detailed study is needed of the whole range of Hardy's
social criticism. It is not to be found in Lerner, Brown or
Merryn Williams. Lerner's and Brown's approaches do not require it. Lerner places Hardy's greatness in his "full rendering of
the life of Gemeinschaft", Brown in his "power to quicken
apprehension of the quality and value of life in the agricultural

community", Merryn Williams in his seeing "what was moving and growing within a whole society". But Brown's "defeat of our peasantry and collapse of our agriculture" has its simple cause in the invasion of the outsider — Fancy, Troy, Wildeve, Farfrae, Fitzpiers: he needs no more detailed social criticism: his social details are the details of what is collapsing, "the seasons of the fair, of the harvest, the sheep-washing", "the bonfire ritual and the wedding rejoicings, the mumming and the fair and the effigy".

Merryn Williams's conclusion is that Hardy

> tended to concentrate . . . on . . . all those who had been con-sidered unworthy of a place in literature up to that time. . . . Hardy's greatness lies in the fact that he transformed into literature a whole area of experience which had never yet been explored . . . the lives of ordinary people. . . . This re-quired an imaginative recreation, from the inside of . . . the thwarted humanity, the inarticulate fullness of emotion, of such men and women as Jude and Tess.

Her method is to describe, rather selectively, the rural England of the period, and when she comes to Hardy's Wessex, rather to re-peat this description, saying that Hardy is accurate; and then to characterise individual novels in a rather general sociological way: in *Under the Greenwood Tree* we are concerned with social adjustment, in *Far from the Madding Crowd* characters are more defined in terms of work, in *The Woodlanders* the community has less capacity for resistance. This makes her largely repeat the literary criticism found in most books about Hardy, and be largely concerned, as Brown was, with Hardy's presentation of Wessex. And just as Brown wrote of Hardy's nos-talgia and the fabular pole of his art, of his treating the collapse "in imaginative form", and Hardy himself wrote of Wessex as "a . . . partly dream country", so she writes of "imaginative recreation". But did Hardy's treatment include adequate social concern about real injustices? Merryn Williams calls Giles, Tess and Jude "representative": "Tess is a representative of ex-ploited and betrayed country girls. Jude is an "obscure" work-

ing man struggling for the educational heritage which has for
centuries been denied to his class." For Hardy's characters to be
representative, "ordinary people", they must be socially realised,
and if they have been "exploited", "denied" and "thwarted"
we must know whether by bad individuals or bad social
institutions.[7]

We should first consider the social phenomena which Merryn
Williams shows to be mentioned by Hardy. There is no social injustice in a merchant buying himself into the landed gentry,
since he may wish to farm; but the Stokes did not do this, since
The Slopes had "not an acre of troublesome land"; and it is not
a new phenomenon, since the Bingleys had done it in *Pride and
Prejudice* and Sir Andrew Freeport when Addison wanted to
wind up *The Spectator*. This is one kind of social mobility. The
ups and downs of Henchard and Oak are another, but still not
unjust. The injustice in the lack of social mobility from which
Jude suffered is the consequence of his lack of education, which
I discuss later in the chapter. Since Hardy does record social
mobility it is difficult to see Alec's seduction of Tess, Fitzpiers's
sexual laxity, or Melbury's "faith in members of long established
families", as expressions of Hardy's indignation about class dis-
tinctions. Melbury here is described as "old-fashioned", just as
Henchard's method of accounting was. The whole business of
the peasant descended from aristocratic stock, which is found
so often in Hardy, is simply a Tringhamesque, idiosyncratic,
antiquarian interest of Hardy's, which is never outside *The
Woodlanders* worked into the motivation: its only effect in *Tess*
is when Angel sees the d'Urberville portraits.[8]

That Oak becomes a "victim of the labour-market" is not
presented as social injustice. Hardy does not consider any other
way of dealing with unemployment.

As to female labour, Hardy himself draws attention to the
fact that Tess's labours at Flintcomb-Ash are untypical: "Female field-labour was seldom offered now" although he adds
"and its cheapness made it profitable for tasks which women
could perform as readily as men". Merryn Williams's statistics
show that the first part of this sentence is true: as to the second,
the tasks Tess performs are not those that women could readily

perform, and when it comes to the reed-drawing Hardy admits this by reintroducing the "two Amazonian [Darch] sisters" and commenting: "They did all kinds of *men's work by preference,* including well-sinking, hedging, ditching and excavating. . . . Noted reed-drawers were they too". And even in regard to Tess's position on the threshing-machine, although Hardy has said that "for some probably economical reason it was usually a woman who was chosen for this particular duty", he is surely also speaking authorially through Alec when Alec says that " 'on all the better class of farms it has been given up' ". In "The Dorsetshire Labourer" he had written that "I am not sure whether at the present time women are employed to feed the machine." The representation of Jude as scaring birds in 1860 at the age of eleven is not inaccurate, but it is not the continuing social injustice of child-labour in 1896, after the passing of the Agricultural Children's Act of 1873.[9]

Hardy ignores the emigration of about six million people from England and Wales between 1821 and 1871. Nobody emigrates except Newson and Tim Tangs: Henchard and Farfrae consider it. Tangs's emigration is presented as to rescue Suke from Fitzpiers: he needn't have gone so far, and anyway this is personal not social: any husband might move house to save his marriage. Migration, the drift to the town, and the related questions of land ownership and the tied cottage, Hardy does consider: these are social phenomena and he shows concern about them, but in a restricted way and submerged by other matters. Lifehold "was already in decline in the nineteenth-century" and originated in the past. Copyhold is likewise because persons "were ousted from their little plots when the system of leasing large farms grew general". In "The Dorsetshire Labourer" Hardy gives qualified approval to peasant proprietorship, but in the novels he advocates neither this nor allotments, though both were the policy of the National Union: the allotment in *Tess* is simply a place where she does her duty to her family and meets Alec. The migration of ordinary labour, except for the young man nearly separated from his girl in *The Mayor,* is not considered at all in the novels, though it is in "The Dorsetshire Labourer", where "this increasingly nomadic habit" means only the loss of the landowner "as a court of final appeal in cases of . . . harsh dismissal . . . by the farmer": otherwise "the artistic merit of their old condition is scarcely a reason why they should have continued in it. . . . Progress and picturesqueness do not harmonise." In the novels it is the departure of the "better-informed class" he regrets, because they were "depositories of the village traditions": here, as in the letter to Rider Haggard, we see the local historian rather than the social reformer. Again, in "The Dorsetshire Labourer", Hardy objects to the tied cottage, "the customary system of letting the cottages with the land" as instability for the labourer, but what happens to Giles and to Tess's family is different. In Tess's case it is presented as natural and almost reasonable: "The father, and even the mother, had got drunk at times . . . and the eldest daughter had made queer unions." Giles's loss of his house is due partly to failure to extend the lifehold, and partly to Felice being a bad landlord, and does not result in his migrating permanently from the Hintocks. Hardy or his characters do frequently complain of the pulling down of houses and although this is partly nostalgic – the loss of the picturesque – it is also social: "There were five houses cleared away last year, and three this; and the volk [including Henchard] nowhere to go.[10]

Hardy's favourite social subjects are marriage, the Church, education and poverty. As to poverty: only small candles are used by the Days, "fourteens", Reuben's trousers have enough material in them to make a waistcoat and more, Mrs Day's concern with appearances is related to her wish to distinguish herself from a beggar, Shiner's friend's new gig and Maybold's silk umbrella and promised piano and pony-carriage give them unfair advantages, and Dick and Fancy are threatened, at least by grandfather James, with being "too poor to have time to sing". A Bath "parson" has gold rings which Parson Thirdly can't afford, and Matthew Moon comments: " 'How unequal things be,' " and £550 makes Fanny Robin, at least in Boldwood's eyes, a bride acceptable by Troy. Elfride's father's marriage to a wealthy widow makes possible immediate publication of her novel, and Lady Constantine's wealth provides Swithin with the equipment he needs for his astronomy. Henry Knight's rooms are in Bede's Inn, which backs on a "crowded and poverty-stricken . . . network of alleys", and Hardy describes "the moral consequences" of this: first that one may see "shirtless humanity's habits and enjoyments" without doing anything about it, and "second, they may hear wholesome though unpleasant social reminders", namely violence and drunkenness. Poverty, reinforced by the economic threat of loss of her cottage, forces Marty to give up her hair and work long, badly-paid hours. There is pressure on Tess herself to make a rich marriage: "Why didn't ye think of doing something good for your family . . .? See how I've got to teave and slave.' " Poverty makes it difficult for Jude as a boy to get books and impossible later to become a university student with or without a scholarship, and as a result poverty dogs him and Sue throughout life. Indeed Jude says: " 'It was my poverty and not my will that consented to be beaten,' " although, since he is a qualified mason and there is no shortage of work, it is really (not that this makes it unrealistic) poverty combined with prejudice against the employment of one "living in sin".[11]

The Mayor, as is natural since it is located in a market town, is much more concerned with money and the lack of it than any of Hardy's other novels. " 'The starvation wages refined folk are likely to pay' " lead Henchard to offer Elizabeth-Jane an allowance; and Henchard's man, after the collision with Farfrae's waggon, refuses to defend himself because " 'I know nothing, sir, outside eight shillings a week.' " The effects of poverty are explored. " 'We be bruckle folk here – the best o' us hardly honest sometimes, what with hard winters, and so many mouths to fill,' " says Coney. And he digs up, with Longways's approval, the ounce pennies: " ' . . . money is scarce and throats get dry. Why *should* death rob life o' fourpence?' " Poverty, but for Farfrae, would destroy the love of the young shepherd and his girl: " 'I can't starve father, and he's out of work at Lady Day. . . . I shall never see e'e again.' " It is because of poverty that money is over-valued and, in a sense, money alone is felt to be real. Thus it was "the sight of real money" that made the spectators take the wife-sale seriously, and Susan thinks she must not desert Newson "when he had paid so much

for me". Hence again the popular admiration for and dislike of
the wealthy, and the general focusing on the money factor.
When Farfrae marries Lucetta, the "great point of interest" on
"kerbstones" etc. is whether he "would sell his business and set
up for a gentleman on his wife's money". And later "as the
Mayor and man of money . . . he had lost in the eyes of the
poorer inhabitants something of that wondrous charm which he
had for them as a light-hearted penniless young man". Instead
of being one of them, singing to their hearts, he is divided
from them by his money.[12]

Henchard is a true hero, representative of his people, in this
respect. He echoes their sentiments about Farfrae's marriage:
" 'tis her money that floats en upward' ". It is, ultimately, his
acquaintance with poverty that causes him to repeat his original
offence by buying Susan back, to "recompense" Lucetta with
"a useful sum" for not being able to marry her, and to pass immediately   from   the   decision   to allow   Farfrae   to   court
Elizabeth-Jane   to   the   thought   of   "a   marriage   portion".
Similarly, Melbury says to Grace, referring to her expensive education: " 'If   you   do   cost   as   much   as   they   [the 'horses and
waggons   and   corn'],   never   mind.   You'll   yield   a   better
return.' "[13]

"A gentleman on his wife's money": the phrase suggests one
limitation to Hardy's social concern about poverty. The rich
generally are or become ladies and gentlemen and do nothing
worthwhile with their money, and this suggests poverty is no
great loss. The money goes on class, clothes, jewelry, grand
houses, and foreign travel. Mrs Troyton, with her £3,500 a year,
acquires a pedigree, a house in town, a carriage in the Row, and
holidays in Torquay, Bath and Paris: half a page is spent in describing her jewels. Wildeve's £11,000 will take him to Paris,
Italy, Greece, Egypt, Palestine, America, Australia, India. And
"in Eustacia's eyes . . . it was . . . sufficient to supply those
wants of hers which had been stigmatised by Clym . . . as vain
and luxurious". Felice buys herself a hair-piece, dines in a gown
hardly higher than her elbows, travels abroad, and yawns.
Fitzpiers and Lady Constantine also yawn; whereas in "upland
hamlets" "no . . . yawns and toilets" delay "the transition from

a-bed to abroad". Knight, Ethelberta and her classy friends, and Paula and *her* classy friends, travel on the Continent: Angel and Lady Constantine's brother pop over to Brazil and back.[14]

The diamond is the folk image of value and class: " 'What a gentleman he is . . . and how his diamond studs shine!" is Elizabeth-Jane's first impression of Henchard. Mrs Durbeyfield notes that Alec " 'wears a beautiful diamond ring' ". Tess acquires and wears Mrs Pitney's diamonds but only to prove that "a peasant girl . . . will bloom as an amazing beauty, if clothed as a woman of fashion". Clym is praised for giving up both diamonds and Paris, and the diamond merchant recurs negatively in comparing Jude's vision of a heavenly city with *Revelation*'s.[15]

The life lived in big houses, whether ancestral or recently acquired by money, is not enviable. Of Stancy Castle and Hintock House as well as High Place Hall it is true that " 'Blood built it, and wealth enjoys it.' " Although the Laodicean Paula wishes Stancy Castle wasn't burnt, Hardy and the hero are glad to leave it "beautiful in its decay": for Paula it has been only a place of idle amusements, with its garden-party, private gymnasium, amateur theatricals, family portraits and ghosts. The lady of Hintock House, ex-actress, absentee, " 'was never in the county till my husband brought me here' ": the curtains are drawn in the daytime, and everything left to the agent. So it is at Enckworth Court, where there is also high-class immorality, till both are reformed by the plebeian Ethelberta. The Stoke-D'Urbervilles' place, The Slopes, has no function in the community: it has "not an acre of troublesome land", and their cottage, " 'good enough for Christians in grandfather's time' " has been turned into a fowl-house.[16]

The other limitation of Hardy's social concern with poverty is that events which might have been ascribed to it are not. One example is the deaths of children. No comment is made on the deaths of Mr Penny's five grandchildren except his own " ''twas to be' ". The death of Sorrow, which, if Kettle's analysis of *Tess* had been right, could so easily have been shown to be due to Tess having to work and feed her baby at the same time and to lack of pre-natal care and proper arrangements for confinement, is introduced by saying that "now that her moral sorrows were passing away a fresh one arose on the *natural* side of her which knew no social law". "Going on the parish" is another theme that Hardy might have developed into social criticism and doesn't appear to. We are told without comment that Gabriel's family did this: combined with the other things that happen to him and Bathsheba the point seems to be to show what ups and downs might naturally occur in Wessex. Mrs Cuxsom's mother " 'were rewarded by the Agricultural Society for having begot the greatest number of healthy children without parish assistance' ": one may read into this brain-washing of the underdog to keep the rates down. Creedle is dismayed by the prospect of being (like Fanny Robin, *verbatim*) "nailed up in parish boards" but Hardy does not think it matters what happens to you when you are dead. And Fanny's poverty (" 'Have you any money?' [asks Troy] 'None.' ") is only social in that her pregnancy, like Tess's, is felt as social shame. She left her job voluntarily, was not dismissed, and in fact left to get married, so her situation is entirely an individual's, Troy's, fault. Again, Gabriel's ruination by loss of his uninsured sheep is not social: he could have insured them: indeed it is out of character for him not to have done, unless one is meant to infer that the wisdom he later shows stems from such disasters. Venn does not become a reddleman from a farmer for social reasons: "He had relinquished his proper station in life for want of interest in it," i.e. from the Wessex equivalent of despair at unrequited love of Thomasin. One has only to think of Smike to realise that Christian Cantle, with "a great quantity of wrist and ankle beyond his clothes" and Creedle with his "cast-off soldier's jacket . . . top-boots . . . picked up by chance, . . . pocket-knife . . . given him by a . . . sailor" are not social criticism. Creedle's clothes are part of the appearance-reality theme in *The Woodlanders*: they tell us something about their previous wearers which can be recovered through "a military memoir . . . a hunting memoir . . . also chronicles of voyaging and shipwreck" but nothing about Creedle.[17]

Finally, the main cause of poverty is low wages. By the time Hardy was writing, they had risen from eight to eleven or twelve shillings, with, as he says in "The Dorsetshire Labourer", rent-free cottage and garden, free fuel, and extra pay at harvest and for lambing and distant carting.[18]

Hardy's real criticism of marriage is not of the social mobility involved in the marriages of persons of different status but, as Mrs Oliphant saw in the case of *Jude*, "an assault on the stronghold of marriage" itself. *Jude* is not, as Hardy wrote to Gosse, concerned only with "the tragic issues of two bad marriages". Within *Jude* we cannot of course escape from the dramatic situation of each particular marriage, but all the marriages are bad. When we are shown Arabella and Cartlett married and unhappy at the Stoke-Barehills Show, the comment is that they are in "the antipathetic recriminatory mood of the average husband and wife of Christendom". It is Jude and Arabella who are absurd in swearing they will always "believe, feel and desire" the same as they do at the moment, Jude who is "licensed by the laws of his country" to love only Arabella, Jude who thinks Sue "does not realise what marriage means", and Sue, "possibly ... unfitted ... to fulfil the conditions of the matrimonial relation ... with ... any man" who thinks it "sordid" to be "licensed to be loved" and thinks "legal marriage" a "vulgar institution". But Jude and Sue are Hardy's mouthpieces. And it is not only *Jude*. In *The Well-Beloved*, Pierston recognizes a couple to be man and wife merely by hearing them quarrel.[19]

Granted Hardy's attitude to Christianity, discussed below, it is hardly necessary to spend time on his attacks on marriage as a Christian institution: the parson who married Jude and Arabella and thought it "satisfactory" because she was pregnant, the vicar who re-marries Sue and Phillotson and "highly approves". Characters as different as Sue, Troy and Fitzpiers agree that a ceremony before a priest doesn't make a marriage: it is a civil contract, not a sacrament. As little as possible is made of normal church weddings. Those of Dick Dewy and Fancy, Oak and Bathsheba, Wildeve and Thomasin, Clym Yeobright and Eustacia, Venn and Thomasin, Fitzpiers and Grace, Henchard and Susan (remarrying), Angel Clare and Tess, and Jude and Arabella, are not described, although Hardy considered himself "churchy". "In a remarkably short space of time the deed was done" is a typical comment. Where possible they take place off-stage, at Bath (Swithin's, and Bathsheba's to Troy) or Port Bredy (Lucetta's), or are planned to be in a registry office (Fitzpiers, Jude and Sue), or by special licence (Clare's, Phillotson's), or do not happen because it is the wrong church or the wrong licence (Troy's to Fanny Robin, Wildeve's to Thomasin, Stephen Smith's to Elfride).[20]

But it is not just marriage as a sacrament that Hardy objects to: it is civil marriage, what Sue calls "legal marriage", being "licensed by the laws", and the "law" itself, which, Arabella says, "if he turns you out of doors, you can get . . . to protect you", he does not want those laws reformed: he only picks on one particular reformable injustice, when Melbury says to Grace of Fitzpiers: " 'He has not done you *enough* harm.' " Even here there is not certainly a reference to the distinction under the Matrimonial Causes Act of 1857, which was not abolished until 1923, that simple adultery was grounds for divorcing a wife but not a husband. In *Jude* both Jude and Phillotson get divorces when they want them. If marriage is to be a social institution it must be protected by ecclesiastical or civil law and it always and everywhere has been, even if by such a loose law as the Roman one of *usus*.[21]

Hardy's statements in his prefaces to *Jude* and *The Wood-landers* confirm that Mrs Oliphant was right. In the Preface to *Jude* he says in reference to marriage, that "in Diderot's words, the civil law should be only the enunciation of the law of nature (a statement that requires some qualification by the way)". There is no law of nature about marriage and Hardy never supplies the "qualification", unless it is, as he also says in the *Jude* Preface, that "a marriage should be dissolvable as soon as it becomes as cruelty to either of the parties", which would lead to obvious difficulties and goes further even than the present principle of irretrievable breakdown. In the Preface to *The Woodlanders* he calls "matrimonial divergence" "the immortal puzzle", and the quotation from Milton's *Doctrine and Discipline of Divorce* in *Jude* further shows the timelessness of the puzzle. Once it is accepted that Hardy is attacking marriage it-

self many other passages fall into place. There is the story of
Bathsheba's father, who could only remain faithful to his wife
by making her take off her wedding-ring and fancying "he was
. . . committing the seventh". There is the opening picture of
Henchard and Susan not communicating: "That the man and
woman were husband and wife . . . there could be little doubt."
There are Grace's reflections, regretting her sarcasm to
Fitzpiers's other "wives": "It was well enough, conventionally,
to address either one of them in the wife's regulation terms of
virtuous sarcasm . . . , fellow-women whose relations with him
were as close as her own without its conventionality." There is
the allaying of the landlord's suspicions that Jude and Arabella
are not married: "Overhearing her one night haranguing Jude in
rattling terms, and ultimately flinging a shoe at his head, he re-
cognized the note of genuine wedlock." We may even feel that
this is one of the points where Hardy sympathises with Eustacia
and Fitzpiers: "Fidelity in love for fidelity's sake had less
attraction for her than for most women: fidelity because of
love's grip had much." She " 'sank into the mire of marriage' ".
"The dance had come like an irresistible attack upon whatever
sense of social order there was in their minds." "The love of
men like Fitzpiers is unquestionably of such quality as to bear
division and transference." Thomasin and Eustacia ought to
have broken up their marriages if circumstances hadn't done it
for them. Henchard was right to sell his wife and ought never to
have remarried her or lost interest in Elizabeth-Jane on finding
she was not the product of his marriage.[22]

There is the same radical rather than social attitude in
Hardy's criticisms of the Church. "Good God! — the eastward
position, and all creation groaning,' " and the fact that "events
which produced heartache in others wrought beatific smiles
upon" Mercy Chant (which Hardy calls the "sacrifice of humanity to mysticism"), do suggest that the Church should be taking an active part in reforming social abuses. In referring to "the
Church of Ceremonies — St. Silas" and probably in his presentation of Angel's "non-evangelical" brothers, Hardy is making the
usual attack on the Tractarians, that they were too exclusively
concerned with ritual and theology. But he also attacks the

socially-conscious Evangelicals and Dissenters. Old Revd Clare *is*
"Evangelical" but it is "the hero under the pietist", "a *man* of
Apostolic simplicity in life and thought" that Hardy admires:
his disciples, Alec and the man with the paint-brush, represent
justification by faith (so you can *do* what you like, as Alec
does) and the inculcation of the fear of a "conjectural" hell.
The Dissenters make two brief appearances in *Jude* when they
expel Jude from the Artisans' Mutual Improvement Society because he's not married to Sue, and welcome Arabella when she
discovers that religion is "righter than gin". But the rustics' preference is for inactive clergy and Hardy never disapproves:
" 'Mr Grinham was the man! . . . He never troubled us wi' a visit
from year's end to year's end.' " Swancourt is criticised for
snobbery but not for being in the mould of Fielding's Trulliber.
Nor are the rustics reproved for not going to church. "The day
was Sunday; but . . . going to church . . . was exceptional at
Egdon." Granfer Cantle hasn't been for a year, Humphrey not
for three. William Worm stopped when he ceased to be employed by a parson. The drill-sergeant reproves the militia:
" 'How can you think of such trifles as church-going at such a
time . . . ' ". Nor do they go to church in Christminster. In
Wessex proper, they sleep, or drink instead: Granfer Cantle does
both: the women go to church to see the men. The church is
only useful for secular purposes, to house the salvage from the
fire at Carriford, or smuggled spirits, or the pikes to defeat
Napoleon. Giles only keeps a Psalter to whet his penknife on.
Bindon Abbey had perished, but the mill still worked. "Unlike
and superior to either of these two typical remnants of
medievalism" – the church and the castle – (but architecturally
like the church) – the Great Barn at Weatherbury is still used
for its original purpose. The clergy are mistaken if not actually
harmful: the rector confirms that Mrs Manston is dead, when
she isn't; Torkingham tells Lady Constantine she's a widow
when she isn't; Tringham having nothing better to do "hunts up
pedigrees" and is thus the origin of Tess's "tragic mischief".
Swithin's father, a clergyman, gives it up for the more useful job
of farming, and is killed in a thunderstorm, allowing Haymoss a
gibe at God.[23]

The only activity for which a clergyman is praised is charity, either of a kind which a layman could practise equally well (Parson Thirdly giving Coggan seed potatoes) or the ironical self-destroying charity of the parson who tells Tess "it will be just the same" if he doesn't baptise or bury Sorrow. It could not be otherwise since charity, as described in 1 Corinthians 13, and the Sermon on the Mount (Matthew 5), are all that Hardy values in Christianity. "The Blinded Bird" and Tess exemplify "apostolic charity", and Jude and Sue agree about it when they agree about nothing else. Tess believes in the *spirit* of the Sermon on the Mount, Cytherea is praised for observing that sermon's doctrines, and Poorgrass refers to it. Clym, like Tess, unites *Corinthians* and *Matthew*: he preaches the eleventh commandment (love thy neighbour) in addresses called Sermons on the Mount, the mount there being Rainbarrow.[24]

It is therefore not necessary to discuss Hardy's paganism and attacks on Christian theology. He saw no place for the Church in society and so could not and did not make or support any proposal for its reform. This is not to say that he was wrong, but merely that this was another field of social criticism which he, unlike for example George Eliot, with her approval of Catholic Emancipation and preference of Anglicans to Dissenters, did not enter.

Unlike marriage and the Church, education is necessarily a social matter, and it was a field in which the nineteenth century was exceptionally active, in legislation, unofficial effort and the variety of its views. Hardy deals with education in *A Pair of Blue Eyes, The Return, The Mayor, The Woodlanders, Tess* and *Jude*, and his overall criticism is the lack of educational opportunities in Wessex at all levels, primary, secondary, and university. It may be improper to import biographical considerations, but it is simplest to see Hardy's difficulty in approaching the subject as connected with his own feeling that after all he had educated himself. As social criticism this feeling, communicated by the many passages in the *Life* where he lists his reading, is not invalidated by the fact that he had received a good education up to the age of sixteen, since he might well not have done. Jude, Elizabeth-Jane, and to some extent Stephen Smith, are, as

Hardy felt he was, self-educated. It makes a difference whether
we are dealing with a woman's or a man's education.

" 'If they only knew what an unfinished girl I am — that I
can't talk Italian, or use globes, or show any of the accomplishments they learn at boarding schools . . . ! Better . . . buy myself grammar-books and dictionaries and a history of all the
philosophies!' " Elizabeth-Jane is not the poorer for being
without those boarding-school accomplishments, which Grace
has acquired before her story begins and which she learns not to
value: " 'I wish I worked in the woods like Marty. . . . I wish
you had never sent me to those fashionable schools.' " Grace
continues her reaction into her revived marriage with Fitzpiers,
forcing him, like Faustus, to burn his books — his "philosophical literature", "old plays" and "French romances".
Elizabeth-Jane does educate herself, although not with a history
of philosophy: beginning with a sound knowledge of the Bible
she reads the Golden Treasury and Ovid, but these are still the
same kind of things as Italian and the use of the globes and they
make no difference to the outcome for her, which is a rich complexion, matronly dignity and serene Minerva eyes. We are told
quite early on of her "wisdom" but if she acquires it during the
novel it is by observing events, "watching", and surely she is the
demonstration that wisdom is impotent to change events. But
Grace's and Elizabeth-Jane's education is only limitedly a social
question, since their destiny is to be wives: it is her own
"happiness" that Grace's education hasn't given her. Tess's case
is not entirely different. She had a good education up to Sixth
Standard at a National School, and intended to be a teacher.
This was interrupted by a social cause: the poverty of her
family which required her to claim kin. Her further education is
by Angel and results in views such as "an ethical system without
any dogma", of which Hardy approves: but she is still regarded
as a wife for Angel, that is, a farmer's wife. " 'The perfect
woman . . . was a working woman . . . not a fine lady.' " The
skill in dairying necessary for a farmer's wife was available to
her and Wessex without formal education. Even Sue is in a
sense self-educated like Tess, although far more widely read:
thanks partly to London and partly to her undergraduate boy-

friend. She doesn't echo Jude's views, as Tess does Angel's, but contradicts them, though like Tess's her position is Hardyan and sceptical until she recants.[25]

We should therefore look at the men. But Stephen is treated rather like the women: educated like Tess at a National School, he has learned chess from a book and so handles the pieces oddly, but he *has* learned it. He pronounces Latin oddly, having learned it by post from Henry Knight, but he can cap, and translate, an obscure quotation from Horace. He is also a successful architect, but that happens off-stage. He has not really suffered from the lack of educational opportunities, but he has a sense of inferiority to people like Knight.[26]

Through Angel's brothers Hardy is really trying to say what he suggests in *Jude*, that the universities, Oxford and Cambridge, are really only theological colleges. In *Jude* he suggests it by having Tinker Taylor speak of " 'them jobbing pa'sons swarming about here" ', but mainly by cataloguing the Christminster worthies as seen by Jude on his arrival there and at his death, and the books he burns. Naturally the books Jude burns are Christian apologists since he has given up trying to become a minister of religion. But the other catalogues also divide almost entirely into good Christians, bad Christians and anti-Christians. The good Christians are Bishop Ken, John Wesley, Dr Johnson, and (probably) Addison, Sir Thomas Browne, Wyclif and Hooker: Ken because his Evening Hymn equated learning to live with learning to die, Wesley because of his concern for the poor, Dr Johnson because of his charitable life, Addison because of his last words and the *Spectator,* one of Hardy's stylistic models, Hooker because he subordinated the Church to natural law. The bad Christians are the Tractarians, Newman, Keble and Pusey, and Arnold because of his "neo-Christianity". The anti-Christians are Gibbon, Shelley, Swinburne and in a sense Bolingbroke, whom Hardy calls 'sceptic'. The only others mentioned are Burton, because of his melancholy, Peel because of the corn laws, Browning because of his mistaken optimism, Ben Jonson, Raleigh and Harvey. The suggestion is both that the universities were more liberal in the old days and that they are now, and to some extent always were (though in the old days all were called Christian) places to go to only to become parsons.[27]

It is only a suggestion. "If Angel were not going to enter the Church, what was the use of sending him to Cambridge? The University as a step to anything but ordination seemed, *to this man of fixed ideas* [Angel's father], a preface without a volume. . . . Perhaps if Angel had persevered he might have gone to Cambridge like his brothers." But he didn't, and being a gentleman was none the worse. But his brothers did, and both became parsons, and one, to enforce the connection between Oxbridge and Church, became Fellow and Dean of a Cambridge college.[28]

So far then there is no social injustice: nobody has lost anything of value by being deprived of formal education. But what about Jude? He is not a gentleman and could not have gone to Oxford or Cambridge. Why not? The sensational letter of the Master of Biblioll ("remain in your own sphere . . . stick to your trade"), combined with the failures of the other heads of colleges to reply to Jude's enquiries (which there is no way of estimating the probability of), take attention away from the real reason, which however Hardy states with perfect clarity: "To qualify himself for certain open scholarships and exhibitions . . . a good deal of coaching would be necessary. . . . [Otherwise] at the rate at which . . . he would be able to save money, fifteen years must elapse before he could . . . advance to a matriculation examination".[29] But Jude has in fact, like Elizabeth-Jane and to some extent like Tess and Stephen Smith, educated himself, and we are meant to accept his quotation from *Job* — "I have understanding as well as you: I am not inferior to you" — as the truth. If Jude had gone to school and known early enough that he wanted to go to Oxford he would have been prepared for, and won, a scholarship to Oxford, just as Hardy himself could have done. Hardy had his parents to thank for his secondary education. If he had met the right people, Jude could have prepared himself for a scholarship even without formal schooling. What made it impossible for Jude was the combination of orphanhood and lack of schooling, even primary schooling.

If we accept Hardy's own dating in the *Life* ("about 1860–1870") taking it to mean that the story opens about 1860, since the main action is ten years later (though the main action itself lasts "eight or nine years"[30] so that Hardy may mean the story opens in 1850 or ends in 1880), there is no improbability in Jude's lack of primary schooling, before the Forster Act. Even after 1870, in some counties the Act was not implemented until about ten years later. Jude at the relevant time was in Mellstock, and, if that is Stinsford, came under the Dorset School Board. But Jude's situation had been remedied by the Forster Act, so there is no modern social criticism here.

There *is* modern social criticism in representing Oxford as not worthy the name Christminster, not the "City of light" where "the tree of knowledge grows", not the "intellectual and spiritual granary of this country", the "great centre of high and fearless thought" but, in Sue's words, "a nest of commonplace schoolmasters whose characteristic is timid obsequiousness to tradition".[31] But is it just? Science began to be studied there about 1850, the year that the Royal Commissions began to investigate it, supported by the then Master of Biblioll, Jowett, the author of the best of Hardy's favourite *Essays and Reviews*. Dissenters were admitted as undergraduates in 1854 and as fellows in 1871. Ruskin was Slade Professor in 1870. Apart from Oxford, the constitution of government departments of Science and Art and Education, the foundation of schools of design, working-men's colleges, teacher training colleges and the National Education League, the foundation and growth of provincial and London universities and extension lectures, the commissions of enquiry into public schools and grammar schools, the Radical bills which preceded the Forster Act — all these things, un-mentioned by Hardy, are signs of the democratisation of education during the period he is dealing with. Hardy's remark in the *Life*, in 1926, that "Christminster . . . is not meant to be exclusively Oxford, but any old-fashioned University about the date of the story, 1860–1870, before there were such chances for poor men as there are now" does suggest the possibility that after publication he pushed the date back because he realised how little modern social criticism there was in *Jude*. But reading the novel, one does not have the impression that it is intended to be a description of obsolete conditions. Most

clearly the mention of Ruskin College and the approval of the
German claim of modernity for Sue, in the 1912 Postscript, suggest the opposite.

"For a moment there fell on Jude a true illumination; that
here in the stoneyard was a centre of effort as worthy as that
dignified by the name of scholarly study within the noblest of
colleges. But he lost it under stress of his old idea."[32] We lose it
too, but it suggests two trains of thought. First, if he had not
lost it, he couldn't have been a parson or a teacher, but he
could, while working as a mason, have educated himself further,
either vocationally through works of the Penny Encyclopedia
kind or liberally through extension lectures and so on. That he
did not consider these possibilities could be put down to his "old
idea" — to get into Christminster — or to the general ignorance
which makes him tragic. Like Tess he learns everything too late.
This is true not only of narrowly educational matters, but of his
innocence about women and ignorance of his own nature.
Orphanhood makes his ignorance more realistic, but himself less
representative. But his experiences might up to a point be those
of many children, even today, children neither orphans nor deprived of primary schooling but whose parents and teachers do
not or cannot take the trouble they should, or who themselves
take the wrong educational decisions. Jude's position is true to
life, rather than true to 1860–90.

The other train of thought leads from this ignorance and
brings us back *via* Clym to education. Jude doesn't know what
marriage is like, whether he can get into Christminster, what he
could learn there if he did, or whether he wants to be a scholar
or a bishop or a licentiate or simply to have a good relationship
with Sue. He doesn't settle in any of these things and so he
doesn't succeed in them. He begins with experiences of dis-
harmony (between the birds and Troutham, between the
Carmen Saeculare and Christminster) and ends "in a chaos of
principles" knowing only that "there is something wrong somewhere in our social formulas". In a way, Jude does settle and
succeed with Sue: "the twain were happy — between their times
of sadness". And Sue says "We gave up all ambition, and were
never so happy in our lives till his illness came." If this were

Arnold or George Eliot or Lawrence we would know what to think of this: turn to private life because the world is ignorant armies clashing by night; or have your private life in one current with a larger duty; or let other activities be judged by whether or not they go with satisfactory human relationships. But Sue's and Jude's happiness is broken by "times of sadness': not only Jude's illness, not only those sadnesses they have surmounted by giving up ambition, but Sue's last pregnancy, the hangings and their consequences. If Hardy were saying that the important thing, at least for Jude and Sue, was a good private life, then the lack of education wouldn't matter. Because we cannot say what career, if any, Jude ought to have had, we cannot say what of value he was deprived of. If we turn to *The Return* we find that there too Hardy's ideas of education can only be stated in general terms: "knowledge of a sort which brings wisdom rather than affluence".[33]

Hardy's omissions reduce his value as a social critic. The period from 1815 to 1870 is called by one historian the Age of Reform, and the period from 1783 to 1867 by another the Age of Improvement. One might sum up the reform and improvement by contrasting Burke's statement in 1795 that "to provide for us in our necessities is not in the power of government" with what the Report of the Royal Commission in 1871 considered "necessary for civilised life": water-supply, drainage, prevention of nuisances, provision of healthy houses, inspection of food, proper burial, suppression of the causes of disease. Many of these applied mainly or wholly to towns, and many were neglected in country areas, but a social critic should be concerned with the neglect. Amongst the things which helped reform and improvement between 1820 and 1880 but which Hardy doesn't mention are: working men's institutes and colleges, public libraries, the Forster Act, the reduction of import duties and increase of imports and of population, the abolition of bull- and bear-baiting, the Tithe Commutation Act, Chartism, the mass emigrations, separate prisons for young offenders and other prison reforms, the repeal of the combination laws and formation of agricultural trade unions, the acquisition by tenants of the right to kill and sell game, the restriction of capital punishment to murder and treason, the growth of police forces, the establishment of county courts, the repeal of the window tax, the extension of the franchise, the abolition of flogging in the army, the spread of contraception, the reduction of road tolls, and the numerous inventions – of chloroform, paraffin, the hypodermic syringe, antisepsis, the thermometer, the sewing machine, the bicycle, the typewriter, and the microphone. And, to go further back, Hardy says, as has been pointed out, nothing about the principal elements of the eighteenth-century agrarian revolution, enclosure and the improvement in winter feeding of livestock.[34]

Even in matters where Hardy feels deeply there is sometimes uncertainty of treatment, for instance cruelty to animals. We have the blinded bird, the caged goldfinch, the dying pheasants, the stuck pig, the rabbit caught in a gin, the dogs drowned and stoned, the horse kicked in the belly. But we also have cheerful pig-killings, and no authorial comment on the birds Swithin catches roosting for Lady Constantine's supper.[35]

Hardy's limitations as a social critic may be indicated by contrasting him with George Eliot. We know that she thinks that agriculture in the Middlemarch area would benefit if landowners would read and put into practice Sir Humphry Davy's *Elements of Agricultural Chemistry* and J. C. Loudon's *Encyclopaedia of Cottage, Farm and Villa Architecture*. We see rick-burning and sheep-stealing in the context of the time: the latter ceased to be a capital offence during the duration of the novel, and after Brooke's protégé was hanged. Knowing of the cholera epidemics of 1831–2 we get the point of a proposal, the year before, to build a fever hospital. Because we are allowed into the minds of educated people, we see the bearing on ordinary lives of the work of Bichat, Robert Brown, Schleider and Schwann on "primitive tissue" and cell nuclei. We know that George Eliot wants coroners to be medically trained and that this is reasonable, as an act to that effect was passed in 1836. We would not expect George Eliot, from our knowledge of her views on society, to approve of experiments like New Lanark, but when she puts a proposal for a similar experiment in the mouth of Dorothea we feel the possibility as part of the social picture as well as knowing that it is not the right way out for Dorothea. We feel the impact of the railways during the dramatic period of the novel and before the first period of railway building through the attack on the surveyors and the attitudes of Featherstone, Mrs Waule, Garth and Timothy Cooper.[36]

Hardy is not George Eliot. His rick burns in order that Oak may minimise the damage: nothing is said about how the fire started. His horse-stealer is hanged, not in order that the law may be changed, but in order that his ghost may appear to his trampwoman on the day she bears his of course stillborn child. Hardy's cholera is merely to lead to the heroic death of his hero and destroy the infidelity of that hero's wife. His railways are either (for instance in *The Mayor*) not there when they should have been; or when they are there, it is to give "intermittent moments of contact" with "secluded" Wessex or make possible "modern unrest" (in *Jude*) and lead to the desolation of roads and unemployment of reddlemen.[37]

The persuasiveness of Brown's argument is owed to the fact that when he pleases Hardy can be extraordinarily accurate, even if he has, as we have seen, to go back into the past and bend dates to be so. He says man-traps "were in use down to the third decade of the nineteenth-century" and "well-nigh discontinued" by 1840, and they were in fact made illegal in 1827. He is right in calling the steam threshing machine "as yet . . . itinerant in this part of Wessex": introduced in the mid-1840s, it superseded flail and horse by 1880. He mentions the repeal of the corn laws, even though only in a Preface, and even though he clearly implies there that Henchard's and Farfrae's buying and selling occurred before it. The lack of church-going – Granfer Cantle and the man at the Chaseborough dance propose to "sleep it off in church-time", and this was what had destroyed medieval Shaston – is in accordance with the census of 1851 which showed that half the country went neither to church nor chapel. Casterbridge Union is in accordance with the New Poor Law of 1834. Farfrae's and Henchard's intentions to emigrate are in accordance with the mass emigrations during the period 1830–1870. Felice smokes cigarettes, which had been introduced to Britain after the Crimean War. One need not be too unhappy about Paula still having her own telegraph in 1881 when private lines had been taken over by the GPO in 1868. Since neither Angel nor Jude was a Dissenter there is no inaccuracy in Hardy's ignoring the admission of Dissenters to Oxford and Cambridge in 1854 and to fellowships there in 1871, but it spoils the argument that there is no point in going there unless you intend to be a parson.[38]

This accuracy is not only chronological, but is found in the detailed presentation of rural life: skills and activities such as the trochar, thatching and cider-making; social life; folkways. And this is important, because, whatever repetitiveness we may find in the characters, language, style, and human situations, the Wessex novels are clearly distinguished from one another by the rural work they describe, work which provides both the essential subject-matter and the poetic tone: sheep and cereals in *Far from the Madding Crowd*, furze in *The Return*, milling in *The Trumpet-Major*, marketing in *The Mayor*, trees in *The Woodlanders*, dairying in *Tess*, and masonry in *Jude*.[39]

We may conclude, then, that Hardy is indignant about poverty, but not always up-to-date or sociological in exploring its bearing; and indignant, but not up-to-date, about the lack of educational opportunity. On marriage, any particular social concern pales into insignificance beside his dislike of the institution itself. Some particular incidents have been given by critics a sociological meaning which they do not carry, and this is sometimes because of the vagueness of Hardy's treatment. Some other evils that he mentions, as well as the lack of educational opportunity, were obsolete when he wrote. He omits some social changes which occurred during his lifetime, and, of those he presents, admits that some are for the better. Poverty, superstition, inefficiency and deceit are part of the old ways. Nevertheless the overall impression is of the loss of much that is of value, though this is partly because of his idealisation, particularly of the rustic characters.[40] The fundamental impulse is neither social reform nor a tragic sense of agricultural collapse, but to record.

3 Ideas

If Hardy is not modern or important by virtue of his social criticism, is he so by virtue of some more general ideas? It seems natural to approach this question by re-considering how and how much Hardy was influenced by other writers, and to divide those influences into ideological, factual and stylistic.[1] I have already suggested[2] that Hardy's impressionism, tentativeness, and insistence on his own ignorance make it unlikely that he should be much influenced ideologically, but I shall consider this question here, and factual and stylistic influence in the following chapter. There has of course been much work done on ideological influences on Hardy, but some repetition is necessary here. In this chapter I shall not repeat the word "ideological" but simply speak of "influences", and I shall only consider Schopenhauer, Von Hartmann, Comte, Darwin, *Essays and Reviews*, Mill, Arnold, and Leslie Stephen. Hardy himself claimed to be more in harmony with Darwin, Huxley, Herbert Spencer, Hume and Mill than with Schopenhauer and Von Hartmann.[3] He also said that he had been "much influenced" by Leslie Stephen's "philosophy"[4] and "much impressed" as a young man by *Essays and Reviews*.[5]

There is no doubt of the presence of Schopenhauer and Von Hartmann in Hardy. In the "Apology" to *Late Lyrics and Earlier* he expressed "respect" for their, and other philosophers', "supercilious regard of hope". They are cited approvingly along with "most of the persons called pessimists" in a letter objecting to Maeterlinck's "vindication of Nature's ways".[6] Almost certainly the "Immanent Will" which destroyed the Titanic and which "stirs and urges everything", and the "circumstantial will" in *Tess* "at work . . . everywhere" which prevents enjoyment, and possibly the "Unfulfilled Intention" in *The Woodlanders* "which makes life what it is" are coined with Schopenhauer and Von Hartmann in mind. There are also passing references, as when old Revd Clare's determination is said to be akin to Schopenhauer and Leopardi, or in a poem, "The Pedestrian, an incident of 1883" where a student of Schopenhauer, Kant and Hegel is given only two months to live. It is probably Schopenhauer's image of happiness that was in Hardy's mind when he made Jude reflect, concerning his plan to become a student at Christminster, "that the whole scheme had burst up like an iridescent soap bubble". It may well be Schopenhauer rather than any other Kantian that Fitzpiers is thinking of when he denies he is in love with any "thing-in-itself".[7]

The question is how important these philosophies were for Hardy, and this is best approached by a reconsideration of his supposed later "evolutionary meliorism". It is not necessary to reassemble the material for the discussion of this problem: it is all in Bailey's article: but I must briefly state my own opinion. There is no doubt that Hardy thought about "evolutionary meliorism": he uses the expression in the "Apology" to *Late Lyrics and Earlier*, and the Hartmannian idea that the will might become conscious and, if so, might either destroy or reform the universe, is present in a number of poems, most clearly "He Wonders about Himself" and "The Sleep Worker". But Hartmann never did more than state the two possibilities, and neither did Hardy. "If way to the Better there be" it is "by the exploration of reality, and its frank recognition stage by stage along the survey, with an eye to the best consummation possible: briefly, evolutionary meliorism"; and the whole discussion ends with "one dares not prophesy". "Evolutionary meliorism" is a woolly phrase, but it does not mean hope, let alone optimism, and the passage that is sometimes quoted (the final chorus of *The Dynasts*) is no help: although not explicitly attributed to them, it must be spoken by the Pities, who have just spoken in two semi-choruses. There are no choruses of all the Spirits in *The Dynasts* and there could not be: elsewhere the Pities are never veridical. The speculation "If Law had consciousness . . ." in the *Life* may have been, as Bailey points out that Hardy claimed in a letter to Edward Wright, his "own idea solely": and so would all the poems be (such as "The Mother Mourns") which are in accordance with the preceding passage in the *Life*: "Law has produced in man a child who cannot but constantly . . . say to such parent that it would have been better never to have begun doing than . . . to have created so far beyond apparent first intention (on the emotional side). . . . The emotions have no place in a world of defect, and it is a cruel injustice that they should have developed in it."[8]

Discussion of "evolutionary meliorism" has, rightly, been confined to the poems and *The Dynasts*. Bailey's argument is that there is no influence of Schopenhauer and Von Hartmann before 1886, and, since Hardy denied the influence of Schopenhauer in the seventies[9] and Schopenhauer was first Englished in 1883–6 and Von Hartmann in 1884, this seems probable. Rutland's approach was: "Having reached a stage of spiritual vacuum by about 1880, Hardy seems to have set about trying to fill it by reading philosophy. . . . It is . . . very interesing to trace the beginning of his philosophical studies in his writing in the mid-eighties." Can we really say that they made any difference to Hardy — a difference which should appear as a difference between *The Woodlanders*, *Tess* and *Jude* and the earlier novels? Rutland cites no passage from these later novels as indebted to Von Hartmann, and only one each from *Tess* and *Jude* as indebted to Schopenhauer:

> "What's the use of learning that I am one of a long row only — finding out that there is set down in some old book someone just like me and to know that I shall only act her part; making me sad, that's all. The best is not to remember that your nature and your past doings have been just like thousands', and thousands', and that your coming life and doings 'll be like thousands' and thousands'."

> "The Doctor says there are such boys springing up amongst us — boys of a sort unknown in the last generation - the outcome of new views of life. They seem to see all its terrors before they are old enough to have staying power to resist them. He says it is the beginning of the coming universal wish not to live."[10]

The former is Tess's reaction to Angel's suggestion that she should study history, the latter Jude's comment on Little Father Time's hanging of the children. The two points made are the denial of the uniqueness of the individual personality, and the denial, or loss, of the will to live. Both points are found in Schopenhauer, in passages in Book IV of *The World as Will and Idea* quoted by Rutland, and they may be connected as they are by Schopenhauer: "Every individual . . . is but another short dream of the endless spirit of nature, of the persistent will to live . . . another fleeting form which it carelessly sketches on its infinite page, space and time." Both Hardy's passages are undoubtedly indebted to Schopenhauer, but the result is not Schopenhauerian.

Schopenhauer discusses the denial of the will to live at the end of Book IV. He regards it as necessary in order to attain peace, his great end, and to escape from individuality. It is achieved by asceticism, and not suicide, which Schopenhauer regards in fact as the *assertion* of the will to live. These ideas of Schopenhauer are completely foreign to Hardy. Hardy is anti-ascetic. This is seen most clearly in *Tess*, where the only characters condemned are those who do not have the "will to enjoy" — Mercy Chant and Angel's brothers. Even Angel is criticised because his love is "less fire than radiance": he wouldn't have left Tess if it hadn't been. Anti-asceticism is also seen in the forgiving attitude to Fitzpiers's "sincerely . . . double and treble-barrelled heart" and there are many other examples of the oft-quoted anti-ascetic Fourier-inspired view of character given in Hardy's letter to *L'Ermitage*:

> I consider a social system based on individual spontaneity to promise better for happiness than a curbed and uniform one under which all temperaments are bound to shape themselves to a single pattern of living. To this end I would have society divided into *groups of temperaments*, with a different code of observance for each group.

While always himself refusing to prophesy, or even to hope, Hardy once permits himself to "*wonder whether*", and several times represents his characters as *asserting that*, there is progress; and if there is, it will take the form of "closer interaction of the social machinery", of the success of "such experiments as" Jude's and Sue's in living together, of Egdon becoming "ripe for" Clym. That Hardy didn't agree with Schopenhauer he showed by putting Jude's comment on the hangings in the mouth of "the Doctor". Like clergymen, doctors in Hardy are sometimes wrong: Fitzpiers in cutting down South's elm, "doctors" in opining that Owen Graye's wound wouldn't heal.[11]

Tess's remarks about the uselessness of learning are typical of the Hardy who believed that "words in *logy* and *ism*" were "but the latest fashion in definition . . . of sensations which men and women have vaguely grasped for centuries": she is expressing Schopenhauer without having read him. They make explicit in an exaggerated form a view implied by Hardy's many comparisons of his characters and situations to historical persons and events. These comparisons are only possible because of the simple view Hardy takes of historical characters, most notably Napoleon who figures in *The Dynasts* only as a military hero and is last seen "blade to blade" with Wellington. They are an example of one of Tess's heroic qualities, imagination. They are like Tess's other discoveries — "the past was past", "outside humanity she had at present no fear" — erroneous apprehensions, infinitely moving because Tess is killed as soon as she has got at the whole truth. They are not the truth: no novelist, however simple his idea of character, could hold such a view.[12]

Hardy has many points in common with Schopenhauer; pessimism, dislike of Christianity, interest in art, desire for stasis and peace (for instance in "According to the Mighty Working"), Hellenism, a sort of spiritualism, kindness to animals. These all appear before he read Schopenhauer. The essential doctrine of Schopenhauer is a metaphysical doctrine of the Will, and it involves a metaphysical distinction between appearance and reality, in which all that is normally called real becomes phenomenal, the real individual will is distinguished from recognisable acts of volition and is identified with the Cosmic Will, and the Cosmic Will is evil. All Hardy does is sometimes to take over the Will as his ultimate power, and sometimes, particularly in *The*

Dynasts, to show individual "phenomenal" wills succeeding or failing because they are or are not in accord with the Cosmic Will.[13]

The thought of Schopenhauer and Von Hartmann is evolutionary in that they describe a process which is supposed to be happening according to law without divine or human intervention. The same is true of Comte, Hegel, Herbert Spencer, Darwin, Huxley and those influenced by Comte such as Mill and Stephen. In Darwin's evolutionary biology, the absence of God appears as the denial of "separate creation", and, as he pointed out, this idea had already appeared in Lamarck, Erasmus Darwin, and Aristotle. Morse Peckham has taught us to distinguish between Darwinism and Darwinisticism by pointing out that accidental change, the control of structure by pattern, and ecological thinking are strict Darwinism, whereas the idea that competition and not co-operative love leads to progress is Darwinisticism. But evolutionary sociology was independent of and prior to Darwinian evolutionary biology, although influencing it (since a human struggle for survival is found in Malthus) and being influenced by it later, in, for instance, Bagehot's *Physics and Politics*.[14] It is misleading to call even Darwinistic ideas which do not find their origin in Darwin.[15]

Hardy never claimed to have read *The Origin of Species* but only to have been one of its "earliest acclaimers". He comments on Darwin in the *Life,* quoting someone who disagreed with the doctrine of "the survival of the fittest in the struggle for life. There is an altruism and coalescence between cells as well as an antagonism." Hardy typically comments "Well, I can't say"; and, of course, in Darwin, as Morse Peckham has pointed out, there is co-operation as well as competition. Later in an ironical and unoriginal (Swiftian) passage in the *Life*, really arguing against blood-sports, he suggests that "the smaller children, say, of overcrowded families" should "be used for sporting purposes. Darwin has revealed that there would be no difference in principle" — Because, presumably, "all animals and plants" may "have descended from some one prototype". The same point, against cruelty to animals, is made in a letter reproduced in the *Life*: "The most far-reaching consequence of the establishment of the common origin of all species is ethical . . . the application of what has been called 'The Golden Rule' beyond the area of mere mankind to that of the animal kingdom"; and in "Drinking Song": "we are all one with creeping things". One other passage in the *Life* uses the term "evolution": "All things merge into one another — good into evil, generosity into justice, religion into politics, the year into the ages, the world into universe. With this in view the evolution of species seems but a minute and obvious process in the same movement."[16] There is only one quotation from *The Origin of Species* in the *Literary Notes*, and that is about the distinctness, although separated only by the isthmus of Panama, of the marine faunas of the eastern and western shores of South and Central America.[17] There is no evidence that Hardy ever read *The Descent of Man*.[18] The "Apology" prefixed to *Late Lyrics and Earlier* complains that "belief in witches of Endor is displacing the Darwinian theory and the 'truth that shall make you free'."[19]

Pinion, Southerington, Webster, Bailey and Stevenson have claimed that Darwin had an important influence on Hardy's novels, particularly *The Return* and *The Woodlanders*, and on his poetry.[20] Although he does not explicitly say so, Dr Pinion must mean that the idea that (because the insects enjoyed the heat which hurt Mrs Yeobright) "cruelty to one species may be ideal for another" is Darwinian. But without the inclusion of natural selection — the idea that in a certain enviroment some species evolve and survive and others die out — it is not. By including Mrs Yeobright among "the larger animal species"[21] Hardy may have thought he was being Darwinian, but in fact all we have are two very old ideas: that animals and plants vary in their needs, and that there is an animal element in human nature. The latter is a favourite idea of Hardy's, and it appears as the assimilation of both humans to animals and of animals to humans. For instance, in *The Mayor* we find a smoking gentleman talking about Susan Henchard (who is for sale) in the same way that the auctioneer has just praised the horse he is selling. Later in the same chapter we are warned not to distinguish between "the peacefulness of inferior nature and the wilful hostilities of mankind": the horses may be rubbing each other's necks lovingly now that Susan and Michael are quarrelling, but one night "mankind might ... be innocently sleeping when these quiet objects were raging loud". Later still we have the expression "sagacious old heads" carefully chosen to cover both the horses and "the coming and departing human guests", both species seeking out "the good stabling and the good ale" of the Three Mariners. In *Far from the Madding Crowd* we have the "delicacy" of a sheep's blush "enviable by queens of coteries", and a dog which drove sheep over a precipice "tragically shot" and compared to "other philosophers who follow out a train of reasoning to its logical conclusion". In *Tess* we have Tess herself often compared to animals, and once, when her breasts are full of milk because her baby has been taken from her, somewhat tastelessly assimilated to the cows, "their great bags of milk swinging under them as they walked. Tess followed slowly in their rear." In *The Woodlanders*, Mrs. Dollery's horse knew the ground "as accurately as any surveyor", and Mr Melbury's horse's "vision" was keener than Fitzpiers's. Cows are similarly upgraded in *Tess*: they like to be sung to before they will yield their milk, and some "had a preference for Tess's style of manipulation". When "snores came from the cart-horse, where some of the men were lying down; the grunt and squeal of sweltering pigs arose from the still further distance", animals and men are again assimilated. This attitude affects our response to the characters of Alec, Arabella and Jude: Alec who oscillated between "animalism" and "fanaticism", Arabella "a complete and substantial female animal — no more, no less", and Jude's "animal passion".[22]

Nor would the conflict in *The Return* be between the worlds of Darwin and Arnold, as Goldberg claims, if it were as he says between mechanical science and natural law and culture and poetry. Darwin found one particular new natural law. He did not invent the idea of science. We do not find in *The Return* either the struggle for existence, or natural selection, or the idea of climatic and geological change. Egdon is "a face on which time makes but little impression".

The untameable Ishmaelitish thing that Egdon now was it always had been. . . . Ever since the beginning of vegetation its soil had worn the same antique brown dress. . . . Everything around and underneath had been from prehistoric times as unaltered as the stars overhead. . . . The sea changed, the fields changed, the rivers, the villages and the people changed, yet Egdon remained.

"It was an obsolete thing . . . in the days of square fields, plashed hedges, and meadows . . . rectangular . . ., artificial grasses . . . turnips": the Agrarian Revolution of the eighteenth century is what it is contrasted with. Its "repose . . . was not the repose of actual stagnation, but the apparent repose of incredible slowness." So it did change, but the change is seasonal not Darwinian: we are told what it is like in March and in summer, when it still "seemed to belong to the ancient world of the carboniferous period". The seasonal preoccupation is made explicit in the description of the effect of the seasons on Thomasin: "The spring came and calmed her; the summer came and soothed her; the autumn arrived, and she began to be comforted." Egdon properly pullulates with fauna – bustards, marsh-harriers, a courser, a mallard, reptiles, rabbits, lizards, grasshoppers, ants, various birds as similes and allegories for Thomasin, heath-croppers, herons, moths and glow-worms, bees, butterflies, flies, snakes, insects, ephemerons, pond-life, wasps, a night-hawk, an adder, a spider, a thrush. Apart from the adder which stung Mrs Yeobright, the thrush, and presumably the night-hawk, none is engaged in acts of violence, let alone the struggle for existence. Even if there are two worlds, of science and poetry, in *The Return*, the unrealistic poetical dimensions are so great and so inclusive of Egdon that Egdon cannot be said to stand for scientific let alone Darwinian truth. Eustacia's, Wildeve's and Clym's choices of partners cannot be described as Darwinian "Sexual Selection", which "depends, not on a struggle for existence, but on a struggle between the males for possession of the females" and is concerned with survival of the species through offspring.[23]

In *The Woodlanders*, the words "existence" and "struggle" do occur, in adjoining sentences:

> She could see . . . trees close together, wrestling for existence,
> their branches disfigured with wounds resulting from their
> mutual rubbings and blows. It was the struggle between these
> neighbours that she had heard in the night.[24]

Another verbal echo of Darwin has been found[25] in the sentence:

> Owls that had been catching mice in the outhouses, rabbits
> that had been eating the winter-greens in the gardens, and
> stoats that had been sucking the blood of the rabbits . . . dis-
> creetly withdrew . . . .

The second passage is the only mention of predatory animals in
The Woodlanders and neither passage is very close to Darwin,
who wrote:

> What a struggle between the several kinds of trees must have
> gone on during long centuries, each annually scattering its
> seeds by the thousand; what war between insect and insect —
> between insects, snails, and other animals with birds and
> beasts of prey — all striving to increase, and all feeding on
> each other or on the trees or their seeds and seedlings, or on
> the other plants which first clothed the ground and thus
> checked the growth of the trees!

There are one or two other passages in *The Woodlanders* expressing the sufferings of trees. Of these the most frequently quoted
is:

> On older trees still than these huge lobes of fungi grew like
> lungs. Here, as everywhere, the Unfulfilled Intention, which
> makes life what it is, was as obvious as it could be among the
> depraved crowds of a city slum. The leaf was deformed, the
> curve was crippled, the taper was interrupted; the lichen ate
> the vigour of the stalk, and the ivy slowly strangled to death
> the promising sapling.

After quoting these passages Lodge comments that "this view of
Nature comes from . . . Darwin" and goes on to speak of "the

evolutionary struggle in nature" in *The Woodlanders*. It happens
that in two of these three passages (but not in the third) one
species is preying on another. But that animals prey on one
another is a well-known and timeless fact, not a discovery by
Darwin. What Darwin did was to connect it with natural selection and the origin of species, for instance:

> How do these groups of species . . . arise? All these results . . .
> follow inevitably from the struggle for life. Owing to this
> struggle for life, any variation . . . if it be in any degree profit-
> able to an individual . . . will tend to the preservation of that
> individual, and will generally be inherited by its offspring.

Hardy is not concerned with variation or its inheritance. And in
all the other passages about suffering trees, the tree suffers from
its own species or the wind. "The breeze was . . . making the
point of each ivy-leaf on the trunks scratch its underlying neighbour . . ." "The wet young beeches were undergoing amputa-
tions [etc.] . . . at every onset of the gale." "Not a bough in
the nine trees which composed the group [all firs, near Clym's
Alderworth cottage] but was splintered, lopped, and distorted by
the fierce weather." "A lingering wind brought . . . the creak-
ing sound of two overcrowded branches . . . rubbing each other
into the wounds." "The wind was so nipping that the ivy-leaves
had become wizened and gray, each tapping incessantly upon its
neighbour." With regard to the expression "the Unfulfilled
Intention" I have already suggested it may have been coined
with Schopenhauer or Von Hartmann in mind, because of the
universality attributed to it: it "makes life what it is" just as the
"Immanent Will" "stirs and urges everything" and the "circumstantial will" is "at work everywhere". Such universality is not
characteristic of Darwin's struggle, which is only concerned
with natural selection, and the operation of the "Unfulfilled Intention" among "the depraved crowds of a city slum" cannot in
itself be held to imply that those crowds are depraved because
they have been worsted in a struggle for existence. The intention is unfulfilled in the sense which is found in poems such as
"The Mother Mourns": "I had not proposed me a Creature . . .
so excelling . . . As to read my defects": or "Discouragement",

where it is "grim . . . to see . . ., where she [nurturing nature] would mint a perfect mould, an ill".[26]

Hardy's object in *The Woodlanders* as elsewhere, and particularly in the contrast between Talbothays and Flintcomb-Ash in *Tess*, is simply to present an unsentimental picture of nature by showing it to be cruel as well as kind. What change there is is seasonal not Darwinian, as in *The Return*. In fact there is more specification of seasons in *The Woodlanders* than in any other novel except *Tess*, and Hardy says: "Almost every diurnal and nocturnal effect in that woodland place had hitherto [before the arrival of Fitzpiers] been the direct result of the regular terrestrial roll which produced the season's changes." The behaviour of the characters is influenced by the seasons. Giles is associated with, and himself dies in, the autumn, Fitzpiers and Grace come together both times in the spring, Felice goes south for the winter and looks to " 'a [second] winter of regrets and agonies and useless wishes, till I forget him [Fitzpiers] in the spring' ". The community's activities are of course also seasonal – Giles's party is at Christmas time, divination of husbands at Old Midsummer; planting, hunting, auctions, barking, cider. At the end life goes on in the most un-Darwinian way imaginable: partly by a demonstration of Fitzpiers's success with women which is no more Darwinian sexual selection than Wildeve's, but mainly by the community reasserting itself, the search-party adjourning to a tavern and swopping stories about matrimony, just as life went on in the marriage at the end of *Under the Greenwood Tree*, the waxing of the ticking at the end of *The Return*, and in the marriage of Bathsheba to the one man who will keep things going right in *Far from the Madding Crowd*. But life also goes on, seasonally and not Darwinistically, through Marty (though she has been said to "suffer from the struggle for existence" in being "compelled to sell her hair to keep alive"). It is Marty, the person who embodies the whole spirit of the novel, and who "looked almost like a being who had rejected with indifference the attribute of sex for the loftier quality of abstract humanism", who will plant the young larches and turn the cider wring.[27]

Professor Bailey says that passages in *The Descent of Man*

"explain Hardy's interest in heredity. In every one of his novels Hardy accounted for his characters' behaviour by commenting on their heredity."[28] But his only example is Tess: "Hardy followed Weismann [*Essays in Heredity* I (1889)] in suggesting that Durbeyfield's body contained a germ-plasm that passed on to Tess traits of her distant, d'Urberville ancestors. . . . At every major crisis in Tess's life, Hardy based her behaviour on the passion, pride and temper she inherited from the medieval d'Urberville knights and dames. Her heritage controlled Tess throughout the novel." Bailey gives three incidents as evidence for his view: Tess telling Angel she is a d'Urberville " 'and we are all gone to nothing' "; Tess not confessing before marriage, said to be due to "something like a reliance on chance, suggested as an inherited trait"; and Angel being deterred from reconciliation by the d'Urberville portraits; and concludes: "Time has not permitted me to point out all Tess's behaviour that was rooted in her d'Urberville ancestry." One wonders whether to wish that it had. I have already argued that Tess's ancestry is a false belief, operative only because it is believed by Angel. In that sense, and in her being sent to claim kin with Alec, her (false) heritage influenced, but did not control, her. Angel's belief, shown in his reaction to the d'Urberville portraits, is not a germ-plasm inside Tess. Hardy does not credit Tess's "ancestors" with passion, pride and temper, but with ruthless lust. Tess does not have a temper in the ordinary bad sense, but strikes and later murders Alec when she is driven beyond endurance. She has passion, is "more impassioned" than the other dairymaids, but this is her heroic participation in "the irresistible universal automatic tendency to find sweet pleasure somewhere". Her pride is self-respect. When she tells Angel "we are all gone to nothing" she is herself saying her ancestry is meaningless, and she says it because she cannot bring herself to make the confession she had started to make. We are told that she drifted like "fatalistic field-folk" and was "in a mental cloud of many-coloured idealities" when courted by Angel and on her wedding-day, but not as a reason for her not confessing: a number of reasons are given for that, including self-preservation and the fact that Angel tells her not to, but never "reliance on chance or fate, suggested as an hereditary trait''. By introducing the d'Urberville coach, Hardy connects heredity with superstition and removes it further from science. Angel's belief in heredity is only one of several reasons why he cannot see Tess as she is.[29]

The harm done by the influence on a major character of a false belief in heredity appears also in *Jude*, where the belief is Aunt Drusilla's absurd one that " 'the Fawleys were not made for wedlock'' '. Of Jude's parents we are only told that they " 'couldn't get on'' ', and of Sue's only that her father "offended" her mother. Of their remoter, gibbeted ancestor — " 'if he *were* one of your family' " — we only know that his wife " 'ran away from him'' '. So we couldn't in any case say what characteristics they are supposed to have inherited. And, as in *Tess*, it is difficult to estimate how much effect Aunt Drusilla's belief had on Jude and Sue: it was one reason for his putting off telling her he was married, and she thinks her own unhappiness with Phillotson illustrates it, and mentions it again as one reason for not marrying Jude when she is free to do so.[30]

In these comparable passages in *Tess* and *Jude* the idea, half-believed by Angel, Jude and Sue, is simply that Jude, Sue and Tess are like their parents or ancestors: this is not Darwinian. The reader may be intended to think of Little Father Time's death as Lamarckian rather than Schopenhauerian: as the inheritance of an acquired characteristic, the will not to live. But this is only an inference from the prominence given to Jude's wish that he had not been born — an inference requiring acceptance of the doctor's account — and even that account is consistent with the boy's vaguely getting the wish not to live directly from his environment: " 'They seem to see all [life's] terrors . . . ' ''. It is much more likely Hardy intended the earlier part of this chapter (VI.ii) to be a representation of the "logical" stages by which a child's mind was driven to the act: " 'All is trouble' ''; " 'It would be better to be out of the world' ''; " 'It's because of us children' ''; " 'We don't ask to be born' ''; " 'I wish I hadn't been born' ''; " 'Whenever unwanted children are born they should be killed' ''; " 'This woman is not my real mother and is deliberately making things worse by bringing in another child, so if I don't act nobody will.' ''

Statements in Darwin such as the one Bailey quotes, that "tastes . . . habits . . . intelligence, courage, bad and good temper . . . genius . . . and . . . insanity . . . run in families", only become Darwinian as part of the argument that man is descended from another species. Bailey leaves us to find our own evidence for his claim that "in every one of his novels Hardy accounted for his characters' behaviour by commenting on their heredity". It is true that Bathsheba, like her father, is fickle and becomes serious; that a Corfiote father combines with conscious memory of Budmouth to produce exoticism in Eustacia; that Paula is like her father in "modernity" and in her very independence, against her father's wishes, in the matter of total immersion. Here Hardy is no more Darwinian than Shakespeare is when he says "Die single, and thine image dies with thee" or Jane Austen when she reproduces parental characteristics in the Bennet children. Darwinian heredity requires remote ancestry, and where this is found, as in *Tess, The Trumpet-Major, The Woodlanders, A Laodicean, A Pair of Blue Eyes* and *Ethelberta*, the points made are simply the antiquity of the family and the decadence of the aristocracy.[31]

The fullest discussion of "Darwinism" in Hardy's verse is still Lionel Stevenson's,[32] under the headings "The Evolutionary Basis of Hardy's Philosophy", "Rejection of the Orthodox Views of God and Immortality", "Immortality through Heredity", "The Riddle of Existence", "Evolutionary Significance of the Immanent Will", and "The Ultimate Hope" (evolutionary meliorism). Hardy's rejection of an orthodox God and immortality is his rejection of Christianity discussed in Chapter 2 and again later in this chapter. It is found in the poems that Stevenson mentions, such as "The Impercipient" and "God's Funeral", but these are not Darwinian: one of them, "The Respectable Burgher on 'The Higher Criticism' " explicitly not. The poems mentioned under the heading "Immortality through Heredity", such as "Her Immortality", "By the Barrows", and "Heredity" do not require us to alter our conclusion that Hardy's treatment of heredity is not Darwinian, and do not justify Stevenson's conclusion that, in Hardy's "purely physical concept of immortality and his purely physical concept of fate . . . he instituted theories based directly on the evolutionary hypothesis and the sciences to which it gave rise".[33] Under the heading "The Riddle of Existence" Stevenson discusses such poems as "The Masked Face", "In a Wood" and "Nature's Questioning". in which Hardy suggests various possible origins of the universe and ultimate powers without choosing between them, or accepts that the matter is incomprehensible, or at least denies that nature is consistently benevolent. But, he says, relying mainly on two passages in the *Life* and "The Mother Mourns", Hardy "blamed the evolutionary process for mankind's unsatisfactory condition". One of the passages in the *Life* is that quoted above, culminating in "the emotions have no place in a world of defect".[34] The other complains that "the human race" and "even the higher animals' are "too extremely developed for [their] corporeal conditions".[35] In the first passage Hardy speaks of the "apparent first intention" of "law"; in the second, and in the poem, of Mother Nature. This is the nature we met in Chaper 1, and the argument is simply that reality does not come up to man's hopes and powers. Stevenson's conclusion, that "The Mother Mourns" "presents a double embodiment of the evolutionary theory: it describes the evolution of the human mind, and it points out that the most recent step in that evolution is the forming of the evolutionary hypothesis"[36] is only justified if by evolution is meant a belief as old as the battle of the Lapiths and Centaurs.

Under the heading "Evolutionary Significance of the Immanent Will", Stevenson discusses Hardy's use of chance and his idea of fate, and the Will, in *The Dynasts*. As I have said, the Will is a metaphysical doctrine and therefore not an explanation. Stevenson says: "Human consciousness – and attendant suffering – was developed through merest accident, by natural selection";[37] but Hardy never says this. Fatalism I have discussed in Chapter 1: it is obviously not Darwinian; but nor, without natural selection, is chance. And in fact the material Stevenson gives as evidence for "The Evolutionary Basis of Hardy's Philosophy" is, like "The Mother Mourns", concerned with the development of civilised man: the references in "Before Life and After" to "the birth of consciousness", in "A Plaint to Man" to his "gaining percipience", in *The Dynasts* to "species slain / By those that scarce could boast a brain."

Hardy, then, in the *Life*, shows knowledge of the idea of what he calls "the common origin of all species", which is Darwinian, but uses it only as an argument against cruelty to animals. And, again in the *Life*, he shows knowledge of the theory of the survival of the fittest, and regards it as Darwinian. But in his fiction he does not set out either to show or to deny that life is a Darwinian struggle, in which the fittest to survive do so either by natural selection or in some other sociological rather than biological way. He does not even present an evolving society, but shows an interest in some particular social changes. In some late poems and in *The Dynasts* he presents as the ultimate reality or power an "Immanent Will" which is evolutionary but metaphysical and not Darwinian; and in some poems he speculates inconclusively about various possible origins and laws of the universe. But his normal practice in both prose and verse is to use the traditional contrast between nature and civilisation, which are to be found both in man (where civilisation is his "consciousness") and outside him, and both of which are mixtures of good and evil.

Hardy's material, visual, practical, empirical, anti-metaphysical and even anti-intellectual temperament explains his hostility to everything in Christianity except the idea of charity and the Sermon on the Mount. We should nevertheless consider how far the form this hostility took is indebted to Arnold, Mill, *Essays and Reviews,* and Comte.

In Arnold's *Culture and Anarchy* there is a chapter entitled "Hebraism and Hellenism", and in his *Pagan and Medieval Religious Sentiment* Arnold says: "The ideal, cheerful, sensuous pagan life is not sick or sorry." So there are at least verbal echoes of Arnold when Sue says " 'I feel that we have returned to Greek joyousness, and have blinded ourselves to sickness and sorrow' " and when Angel says that " 'it might have resulted better for mankind if Greece had been the source of the religion of modern civilisation and not Palestine' ": especially as Hardy copied the "sick and sorry" sentence into his notebook. In *Jude,* but not in *Tess*, the two strands of Hellenism and Hebraism are

held throughout the novel, in the lack of "harmony between
this pagan literature [the *Carmen Saeculare*] and . . . Christminster", in the fact that at Christminster, for Jude (loving Sue),
"the atmosphere blew as distinctly from Cyprus as from
Galilee", in the "contrasting ideas" which the images of Venus,
Apollo and Christ awoke in Sue, in Sue's calling the saints
Jude's "Pantheon" and comparing Jerusalem adversely with
Athens, and in the Houses of Atreus and Jeroboam, offered as
parallel examples of tragic doom.[38]

In *Tess*, the alternative to Christianity is paganism, not
Hellenism, and Christianity is assimilated to other superstitions.
Even when Apollo is meant ("a golden-haired, beaming, mild-
eyed God-like creature") he is not named, he is part of the sun-
light-colour-atmosphere complex, and he is an example of the
pluralised" old-time heliolatries". The "Benedicite" is really for
Tess a memory of her ancestors' "pagan fantasy". Alec's condition before he got religion was "paganism", equated with
"animalism". Angel too experiences "pagan pleasure in natural
life and lush womanhood". He knows Tess's beliefs were really
"Pantheistic", and she finally accepts that she is "a heathen".
Angel is the pagan god of Tess's world: he was so "godlike" that
her "religious sense" of the validity of the "union" with Alec
was overcome. She prayed to Angel, and it was her "religion" to
be faithful" to him. Marcus Aurelius, though he wrote in Greek,
is called "the Pagan [not Hellenic] moralist". This is the termi-
nology of the earlier novels: at the gipsying in *The Return*
"Paganism was revived in their hearts, the joy of life was all in
all": Somerset studies Gothic architecture independently in
(glancing at Arnold's "neo-Christianity") "these neo-Pagan
days".[39] Sometimes, not only in *The Woodlanders*,[40] the alternative to Christianity is *Norse* mythology. "Fragments of
Teutonic rites" occur on Egdon, and the Casterbridge amphi-
theatre might, since it was in fact neolithic in origin, be "called
the spittoon of the Jötuns". In *Tess*, only Angel "had per-
sistently elevated *Hellenic* paganism at the expense of Christianity", and it is to Angel and the similar persons who are
Hardy's readers that an Aeschylean phrase, the President of the
Immortals, is addressed.[41]

Christianity is assimilated to other superstitions in *Tess*. This is done, firstly, by representing Christian acts as superstitious: Tess imagining "the arch-fiend tossing [her baby] with his three-pronged fork . . . ; to which picture she added many other . . . details . . . sometimes taught the young in this Christian country"; the idea that cattle kneel on Christmas Eve which for Angel " 'carries us back to medieval times, when faith was a living thing!' " Secondly, it is done by presenting the other (non-Christian) superstitions, such as witches and fairies, the *Fortune Teller*, the half-belief in Conjurer Trendle's son, the story of Guenever's robe and the legend of the d'Urberville coach, and representing the heroine as "steeped in . . . superstitions". And thirdly it is done by representing Christianity itself as a matter of belief, where believing means, or can be taken to mean, superstitious belief, belief without evidence, mere theory, not knowledge. This is most explicit when Angel says the Church " 'refuses to liberate her mind from an untenable redemptive theolatry' " and in his denial of Article Four. It is also seen in the continual use of the word "dogma": Felix is " 'a contented dogmatist' "; Angel cannot accept his father's "narrow dogma", Tess accepts, and exemplifies (as Angel does not), " 'the religion of loving-kindness [that is, charity again] and purity . . . an ethical system without any dogma' ". The unbaptised, drunkards and suicides are *"conjecturally* damned". The words theology, mysticism and faith have the same effect: Alec, now animalist again, speaks of the time " 'when I was theological' " not "when I was religious". Earlier Tess had "tried to tell him that he had mixed . . . theology and morals, which in the primitive days of mankind had been quite distinct". Angel's mother, a parson's wife, in language which fits into the theme of the "will to enjoy", asks: " 'What woman . . . believes the promises and threats of the Word in the sense in which she believes in her own children, or would not throw her theology to the wind if weighed against their happiness?' " Mercy Chant's belief in the value of suffering is a "sacrifice of humanity to mysticism", not to religion or God. Alec's sermon is on justification by faith, and Tess, again fitting into the theme of enjoyment, objects to " 'securing your pleasure in heaven by being converted' ", i.e.

by faith not works. All this is the point of her aposiopesis " 'But I don't believe –.' " She has just said she doesn't believe in anything supernatural. She just doesn't believe, she feels and knows. The Cross-in-Hand is a very good image of Hardy's atti-tude. It *is* just "a strange rude monolith", a "stump". It is variously *believed* to be a boundary stone and the remains of a cross, "the site of a miracle or murder, or both"; and, if of a murder, a judicial murder, of a man who " 'sold his soul to the devil, and . . . walks' ".[42]

Hardy in *Jude* confronts Hellenism and Hebraism in his own and not in Arnold's way. Hardy has not used any part of Arnold's argument in *Culture and Anarchy*.[43] It could not be otherwise since Hardy did not accept Arnold's "neo-Christianity".[44] Arnold used the two terms "Hebraism" and "Hellenism" because, as he said, "they very often are con-fronted". They were so because Hellenism and Christianity are the two Western cultural traditions: until 1840 some English grammar schools were forbidden by their statutes to teach any-thing except Latin and Greek. Nobody's influence was needed to turn Hardy towards Greek ideas. The choice of paganism as the normal contrast with Christianity may have been influenced by Arnold's *Pagan and Medieval Religious Sentiment*, but the treatment of Christianity as superstition seems rather Comtian if anything.

The Greek tradition is also an element in *Essays and Reviews*, which was also an argument for "neo-Christianity". I suspect that what "impressed" the sensationalist simplificatory extre-mist in Hardy was the label, "The Seven Against Christ". The Greek tradition is an element in the essays by Temple and Williams: Temple discusses the contributions of Greece, Rome and Judea to Christianity, and – as followed by Arnold – says the Church revived Judaism in self-defence: Williams says the religions of Hellas and Latium as well as Christianity and others appealed to the better side of our nature. These essays do not appear to have influenced Hardy.

Rutland and Webster alone discuss the Seven in any detail, and these discussions are mostly expositions of the Seven's views. Rutland implies they turned Hardy from ordination, and

Webster says "they undermined his faith".[45] Rutland thinks Hardy must have been impressed by Jowett's essay "On the Interpretation of Scripture", and by "the method, which was imported from science". That method is seen most clearly in the essays by Baden Powell "On the Study of the Evidences of Christianity" and Goodwin on "Mosaic Cosmogony". Goodwin discusses the geological evidence at some length, and Baden Powell mentions modern astronomy and geology and Darwin. There are a great many geological terms in Hardy, and a famous trilobite in *A Pair of Blue Eyes,* and the Valley of the Great Dairies was "a level landscape compounded of old landscapes long forgotten", "loam . . . brought there by the river when it was as wide as the whole valley".[46] These only prove Hardy had some knowledge of geology, knowledge which in fact he generally used, along with his knowledge of human history, in the service of his own strong sense of the great length of past time in contrast with the brief span of human life.

Since neither Rutland nor Webster quotes a single passage from any of Hardy's works as showing the influence of *Essays and Reviews*, and since his literary notebooks do not contain a single extract from it, the critic might seem not to need to pursue the matter further. There is however in Hardy much misapplication of scripture, and it does need to be said that this is almost all of a different kind from that discussed by Jowett. Jowett objected to the selective application of Christ's words, that is, the overuse of the authority of such commands and statements as "Render unto Caesar . . ." and "The powers that be are ordained of God" and the disregard of less convenient ones such as "Sell all thou hast" and "I call not the righteous but sinners to repentance." He also complained that particular statements by Christ have been taken out of their contexts and treated as the whole truth on particular subjects: for instance, on divorce, His statement "that whosoever shall put away his wife, saving for the cause of fornication, causeth her to commit adultery: and whosoever shall marry her that is divorced committeth adultery." Jowett also objected, as did Rowland Williams, to the allegorical interpretation of scripture, and praised the "lyrical passion" of 1. Corinthians 13 (the charity passage). The

latter is too well known for Hardy to have learned of it from
Jowett, and there is only one reference to the allegorical interpretation of scripture in Hardy, Sue ridiculing "The Church pro-
fesseth her faith" as an explanation of the *Song of Solomon*.[47]

There are only three quotations from the Bible by characters
in Hardy, all in *Tess* and spoken by Alec, which could even
appear to be influenced by Jowett's essay. "The unbelieving
husband is sanctified by the wife, and the unbelieving wife is
sanctified by the husband."At this point Tess is the unbeliever
and Alec is monstrously offering to sanctify her, being himself
at this point in transition, as it were, between God and sex, and
hoping to escape the choice and unite them in matrimony; and,
since he fails, sex triumphs. The Biblical context (converts in
the early Church) is inapplicable to nineteenth-century England.
And it is again Alec who quotes *Hosea*: "she shall follow after
her lover, but she shall not overtake him; . . . then shall she say,
I will go and return to my first husband; for then was it better
with me than now." This passage is interpreted by the rubric as
metaphorical whoring, "the idolatry of the people", but even if
it is about *real* whoring, Alec of course misapplies as well as mis-
quotes it (there are plural lovers in *Hosea*) to Tess, as he does
the expression " 'you dear damned witch of Babylon' " (*Revelation* has "whore").[48]

But what Hardy is doing here is having the Devil quote scripture, which is a proverbial and therefore familiar idea (expressed usually slightly differently from its apparent source in
Shakespeare) and needs no reference to Jowett. Alec, like other
characters in Hardy — Fitzpiers, Percomb, the South Carolina
gentleman — is occasionally typed as the Devil: indeed the
parallel with *Paradise Lost* requires it: and once he calls himself
"the old Other One". That Hardy is thinking of Alec as the
Devil quoting scripture is shown by a remark by Ladywell in
The Hand of Ethelberta in reply to a garbled quotation by
Neigh from Thomas Hood's *The Bridge of Sighs*: " 'I would
have burlesque quotation put down by Act of Parliament, and
all who dabble in it placed with him who can cite Scripture for
his purposes.' " Any Jowettian dimension to the *Hosea* quotation is rendered further unlikely by its having been used once al-

ready by Ethelberta to Ladywell to delay her answer to his proposal of marriage. Ethelberta quotes it correctly, as to plurality
of lovers, but omits the last word — "husband" — and ends with
an aposiopesis: the quotation is inappropriate since she doesn't
have a husband, and can't return to her first husband as he is
dead.[49] Why does Hardy misquote the same passage twice? One
critic has complained about both Angel and Alec calling Alec
Tess's "husband in nature' ": "According to what ethical standard or law is the first male to have sexual relations with a
woman her husband?"[50] But it does seem to be a development,
albeit paradoxical, of the idea that a woman must be a virgin
when she marries. When she ceases to be a virgin she should
marry the man. The man she should marry is her "husband",
and if she "marries" again, her "first husband". In *Tess*, Hosea
is misapplied, and the misapplication is part of the unfair social
pressure on Tess. In *The Hand of Ethelberta* Hosea is sympathetically applied by Ethelberta to herself: since she once
wishes she was dead, she may be wanting to rejoin the late
Mr Petherwin, or she may be thinking of her first lover,
Christopher Julian, who, sadly, wasn't and wouldn't be, her first
husband. Hardy's basic idea is simply his criticism of forced
monogamy. When Troy calls the dead Fanny Robin " 'in the
sight of Heaven . . . my wife' " it might seem merely his
"romanticism". But Lucetta also "had been so far compromised
with [Henchard] that she felt she could never belong to another
man" yet does marry Farfrae. And Sue is clearly wrong when
she says that, by her not marrying Jude, " 'we have . . . avoided
insulting . . . the solemnity of our first marriages. . . . I am still
his [Phillotson's] wife.' "[51]

But the characteristic misapplication and misquotation of the
Bible in Hardy is by Hardy. Instead of God, "the fettered gods
of the earth say, let there be light": *Genesis* adapted to attack
monotheism, just as Tess's praise of the created world was really
a "Fetichistic utterance" although its "setting" — the words of
the "Benedicite" — was "Monotheistic". Jude, saying that
" 'you are my dear Sue, from whom neither length nor breadth,
nor things present nor things to come, can divide me!' " is saying about the love of Sue what *Romans* says about the love of

God. When Troy's expression of love for the dead Fanny Robin is described as "the τετέλεσται of [Bathsheba's] union with Troy" Hardy is seriously applying Christ's words to Bathsheba's "crucifixion". Sometimes Hardy turns the Bible against society, as when he makes Jude use the language of *Corinthians* and *Judges* to complain that he can't go to Alfredston, Melchester, Shaston or Christminster " 'though "we have wronged no man, corrupted no man, defrauded no man!" Though perhaps we have "done that which was right in our own eyes." ' " In *Jude, The Mayor* and *The Return* the un-Christian state of despair is justified from *Job*.[52] In such passages one cannot say whether Hardy thought of himself as the Devil quoting sculpture, or was influenced by Jowett.

There remain, as possible influences on Hardy's treatment of Hellenism and Christianity, Mill and Comte. The most claimed for Mill in this context is that Jude and the earlier Sue glimpsed that "Greek self-development which the Platonic and Christian ideal of self-government blends with", in Mill's phrase in *Liberty*.[53] Self-development is glimpsed by Sue when persuading Phillotson to let her leave him. She quotes von Humboldt's ideal, which Mill approved of, "human development in its richest diversity". There is no blending of this with a Platonic and Christian ideal of self-government. What there is in *Jude* is a youthful, and Hardy means natural or inborn, requirement of harmony in the world, something like Tess's wanting to know "why the sun do shine on the just and the unjust alike". We are told of Jude's "sense of harmony" very early, but only after it has been "sickened" by his inability to show mercy to the birds without cruelly depriving man of food. Of Sue we are not told until after her recantation, that "in the days when her intellect scintillated like a star" she had imagined "that the world resembled a stanza or melody composed in a dream". Music is present in *Jude*, rather as in *Twelfth Night*, to keep the idea of harmony before our eyes, and the idea is connected with Jude and Sue, when they are listening separately but simultaneously to choral singing in Cardinal College: "The girl . . . was . . . ensphered by the same harmonies as those which floated into his ears; and the thought was a delight to him." But no actual harmony between Greek and Christian ideals is discussed: on the contrary, "there seemed little harmony between this pagan lite-rature [Caesar, Virgil, Horace] and the medieval colleges at Christminster".[54]

We do find in Hardy's use of the terms "fetichism", "poly-theism", "pantheism" and "theology", as part of his treatment of Christianity and paganism, probable traces of Comte's "theological" stage. Tess singing the "Benedicite" "probably ... was a Fetichistic utterance". To Sue, Christminster "is a place full of fetichists and ghost-seers". Henchard must have "a fit place and imagery" for his oath, "for there was something fetichistic in this man's beliefs". Listening to the wind on Egdon Heath in "fetichistic mood" might lead to a religious in-terpretation of the phrase "the spirit moved them". "There is no fetichism" in a man's attitude to his clothes. There are several extracts from Comte in the *Literary Notes* mentioning fetichism, in particular: "The doctrine of Polytheism (Greeks) is less poetic than that of Fetichism (worship of material things) which could better idealise the External world." This idea seems to harmonise with the material, visual and physical ele-ment in Hardy's attitude to life, and with such poems as "The Garden Seat", "The Whitewashed Wall", "The Six Boards" and "The Workbox".[55]

There are also in the *Literary Notes* extracts from Comte about polytheism, monotheism, and pantheism, which find echoes in *Tess* and *Jude*. Tess's beliefs were "Tractarian as to phraseology and Pantheistic as to essence". Jude reads the *Carmen Saeculare* "under the sway of a polytheistic fancy". To call "Theology ... the last grotesque phase of a creed which had served mankind well in its time" is Comtian. But Hardy's normal terms for non-Christian belief both in *Tess* and *Jude* and in the other novels are "pagan" and "Teutonic" which Comte does not appear to use, and "Hellenic" which is common to Arnold, Mill and others. Moreover, *pace* Hyman, Hardy does not have Comte's law of development through three stages: he does not have the remotest vestige of a "metaphysical" stage, and while he cannot be expected to disagree with the definition of the Positive stage — the stage of taking an exact view of the real facts — he never uses the term in his fiction. He has in other words not taken any ideas from Comte, but taken only expressions convenient to that hostility to all forms of religious belief which, however much we may analyse it today in terms of archaeology and geology and evolution and biblical criticism, was so much in the air at the time and common in one degree or another to so many thinkers — Comte, Mill, *Essays and Reviews*, Leslie Stephen, Arnold — that it is not necessary to look for a source for it when we find it in Hardy.[56]

What further influence did Comte have on Hardy? There are thirteen pages of extracts from the *Social Dynamics* in the *Literary Notes*, and Hardy possessed the *General View of Positivism*. The "Apology" to *Late Lyrics and Earlier* and the essay "Candour in English Fiction" approve of Comte's looped orbits as an image of progress, but they do not appear in the fiction. In the *Life* he seems to accept the religion of humanity: "If Comte had introduced Christ . . . into his calendar . . . thousands who . . . hold Positivism to contain the germs of a true system . . . would have been enabled . . . to modulate gently into the new religion."[57]

But he also explained the attribution of *Far from the Madding Crowd* to George Eliot by saying that some of Comte's expressions must have passed into his vocabulary, and so one should deal first with influences which are, like those on Hardy's treatment of Christianity, either verbal or, if more than verbal, isolated and particular. Hardy may have been thinking of Comte's three successive states of morality — "personal", "domestic" and "social" — when he made Oak disregard "interests . . . which affected his personal well-being", and Elizabeth-Jane willing "to sacrifice her personal comfort . . . to the common weal". There are references to "stages" and "phases" in *The Return* and *Tess*, though they do not seem to be Comtian ones: "In passing from the bucolic to the intellectual life the intermediate stages are usually two at least . . . ; and one of these stages is almost sure to be worldly advance." The main divisions of *Tess* are entitled "Phases" and we are told that "phases of her childhood lurked in her aspect still". Hardy's references to "social ethics", "social sympathies", and "self love" may be influenced by Comte; the most substantial are in *Two on a Tower* where the Preface refers to "the growth of social sympathies", and where we are told of Lady Constantine: "She strove hard, and made advance. The self-centred attitude . . . was becoming displaced by the sympathetic attitude, which . . . gave her . . . a . . . sense that she was rising above self-love." And later: "Her altruism in subjecting her self-love to benevolence . . . was demolished by the new necessity [her pregnancy]." Separated from her, we see Swithin "from an intersocial point of view" and find him with "little food for the sympathetic instincts". And, in *The Return*, "As far as social ethics were concerned Eustacia approached the savage state." There may be reference to the Religion of Humanity in Angel's views, as when he answers his father's question — what use is a university education " 'if it is not to be used for the honour and glory of God' " — by saying " ' that it may be used for the honour and glory of man' ". Concerning Hardy's uses of the terms "altruism" and "loving-kindness", I do not follow Dr Hyman even to the extent of treating them as verbal echoes since Comte does not appear to have used either. Instead of "altruistic" he says "social", "benevolent" or "unselfish".[58]

Dr Hyman credits Comte with a much more wide-ranging influence. She sees Comte in effect as the determinant of the central characterisations and developments in all the novels. The short answer to this is that, although Hardy's use of terms such as "fetichism" and "social ethics" almost certainly shows the influence of Comte, those terms, and indeed the whole Comtian description of the ages of progress, refer to ideas which are not sufficiently distinct from ordinary concepts to affect the novelist's normal concern with goodness and badness and change and suffering and happiness. Being socially ethical is being unselfish and being unselfish is being good.

One of Dr Hyman's ideas is that Hardy's characters develop in a Comtian way from the personal through the domestic to the social state. This becomes less plausible when so many of them relapse or fail to develop; and it leads to many unacceptable judgements. Thus Henry Knight, whose "eyes passed . . . from deep love to fellow-man's gratitude" is said by Dr Hyman to progress from personal to social but to relapse in rejecting Elfride. Tess "is drawn to an intellectually and socially superior mate and is transformed by the process of interaction with her lover", "beginning as a natural creature . . . she moves toward the human world . . . but ultimately relapses". The "altruism" of Venn and Thomasin is "limited and obsolete". Henchard is "the egotist who is unwilling or unable to make the necessary adaptation to the next stage of development". Eustacia, "blaming . . . some . . . Prince of the World", is at "the 'theological' phase of development". After all, to relapse or fail to develop is merely to be selfish, or to be unselfish at one point and selfish at another.

The search for Comte leads to unacceptable judgements. "Through his interaction with Eustacia . . . Clym . . . has created a new kind of altruism . . . disciplining his sorrow to socially useful ends." In fact he is socially useless at the end, and his own verdict — that he has killed two women — is not without some truth. It is unfair of Dr Hyman to simplify the situation in *The Mayor* by merely blaming Henchard for egotism in selling his wife, selling bad grain, and using Farfrae. The wife's nullity, and Newson's money, bear their share of the blame for the wife-sale; the bad grain is part of the inefficiency of old Casterbridge; and Henchard doesn't merely use Farfrae, he loves him. It is equally unjust to describe Farfrae, who is represented as repulsively successful (especially in his separation of the commercial from the romantic) as "the more advanced altruist". The accounts of Tess, Angel, Jude and Sue are particularly misconceived. Tess is said to be transformed by Angel, but this is to ignore the real movement of the novel: " 'by experience . . . we find out a short way by a long wandering' ". Tess is not transformed at all; her various experiences, such as the deaths of Prince, Sorrow and her father, Alec's rape, the loss and recovery of Angel, and working at Flintcomb-Ash, lead to her adopting a succession of hypotheses and finally acquiring understanding which her execution prevents her living her life by. Dr Hyman is also wrong in treating Tess's decision "to be their [her brothers' and sisters'] Providence" as "a determination to move into the sociological stage" (she had always been the mainstay of the family), and in calling her "passive responsiveness" to Angel "retrogression" and "the dead end toward which idealistic love leads": on the contrary, her unselfish love is part of her heroism, and her wish "to snatch ripe pleasure" part of "the 'appetite for joy' which pervades all creation". Dr Hyman is equally wrong in regarding Angel's "horror" that Tess's "affection . . . had apparently extinguished hor moral sense" (in murdering Alec) as a sign that he is "moving forward", and in regarding his final "tenderness" and vow to "protect" her as a sign that he is "at last adequate". The murder of Alec did not mean that Tess's moral sense was extinguished:she always had a high sense of responsibility, took the blame for the death of Prince, and considered herself "wickedly mad" for killing Alec: Hardy's expression of Angel's "horror" indicates Angel's persistent blind intellectualism. As to his tenderness and protectiveness, look at the passage:

> But anyhow, here was this deserted wife of his, this passionately fond woman, clinging to him. . . . Tenderness was absolutely dominant in Clare at last. He kissed her endlessly with his white lips, and held her hand, and said –
> "I will not desert you! I will protect you. . . ."

He cannot protect her, since she has committed murder, and in fact he indicates her to the police at Stonehenge: "they saw where she lay, which they had not done till then". His "tenderness" is a euphemism for his lust, his only expression of it endless kisses with his repulsive white lips in a context of triumphant male sexuality: "But, anyhow . . . this passionately fond woman, clinging to him." Dr Hyman is equally insensitive in calling Alec altruistic because he says " 'I . . . try to help you.' " Alec's "help" is obviously interested.[59]

Dr Hyman criticises Jude and Sue for behaving like lovers at the Great Wessex Agricultural Show and neglecting Little Father Time: this shows they have not passed from the personal to the domestic stage, she says. On the contrary, they do not neglect him and they are favourably contrasted with Arabella and Cartlett. Dr Hyman says that Jude's and Sue's criticism of marriage shows their "inability to move beyond the courtship stage", that "Sue cannot pass into the domestic or 'sociological' stage by becoming a wife and mother" and that Jude is egocentric in " 'following inclinations which do me and nobody else any harm, and actually give pleasure to those I love best' ". It is Jude's tragedy, not his fault, that he has not become a useful member of society; but Dr Hyman's remarks about marriage show a more serious blindness to the difference between Hardy and Comte. For Comte marriage was an essential step in the development from personal to social: first (in order of a person's development) filial love, then brotherly, then conjugal "secured by the reciprocity and indissolubility of the bond". Hardy states quite clearly, in the 1912 Postscript to *Jude*, "that a marriage should be dissolvable as soon as it becomes a cruelty to either of the parties"; and he also there quotes with approval a German critic's praise of the novel as a delineation of the bachelor girl "who does not recognize the necessity for most of her sex to follow marriage as a profession, and boast themselves as superior people because they are licensed to be loved on the premises".[60]

The fact that there are a large number of extracts from Comte in the *Literary Notebooks* is not in itself significant: the question is what use Hardy made of them. Apart from those I have discussed, Björk only suggests that seven short extracts were used in imaginative works. In connection with two passages referring to St Paul, he collects references to St Paul in *Tess, Two on a Tower, The Return* and *The Dynasts*; but apart from suggesting that Hardy may have remembered Comte's linking of St Paul and Aristotle Björk does not assert influence, and there is no reason to suppose Hardy derived his idea of St Paul from anyone but St Paul. Clym, saying there can be progress without uniformity, is supposed to be contradicting Comte, but Comte is talking about progress as the development of human unity, that is, that we are all part of humanity; whereas Clym appears to mean that he can bring wisdom to Egdon even though affluence will arrive before it elsewhere. Björk sees a reference in *Ethelberta* to "meditative" and "active faculties" as possibly influenced by Comte, but these are terms in common use. This is also the case with the statement in reference to Bathsheba, that "the soul is the slave of the body", which Björk says may possibly be influenced by a statement by Comte that nobler phenomena are subordinate to grosser. About the description of Alec when he gets Paulinism, Björk only says it "may conceivably" be similar to Comte's idea that under strong passion one may regress to the theological stage.[61]

Finally, there are vast areas of Comte which Hardy shows no knowledge of: Comte's attitude to women and the working-class and what he calls "philosophers", and his demand for a controlled and uniform system of education throughout Europe, a totalitarian spiritual power, and compulsory festivals.

What influence of Arnold and Mill can we find other than in the matter of Hellenism and Christianity? In that matter I have tried to treat the possible influences collectively, as de Laura does, but my conclusion is that such collective influence is not influence at all. Normally I examine each "influential" writer separately, and this method may not do justice to the complexity of the influences, especially where Arnold, Mill and Stephen are themselves a complex of influences, particularly the influence of Comte. De Laura's method, on the other hand, by stringing Pater, Shelley, Carlyle, Frederic Harrison, Fichte, Spinoza, Schelling and S. Simon together with those already named, may suggest a complexity of influence, and therefore a degree of intellectuality in Hardy, which is not really there. So it is worth quoting de Laura's comment on Fitzpiers's throwing away of his "philosophical literature": "So much, Hardy seems to say, for the 'modern' Dr Fitzpiers and for modern thought"; and his overall conclusion, that:

> It is very difficult to locate the affirmative ethical centre of Hardy's exploration of the complex "modern" theme. Fairly clear as he is concerning what he respected in English life, his positive ideal is finally the simple endorsement (predictive of Lawrence) of freer relations between men and women . . .;

and that: "Hardy's major ethical contrast . . . is . . . between an unspecified 'Nature' . . . and 'Civilisation.' " I have discussed

Fitzpiers's "so-called culture" in Chapter 1, and that eliminates Fichte, Spinoza and Schelling, and I discuss Shelley and Carlyle in Chapter 4. The heart of de Laura's case is really Arnold and "neo-Christianity". Apart from that, there is the quotation from *Pagan and Medieval Religious Sentiment* in *A Laodicean* about the "modern spirit" and "imaginative reason"; but it is not integrated into the novel. There is de Laura's wrong inference from *Robert Elsmere* and Hardy's dislike of neo-Christianity, that we are not meant to accept Tess's version of Angel's viewpoint: an "ethical system without any dogma . . . the religion of loving-kindness and purity", which de Laura calls "natural supernaturalism" although Tess has just said "I don't believe in anything supernatural' ". The loving-kindness is demanded authorially in the "Apology" to *Late Lyrics and Earlier* and is the same as charity; the purity is not, as de Laura says, "Victorian idealism" but the purity which is thematic in this novel; and the irony of "ethics without dogma" is, as I have said, that Tess exemplifies it and Angel doesn't. And finally there is de Laura's claim that a sentence in *The Return* ("A man who advocates aesthetic effort and deprecates social effort is not likely to be understood by a class to which social effort has become a stale matter") "sums up whole chapters" of *Culture and Anarchy*. The bearing of the sentence in *The Return* is obscure since Clym wants to confer "wisdom rather than affluence": is wisdom produced by aesthetic and affluence by social effort? Arnold wanted "a resurrection now", a best self, "something inward", not instead of social effort, but because social effort was not enough; but without reference to Arnold's detailed argument, Hardy's sentence cannot be understood to be even an answer to Arnold.[62]

And what, apart from Hellenism and Christianity, of Mill? Ethelberta quotes extensively from *Utilitarianism* to justify "marrying for the good of her family": the utility principle means that the standard of conduct is not one's own happiness but that "of some few persons". But Hardy's treatment is uncertain here. When he comments: "that these few persons should be those endeared to her by every domestic tie, no argument was needed to prove", we think we have the familiar con-

tempt for "logies" and "isms": all she's got from Mill is the obvious advice to act morally, to put others before yourself. But
later Hardy calls her "a pseudo-utilitarian" who had gravitated
to "distorted Benthamism", suggesting that Mill had really had
a bad influence on her. However, this doesn't alter the fact that
it does not need Mill to teach us to put others' welfare before
our own. Sue quotes twice from Mill *On Liberty*, in support of
(Hellenic) "self-development in . . . diversity" as we have seen,
but also, and from the same chapter: " 'She, or he, "who lets
the world, or his own portion of it, choose his plan of life for
him, has no need of any faculty than the ape-like one of imitation." ' " The quotation is inapposite, in the context of her asking Phillotson to release her, since neither she nor Phillotson has
allowed the world to choose their plan of life — each chose to
marry the other; but what Hardy means is that marriage itself is
the world's plan of life, and since you do not know what it is
like till you marry you do not really choose it. This quotation
from Mill, in itself, adds nothing to the theme of unconventionality discussed by Hyde, but the fact that Sue quotes Mill
adds to the persuasiveness of Hyde's suggestion of a more complex influence — that of the idea which Mill develops both in
this same passage in *Liberty*, and in *The Nature and Utility of
Religion*, that those who have "strong desires" have "more of
the raw material of human nature", and:

> It is only persons of a much higher degree of natural sensi-
> bility and intellect combined than it is at all common to meet
> with, whose feelings entwine themselves with anything like
> the same force around opinions which they have adopted . . .
> later in life.

This goes beyond the demand in the *Life* for "a social system
based on individual spontaneity" which I have quoted above
and called "Fourier-inspired" because of the knowledge of
Fourier shown in the *Literary Notes*, and beyond de Laura's
conclusion that Hardy is for freer personal relations. It is an
idea which Hardy carries out, as Hyde says, both in the weakness of Sue's unconventional desires, and in the strength of the

desire for very ordinary kinds of liberty shown by Arabella, Villbert, and the "common" people who alone applaud Phillotson for releasing Sue. But this is the whole extent of Mill's influence.[63]

Hardy himself described Leslie Stephen (referring to his first meeting with him in 1874) as "the man whose philosophy was to influence his own for many years, indeed more than that of any other contemporary", and wrote that, by the summer of 1879, he "had been much influenced by his philosophy, and also by his criticism", giving, as an example of the latter, Stephen's opinion that the poet should touch our hearts by showing his own and not by exhibiting his learning, taste or skill in imitating his predecessors. He also quotes a letter in which Stephen, in 1876, advised him not to read criticism (except Sainte-Beuve's and Arnold's) and not to "bother . . . about critical canons", and, in 1901, Stephen's opinion that "we cannot write living poetry on the ancient model". In the seventies, as editor of *The Cornhill*, Stephen commented on *Far from the Madding Crowd*, *The Hand of Ethelberta*, *The Return of the Native*, and *The Trumpet-Major*, and some of these comments of course involved critical principles. The extracts from Stephen in the *Literary Notes* are from his *History of English Thought in the Eighteenth Century* (1876) and from articles in the *Fortnightly* for 1880 and the *Cornhill* for 1881. Of these the only philosophically or literarily significant ones are to the effect that many supposed innate differences between persons are really produced by circumstances, and that Darwinism relieves us from having to accept a fixed order with a supernatural sanction and allows us to "recognize in society, as in individuals, the development of an organic structure"; and a long extract from Stephen's article "The Moral Element in Literature".[64]

Most critics discuss only Hardy's relation with Stephen as editor. Some call him his "mentor". Some quote his superlative acknowledgement of Stephen's influence: only Dr Björk, Professor Southerington and Dr Hyman explain it as other than the function of editor and general mentor. H. C. Webster indeed concluded that "a careful comparison of the works of the two men fails to show that Stephen influenced the shape of any of

Hardy's fundamental ideas . . . Hardy . . . believed in all of Stephen's fundamental premises before Stephen published ['Are We Christians?', *An Agnostic's Apology, The Science of Ethics*] . . . or made the novelist's acquaintance." Similarly, on one particular point, Dr Pinion wrote: "Leslie Stephen's observations on the poetic folly of mimicking the notes of one's predecessors merely confirmed Hardy's earlier convictions."[65]

Björk, while finding Stephen's "profound impact . . . on Hardy . . . not easy to particularize because of its broad and general nature in aesthetics, religion and philosophy", claimed that "The Moral Element in Literature" showed "considerable harmony with Hardy's own aesthetics", in the following respects: that the novelist is the true historian of his time, that he should convey the emotions and thoughts of his contemporaries, that his work's value depends on his moral qualities, that "emotional sentiment" is superior to cleverness, and that literature humanises the reader. One may object in particular that what Hardy says about the novelist as historian ("the best fiction . . . is more true . . . than history") comes, as his editor says, from Aristotle (perhaps through Fielding, I add) not from Stephen, and that Hardy does not say that the novelist should convey the emotions and thoughts of his contemporaries but that "a poet should express the emotion of all the ages and the thought of his own". But the two important objections to detecting Stephen's influence here are general and connected with one another: such statements are commonplaces and vague in their bearing, and the similarities are between Stephen and Hardy's essay "The Profitable Reading of Fiction" and his *Life*, and not between Stephen and Hardy's creative performance.[66]

Stephen plays a small part in Southerington's view of "Hardy's vision of man". Southerington quotes the extract in the *Literary Notes* about Darwinism, and comments: "Such a development . . . could only be the result of combined human effort. . . . It seems to have been through a process of thought similar to this that Hardy reached the notion of equilibrium, a state in which mortals might influence the development of their environment. . . . Yet his own view was formulated on premises which were different from Stephen's": and Southerington then

quotes a sentence from *The Science of Ethics* to the effect that
pain is tension and pleasure equilibrium, whereas "Hardy . . . regards the intellect as the most fruitful source of change." But
Stephen also says, in *The Science of Ethics*, that "every being or
collection of beings which forms a race or a society is a product
of the continuous play of a number of forces constantly shifting
and re-arranging themselves in the effort to maintain the general
equilibrium", so the "blossoming" of the "perception . . . that
intelligence lies . . . in . . . the recognition that change is in-
evitable . . . may be due to Leslie Stephen", though its "root
. . . is from Darwin".[67]

It cannot be regarded as Stephen's influence — Hardy disagreeing with him — that Hardy regards the intellect, Stephen
the feeling of pain, as the source of change; and indeed there is
nothing particular to Hardy which can be called regarding the
intellect as the most fruitful source of change. It is just a question of epistemological language. We commonly mean by the
will that which leads to action, and consider action as either
reasonable or unreasonable: if it is reasonable, then reason, intelligence, the intellect, has determined the will, by seeing the
desirability of the action, which may, reasonably, be to escape
pain. Stephen's two equilibria are different from one another
and from Hardy's: pleasure as equilibrium in Southerington's
extract from Stephen is a state of the individual in which there
is no motive to act, while his general equilibrium is a stable condition of society. Hardy's is a state of "the mighty necessitating
forces" in which pain may be reduced "by loving-kindness,
operating through scientific knowledge, and actuated by the
modicum of free will conjecturally possessed by organic life",
that is, a state in which change is possible. Hardy's tentativeness,
discussed at the end of Chapter 1, agrees with "conjecturally"
here and means one cannot take the matture further. There is
no evidence that he read *The Science of Ethics*, published in
1883 after the period when Hardy claimed he had been influenced by Stephen's philosophy, and there is no trace in
Hardy of its basic idea that moral qualities are transmitted
through the "social tissue" of the race, which they evolve to
preserve.[68]

Even if Björk's and Southerington's arguments are accepted,
they do not make Stephen into the man who influenced Hardy
more than any other contemporary. The confusions of Stephen's
thought,[69] and his debts to others such as Comte, Mill, Spencer
and Darwin[70] make the detection of his influence difficult.
Hardy may be exaggerating, and it is unlike him to speak of
himself as having a philosophy, and inconsistent with his refusal
in 1899 to join the Rationalist Press Association (with which
Stephen was associated), because it "would naturally compose
itself rather of writers on philosophy, science and history, than
of writers of imaginative works";[71] but some explanation of his
tribute must be found. Philosophically I believe Stephen's influence was, in one word, his agnosticism. Hardy had read
Stephen's article "Are We Christians?" in 1873, before they
met.[72] Stephen uses the word "scepticism" rather than the
recently coined "agnosticism"; says the essential articles of the
Christian creed can have no meaning for this day when people
must take reason for their guide; and attacks dogma and "supernaturalism", and in particular the ideas of eternal damnation
and redemption and the divinity of Christ. The Sermon on the
Mount is one of the "meanings of some value" that Christianity
may have for us. I cannot conceive of Hardy without his agnosticism, and the points that Stephen makes in this article must be
covered by any rationalistic attack on Christian belief, but the
fact remains that they are all in Hardy, in the reference to the
"conjecturally damned" among whom Sorrow was buried,
Angel's objection to Christianity's "untenable redemptive
theolatry", his brother's "contented dogmatism", Tess's belief
in the Sermon on the Mount, and so on. It is *A Counterblast to
Agnosticism* that Angel's brothers read. In exaggerating
Stephen's influence, Hardy may also have been affected by having witnessed Stephen's renunciation of Holy Orders: it would
be characteristic of him to make much of an actual human contact, an event in life, not merely something read in a book. And
I think that his friendship and frequent contacts with Stephen
made Hardy exaggerate his intellectual influence. He liked and
admired Stephen who was like him in many ways,[73] and who
when Hardy was unknown no doubt treated him with the same

unpatronising simplicity he used to everyone. Hardy divides his influence into "philosophy" and "criticism". By "criticism" he might mean no more than Stephen's criticisms of the novels submitted to *The Cornhill*, many of which (but not all) Hardy acted on; but here again I think the exaggeration was due to an event in life: he *felt* that Stephen, whose magazine publication of *Far from the Madding Crowd* brought Hardy fame, had made him a novelist.

This does not quite exhaust the debt. There are, first of all, a number of possible thematic and factual borrowings from Stephen of the kind discussed in the next chapter. Stephen's article "A Bad Five Minutes in the Alps" may have given Hardy the idea of Knight's cliff-hanging in *A Pair of Blue Eyes*. Toland's explanation of the biblical pillar of cloud, extracted into the *Literary Notes* from Stephen's *History of English Thought in the Eighteenth Century*, may have given Hardy the idea of the bonfire making the pillar of cloud intelligible to Tess.[74] The expression "the cogency of direct vision" which occurs in the extract in the *Literary Notes* from Stephen's "Moral Element in Literature" is also found in *A Laodicean.*[75]

But there is also Stephen the historian of the eighteenth century, who by 1880 had not only published the history of its thought — the Deists, Butler, Hume, Shaftesbury, Mandeville, Hutcheson, Hartley, Paley, Adam Smith, Bentham, Burke — but substantial studies of Defoe, Richardson, Pope and Johnson, and was later to publish books on Swift and Hobbes and on *English Literature and Society in the Eighteenth Century*, and essays on Fielding, Gray, Sterne, Horace Walpole and Crabbe; and whose own thought had the rationalism, and his style the clarity, of the period.

The eighteenth-century element in Hardy is not merely the consequence either of his early dramatic dates or of the timelessness of his themes,[76] although timelessness was an eighteenth-century concern, as Stephen no doubt pointed out to Hardy.[77] Hardy's eighteenth-century reading began early, and many critics have considered that his attitude to life was established early.[78] He notes that his grandmother "knew the writings of Addison, Steele and others of the *Spectator* group almost by heart and was familiar with Richardson and Fielding". As a child he read, or possessed, Isaac Watts, Dryden's Virgil, *Rasselas, Paul and Virginia* and Walpole's letters. His first novel imitates Defoe. By 1874 he prefers Fielding's country humour to George Eliot's and by 1875, when he is most under Stephen's influence, he "reads again Addison, Macaulay, Newman, Sterne, Defoe, Lamb, Gibbon, Burke, *Times* leaders, etc., in a study of style". In 1878 he shows familiarity with Richardson's "letter-system"; in 1880 records advice to read Swift for "narrative style"; in 1890 includes Swift and Moliere, Voltaire, Dryden, Fielding and Smollett in a list of reading, "mostly the satirists"; and in 1895 writes of the "Fieldingism rather than Zolaism" of some scenes in *Jude*. He lists the eighteenth-century plays William O'Brien acted in, is interested in the associations of places in London with Garrick, Johnson, Reynolds and the Burneys. He makes Ethelberta perform in the manner of Defoe, and creates in Sue a "child of the Eighteenth Century". He is critical of Shelley, almost ignores Byron, Keats and Coleridge, and disagrees with and minimises his debt to Wordsworth. Indeed how much he owes to Wordsworth is doubtful. A poem like 'Domicilium' is Wordsworthian. Some of the arguments in the "Apology" to *Late Lyrics and Earlier* are from the Preface to *Lyrical Ballads*. Between Wordsworth's and Hardy's ballads there is little similarity. He objects to expressions of mystical pantheistic optimism, such as "Nature's holy plan", "trailing clouds of glory" and "that immortal sea which brought us hither", but never discusses it, and never gives Wordsworth credit for the concern with ordinary people which is his own starting point. To make no distinction between fancy and imagination, and require poetic diction and not the language of common speech in works of imagination in verse, is to disagree radically with Wordsworth.[79]

It was Stephen who wrote:

> I would never abuse the century which loved common sense and freedom of speech, and hated humbug and mystery: the century in which first sprang to life most of the social and intellectual movements which are still the best hope of our

own; in which science and history and invention first took
their modern shape; the century of David Hume, and Adam
Smith, and Gibbon, and Burke, and Johnson, and Fielding.

Common sense, hatred of humbug and mystery, the intellectual
movement which is still the best hope of the nineteenth century,
Hume and Gibbon are, in one word, agnosticism. In Jude's calling Sue "Voltairean" and remembering Gibbon's sarcasms about
Christian miracles, in Sue's reading Gibbon on Julian the
Apostate, and "The Respectable Burgher" finding Voltaire
"moderate" compared with the Higher Criticism, and probably
in his inclusion of Hume – the author of the essay on miracles
– with Darwin, Huxley, Spencer and Mill as "more in harmony"
with him than Schopenhauer, Hardy acknowledges the
eighteenth-century source of his agnosticism.[80]

The prerequisite of the characteristics of the period which
Stephen lists was the empiricism of Locke, Berkeley and Hume.
This empiricism, and not only Hardy's visual imagaination, is
seen in the insistence throughout his work, but particularly in
Tess, that what we experience is only appearances; and it may
well be derived from the author of the *History of English
Thought in the Eighteenth Century*. We are not only concerned
with Tess's sufferings but with the development of her consciousness – her attempts, as hero, to make sense of her experience. " 'By experience we find out a short way by a long
wandering' [which] unfits us for further travel." "Experience
unteaches – (what one at first thinks to be the rule in events)":
Tess unlearns superstition, dogma, the desire for the society of
"that cold accretion called the world", the will to live. Her un-
learning is supported by Angel's: he had "made the mistake of
allowing himself to be influenced by general principles to the
disregard of the particular instance": and by the criticism of
Angel's father that, like Arnold, "he had made up his mind once
for all on the deeper questions of existence". But Tess comes up
against "life's contrarious inconsistencies": the cruel lover, the
sun shining on the just and the unjust, nature opposed to the
social law, opposite views on whether we meet again after
death; and, until the end, makes various wrong inferences from

her experience, that "the past was past", or that "outside humanity she had nothing to fear", or that, not being mangled, she was better off than the pheasants.[81]

Hardy does not follow the professional philosopher in going on to show that by induction we can have a highly probable knowledge of the external world. He stops at showing that our experience is of contradiction and uncertainty. To remind us that what we experience directly is sense-data, colours are mentioned over three hundred times in *Tess*, and the associations of colours are confusing: red is not only the colour of both love and violence but of Talbothays and the reaping-machine: blue the colour of romantic distance and Alec's unromantic cigar-smoke, white the colour of purity and vacuity. Light is the condition of experiencing colour, and it varies from the sun, which can be both "mild-eyed" and "pitiless", to a candle, which can be "kindly" or "sinister". Mist, fog and atmosphere increase the unreliability of appearances. Words like "seem", "aspect", "indistinct" and "mask" are common. Darkness, blackness, the absence of light, is the absence of consciousness; so Tess sleeps at her seduction, in the stone coffin and at Stonehenge, faints when reed-drawing, and feels the "petite-mort" on learning about the Cross-in-Hand, to prepare for the end of her "short way" — the final loss of consciousness in death — well signalled by the black flag. One is also aware of Hardy's empiricism when he says that "ideas" are the "definition . . . of sensations", that Tess "was in a dream wherein familiar objects appeared as having light and shade and position, but no particular outline", and that "the light from the water-bottle was merely engaged in a chromatic problem. All material objects announced their irresponsibility."[82] Hardy may well have found out about empiricism, of which he makes such imaginative use in *Tess*, from Stephen.

There are eighteenth-century elements in Hardy's characters: his view of rustic character is indebted to Gray's "Elegy". They are not Hodge but "varied fellow-creatures . . . some mutely Miltonic, some potentially Cromwellian"; Marty's "fingers which clasped the heavy ash haft might have skilfully guided the pencil or swept the string"; in London, Jude might have become a "statuary". Hardy's actresses — Matilda Johnson, Felice

Charmond, Eunice Manston − are immoral, not far from the whores and orange wenches of Covent Garden. Dr Chestman, wrongly predicting that Owen Graye will get worse, is like Fielding's surgeons. Revd Swancourt with his horse-, pig- and cow-medicines recalls Trulliber. Dislike of foreigners, particularly the French, reiterated in Hogarth and eighteenth-century literature (Farquhar's Foigard, Dryden's Melantha and Sir Fopling) reappears as foreign blood in the veins of baddies such as Troy, Eustacia, Lucetta, Farfrae and Felice, and the use of foreign terms to describe them: *weltbürgerlich*, a *femme de trente ans* (Felice), *guindée* (Mercy Chant), *Weltlust* (Alec), *Perruquier* (Percomb): whereas Hardy's contemporaries (Carlyle, George Eliot, Arnold), so far from disliking foreigners, channelled French and German ideas into English culture. Richardson's, Fielding's and Jane Austen's distrust of the morals of the upper classes (Mr B., Lovelace, Beau Didapper, Lord Fellamar, Hon. Yates) is echoed in the creation of Troy's father, Mountclere, Captain de Stancy, Sir Blount Constantine and Fitzpiers. Hardy praises Thackeray for not drawing perfect characters, which is Pope's defence of Homer. Hardy frequently gives his characters the sort of names we find in Restoration and eighteenth-century comedy: Boldwood, Bridehead, Callcome, Cantle, Charmond, Chestman, Fairway, Frankland, Heartall, Lackland, Ladywell, Leaf, Maybold, Menlove, Pennyways, Seamore, Seedling, Springrove, Tangs, Tipman, Trendle, Weedy, Whittle, Wildeve, Winwood, Woodwell, Worm, Yore.[83]

Some of Hardy's minor themes seem to originate in the eighteenth century. Fashionable people express amusement by "a slight laugh" rather than the "Ha-ha-ha! and . . . shaking of the shoulders [found] among the minor traders of the kingdom": Lord Chesterfield had advised that "there is nothing so illiberal and so ill-bred as audible laughter". Fancy, like Sophia Western, does not want to marry without her father's consent and manages to make him consent.[84] Elfride's and Eustacia's telescopes are not only memory of Hardy's father's: they are contrasted with microscopic vision − Knight's trilobite and the "curious microscopic life" half-blind Clym leads among the bees and grasshoppers. More clearly in *The Return*, the contrast is

between Eustacia's romantic interest in the distant and Clym's
satisfaction with the real and local: following Bacon, the
contrast between the telescope and microscope was frequently
made in attacks on and defences of the Royal Society, and by
Addison. Not "the ache of modernism", but Squire Western's
objection to Sophia's "sighing and whining and languishing and
writing" stands behind William Dewy's perception that his son
is "all in a mope . . . studding and thinking as if 'a were going to
turn chapel member".[85] Possibly Gay's letter mentioning that
John Hewet ranged the cows for Sarah Drew gave Hardy the
idea of Angel's doing it for Tess. The French romances, dislike
of which was shared by Pope, Addison, and Fielding, appear
jumbled up with serious works in Fitzpiers's library as they did
in Steele's "female library" and Addison's Leonora's library.
Criticism of the "double standard" of sexual morality, which
is perhaps the main moral theme of *Tess*, is found in *Jonathan
Wild* and *Tom Jones*.[86]

Hardy's repeated statements that fiction should "strike the
balance between the uncommon and the ordinary" or "reconcile the average with . . . uncommonness" recall the quotation
from Pope with which Fielding sums up his discussion of this
topic; "The great art of all poetry is to mix truth with fiction,
in order to join the credible with the surprising." In the first
versions of *The Return* and *Tess*, Hardy used the mock-marriage
common in Restoration comedy and the eighteenth-century
novel; and he sometimes follows Fielding in developing an incident as if he were writing a play and not a novel, a habit more
acceptable in the ex-dramatist "founder of a new province of
writing". When the bishop arrives unexpectedly at Swithin's
tower, Lady Constantine hides behind the bed curtains, like
Fielding's Square, Lady Bellaston and Honour. Ethelberta's
hotel at Rouen is the scene of complicated exits and entrances
by her various suitors.[87]

The eighteenth-century element in Hardy's language has
often been noticed. Lionel Johnson wrote that "Mr Hardy's
praise of nature is in the very dialect of the Eighteenth Century." Dr Gittings sees his moral reflections or aphorisms as "a
legacy from his reading in eighteenth-century authors", parti-

cularly Fielding and Horace Walpole's letters. S. F. Johnson showed that *The Return* exemplifies the various categories of Burke's Sublime: but just as Hardy there says that "a *more recently* learned emotion . . . responds" to Egdon's "sublimity", not to "beauty", so in *Tess* he speaks of "a *new* kind of beauty, a negative beauty of tragic tone": why should not all such passages, and Stonehenge, and the fires in *Desperate Remedies, A Laodicean* and *Far from the Madding Crowd*, the storm in *Far from the Madding Crowd*, the cliff in *A Pair of Blue Eyes*, the isolation of Endelstow, Little Hintock and Marlott, and Swithin's tower, be seen as exemplifying Burke?[88]

Hardy is fond of the sort of Latinism we associate with Johnson and Gibbon: "palpable confederacy", "amatory salutes", "peristaltic and vermicular motion", "spirituous delectation", "dolorifuge", "congelation". Sometimes such expressions recall particular authors. Tess is described by a favourite word of Swift's as "untinctured by experience". A footnote from the "Magnificat" at the end of *The Dynasts* in the decent obscurity of a learned language might suggest Gibbon. The comparison of Winterborne's hearth to "a vast scorching Sahara, with red-hot boulders lying about" is like Pope seeing China's earth in a coffee cup. Gray's sentiment that "ignorance is bliss" is paraphrased as "blindness may operate more vigorously than prescience". In Boswell's Ode, Johnson is made to describe himself as "Thrale's Entire" and Dare describes Paula as 'Cupid's Entire XXX" with perhaps some help from Racine. Johnson's dictionary definition of network may have suggested Winterborne's reticulated tablecloth, Mother Cuxsom's reticulated face and Tess's reticulated pinafore. Songs of the period, too, naturally survive in rural Wessex — "Malbrook" and "The Roast Beef of Old England". Coggan's song, "And while peace and plenty I find at my board" is, with its biblical reference to "sickness and sorrow", probably by Hardy, but sounds like Goldsmith or Sheridan or Gay. The use of "object glass" for "lens", "pencil" for "paintbrush" and "buckle" for "curled hair", also takes us back to the eighteenth century.[89]

Some motifs suggest Jane Austen. Questionable outsiders come from the North: Stokes, Farfrae, Bingleys, Churchills.

Knightley is for "truth and sincerity", Knight for "a soul truthful and clear".[90] The bishop's proposal to Lady Constantine is like Mr Collins's to Elizabeth Bennet.[91] The end of *Far from the Madding Crowd* (Chapter LVI), recommending "substantial affection" and "*camaraderie*" rather than love, is like *Pride and Prejudice* (III. iv) which contrasts "gratitude and esteem" with "what is so often described as arising on a first interview". Captain Flower in *Ethelberta*, in commissioning a painting of a ship, had attended to Admiral Croft's criticisms.[92]

If Hardy frequently escapes from his age into the past, it must also be said that much of the impression of his not so escaping is caused by what are in fact merely topical, not social or ideological, references. The reference to Velasquez in *Tess* just after a book about him had been published, is dramatically topical, an example of Angel's brothers' lack of integrity that they follow the fashion[93]. Comets and exploration in *Two on a Tower* do not have this excuse. It was published in 1882, shortly after one transit of Venus and actually before another, and Tebbutt's comet and Professor E. C. Pickering's paper on variable stars appeared while it was being written.[94] Places visited by Livingstone are visited by Sir Blount, and probably Livingstone's travels gave Hardy the whole idea of Sir Blount.[95] Other examples are: the arrival of the South Carolina gentlemen because of "the failure of the Southern cause"; the Turkish knight dying hard like the Ottoman Empire; and Tess's doubt whether the diamonds "were absolutely hers", which reflects the Married Women's Property Act of 1882. In one case topicality leads to anachronism: when Pierston in 1850 refers to Newman's *Apologia pro Vita Sua*.[96] Since easier divorce is not the point in *Jude*, may we not see Parnell's divorce and *Reg.* v. *Jackson*, in 1890 and 1891, as topical influences on the treatment of marriage in that novel?[97] But wherever an ideological influence has been shown not to have been realised, such as the reference to Arnold at the end of *A Laodicean*, it becomes merely topical. Another example of this is Tess's two "merciless polemical syllogisms": we are told nothing of the first, then: "She gave another, which might possibly have been paralleled in many a work of the pedigree ranging from the *Dictionnaire*

Philosophique to Huxley's *Essays*." Since the reference to Huxley is not developed, it adds nothing to the reference to eighteenth-century scepticism.

Nineteenth-century ideologies, then, had little effect on Hardy and all the less for the eighteenth-century elements in him, whether these were inspired by Stephen or not.

4 Invention

I do not claim the discovery that Hardy is repetitious. Professor Hillis Miller, for instance, said that "the novels repeat not only external situation, theme, and motif, but also the deeper organizing principles".[1] But I argue that the repetitions, especially taken with the use of autobiography and the stylistic and factual use of other writers, are a sign of limited power of invention. The volume of the repetitions and borrowings and uses of his own experiences is an essential argument for this conclusion. It makes critical discussion of all the examples impossible, but they do not bear out the theory that Hardy is merely developing and varying certain rich ideas, as Shakespeare does the idea of love and Conrad the idea of fidelity. Nor is he merely re-using the language and ideas of novels such as *Desperate Remedies* and *A Pair of Blue Eyes*, which he might regard as quarries for later work since they had not been widely read.

There is of course repetition justified by the importance of the idea repeated, such as the suicides and death wishes and references to education and love-destroying marriage discussed in Chapters 1 and 2 above. The iterative imagery of trees and man-traps in *The Woodlanders*, of colour, light, atmosphere, joy, dreams, constraint and suspense in *Tess*, and of pigs, hands, windows, photographs, pictures, roads, and parallel lines in *Jude*, noticed by critics, enrich these novels. So do other iterations not noticed by critics, such as the references to leaves, respectability, old-fashionedness and mechanicality in *The Mayor*, and even, in *Desperate Remedies*, the repetition of the word "parish". We all do fall as a leaf, and the leaves in *The Mayor* lead to their last appearance at Henchard's death. The repeated references to respectability are connected with Elizabeth-Jane's stigma of illegitimacy and its removal through her and her mother's marriages. To call behaviour mechanical reminds us of the Will. Old-fashionedness is related to the theme of old and new. "Parish" in *Desperate Remedies* at least stresses concern with a community.[2]

There are of course many more ideas in Hardy important enough to be repeated from novel to novel: fear of the future, misremembering history and myth, homelessness, evil that ceases as soon as it has done its work, the peasant who is not a stereotype, the heroism of admitting a sexual error, the difficulty of achieving individuality *sub specie aeternitatis*, the unendurable (expressed by saying this or that is "more than I can bear"), are in this way legitimately repeated. Dead leaves contribute to the seclusion of Little Hintock and are an image of Tess's past coming to light – they are not merely repeated from *The Mayor*. One has only to think of words and expressions such as harlican, maphrotight, projick, randyvoo, Peter's Finger, Cubit's thighs, Oliver Grumble, and King Norman, to see the richness of the idea that Wessex preserves in garbled forms some knowledge of central history and culture.[3]

The repetitions which most strongly suggest lack of invention are where passages are repeated *verbatim* at some length from an earlier work, and where the observation or expression repeated is idiosyncratic. Many *verbatim* repetitions have already been noticed by critics: a description of winter from *Desperate Remedies* in *The Trumpet-Major*; two sentences on a sunset, and a description of the effect of landscape on character, from *Desperate Remedies*, in *The Return*; a description of Ellen Terry from a notebook, applied to an unnamed actress in *The Well-Beloved* and quoted in the *Life*; descriptions of Hodge, a ridding, and an old shepherd at a hiring fair from "The Dorsetshire Labourer", in *The Mayor* and *Tess*; thirty-six lines of *A Pair of Blue Eyes* in *The Queen of Cornwall*; a description of Blackmore Vale from a review of Barnes's poems, in *Tess*; the description of the death of Miss Aldclyffe from *Desperate Remedies* in *An Indiscretion*. To these must be added, from *The Trumpet-Major,* "A Committee Man of the Terror" and "A Changed Man" respectively, the description of the beacon-tenders' hut, the hussar's pelisse, and the guarding of George III at Weymouth, in *The Dynasts*, and, from *Under the Greenwood Tree*, Somers's advice to Pierston in *The Well-Beloved* ("When you have decided to marry, take the first nice woman you meet. They are all alike"). A description in *Tess* of the arrival of strange birds at Flintcomb-Ash paraphrases a description in *The Return* of the arrival of a wild mallard on Egdon: "unconceived regions" reappear as "unknown regions", "the home of the North wind" as "the North pole", "glacial catastrophes" as "the crash of ice-bergs", "snowstorm episodes" as "the slide of snow-hills", and "glittering Auroral effects" as "the shooting light of the Aurora"; and in both novels the birds prefer Wessex and forget, or dismiss from their minds, their polar homes. The two passages near the end of *The Well-Beloved* are a special kind of self-plagiarism: two pages of the magazine version are repeated in the book version, but in the former they describe the hero trying to commit suicide, in the latter Avice III and her boyfriend trying to escape to Budmouth. The editor of the New Wessex *Desperate Remedies* has noted some briefer repetitions from it in later work: of a Leyden jar and of the phrases "outer chamber of the mind", "Cliff without a Name" and "it never looks like summer". We also find, in *The Mayor*, that "to the liege subjects of labour, the England of those days was a continent, and a mile a geographical degree": and in *Tess* "to persons of limited spheres, miles are as geographical degrees, parishes as counties, counties as provinces and kingdoms". In *The Mayor*, tumuli are compared to "the full breasts of Diana Multimammia supinely extended there": in *Tess* they are "as if Cybele the Many-breasted were supinely extended there": in "By the Barrows" they are "bulging as they bosoms were / of Multimammia stretched supinely there."[4]

Hardy repeats not only pages, paragraphs and sentences but general ideas, themes and motifs, the same elements in his presentation of Wessex, and the same favourite words and stylistic and rhetorical elements. He is "idiosyncratic": it is itself one of his favourite words: and I begin with repetition of observations which, in Hardy's own words, "illustrate the author's idiosyncratic mode of regard", because such repetitions seem particularly inartistic: we thought the author was sharing with us a new idea, and find he is only saying what he always says. Repeatedly in Hardy, flames flap, raindrops rap, hedges are compared to

strainers, embers to deserts, ponds to eyes, footpaths to meridians, ivy-leaves to neighbours: German soldiers are sad, dark
skies are darkened further by buildings, gowns are blue, heads
are haloed, light casts shadows upward, eye-sockets are fingered,
insides of mouths inspected, the Duchess of Richmond's ball is
precisely located, Adam's thoughts about the first sunset con-
jectured; the richness of the soil is the product of more than
human time; things are seen as drawings, outlines or profiles;
speech is unnecessary; nature is an Aeolian harp. Only space and
consideration for the reader's patience prevent the examination
of all these cases.[5]

In Tess, the halo is part of the system of iterative imagery.
Tess herself is in a sort of halo or "photosphere" made of her
own hopes, Angel's love, and the sunshine; and this relates her
to the party returning merrily from the Trantridge dance, who
have individual haloes in the moonlight, and to the "sort of halo
or occidental glow" which "came over life" at Rolliver's. But
we have already had haloes round Elfride, Christopher Julian,
Clym, Paula, Lucetta and Phena, not to mention the actual saints
in Stephen Smith's notebooks, the haloes round the candles at
the Dewys' dance and one hanging over Casterbridge; and we
are to see them again round "he, she, all of them" in "During
Wind and Rain", a "halo or glow-fog overarching" Christminster
— as it had Casterbridge — and others surrounding Paris and
London by night.

"Distinctness" is the quality of line-engravings and architec-
tural drawings which lightning and the early morning light confer on hedges and bushes in the storm at Weatherbury and on
old buildings in Sherton and Christminster. Also, Wintoncester's
buildings are seen "as in an isometric drawing": a yew appears
"as if drawn in ink" and creepers "as if drawn in charcoal"
against house walls. Trees at Mellstock, Dick's profile, and the
whole Mellstock Quire are seen as black, flat outlines. Elfride,
Charlotte de Stancy, Eustacia, Henchard, Tess, the band at the
gipsying on Egdon, the passengers in Mrs Dollery's van, and the
cows at Talbothays, are seen in profile or outline. The explanation may be clarity and visualisation, but it happens too often.

The idea that speech is unnecessary because there are other

means of communication is important to and characteristic of Hardy, since it is related to his "ache of modernism", "the modern vice of unrest", the speculative "thought [which] is a disease of the flesh". Nevertheless it too is repeated in an idiosyncratic way with inartistic frequency, generally as a comic yet respectable Wessex trait. Reuben Dewy's "deliberateness in speech" had "more to do with the machinery of the tranter's throat than with the matter enunciated". The "long acquaintance" between Geoffrey Day and Enoch "rendered words between them almost superfluous as vehicles of thought". So with Miller Loveday: "Every time that he poked his fire they knew from the vehemence or deliberateness of the blows the precise state of his mind." The point is made again about the farmers at Casterbridge market: "Not to hear the words of your interlocutor in metropolitan centres is to know nothing of his meaning. Here the face, the arms, the hat, the stick, the body throughout spoke equally with the tongue"; and Hardy goes on for another ten lines to explain how satisfaction, wonder, deliberation and a sense of tediousness were so expressed. Again, it is said of Winterbourne's silence that "the infinitesimal movement of muscle, curve hair and wrinkle which when accompanied by a voice goes unregarded, is watched and translated in the lack of it"; and of Angel when "getting to behave like a farmer" that "the muscles of his face had grown more expressive; his eyes looked as much information as his tongue spoke, and more". And in contradiction to what *The Mayor* says about metropolitan centres, Mrs Swancourt in London is " 'a listener ... not to the narratives told by my neighbours' tongues, but by their faces' ".

The Aeolian harp was the favourite toy of the Romantic poets: Goethe and Coleridge wrote poems about it. It is important in and characteristic of Hardy to say that by the action of the wind in trees and undergrowth nature herself expresses the sadness of life, but he does it far too often. There is an actual Aeolian harp in *The Trumpet-Major*, and "Aeolian modulations" and "Aeolian improvisation" from the wind in the grass and tent-cords in *The Mayor*. In *The Woodlanders* — the "Gregorian melodies" from South's elm — and in the "regular antiphonies of a cathedral choir" from the trees in *Far from the Madding Crowd*, the Aeolian and Gregorian ideas are combined. In *The Return* we learn of the "muttered articulations of the wind" like "souls" in "Limbo", of its "strumming upon the furze bushes", of the wind in the reeds making "sounds as of a congregation praying humbly" and of its "treble tenor and bass notes" especially in the holly and the "mummied heathbells". Three times it blows among pine-trees: once (in *A Laodicean*) sighing " 'like ten thousand spirits in trouble' " (that is, souls in Limbo), and twice in *Two on a Tower*: once merely breathing stertorously, while the other time its "peculiar dialect" is "enough to say what trees they were". It sighs again in *Tess*: "the occasional heave of the wind became the sigh of some immense sad soul": and it is also Aeolian, and Angel-ic, at Stonehenge: "the wind, playing upon the edifice, produced a booming tone like the note of some gigantic one-stringed harp". In *Ethelberta* it speaks in the trees "in . . . melancholy moans and sobs". In *The Mayor* it " 'makes a peculiar poetical-like murmur" ', says Jopp (it was really the skimmity). In *The Woodlanders* there is "music in the breeze" and a wind "vocalises" the "sorrows of the trees", and the pines "sigh" when planted, as they do in "The Pine Planters", "The Mother Mourns", and "Yellham-Wood's Story". In "A tryst at an Ancient Earthwork", winds play upon the grasses "as upon a harp": in *A Laodicean*, the wind plays on a telegraph wire. The "rhythmic tidal lyres" of "The Convergence of the Twain" are an underwater Aeolian harp. Finally, Tess and Sue themselves behave like Aeolian harps, Tess like a harp to a harp: when Angel played, "the harmonies passed like breezes through her, bringing tears to her eyes"; and when Little Father Time cries Sue cries too, "being a harp which the least wind of emotion from another's heart could make to vibrate".

Among the less idiosyncratic ideas that Hardy repeats are: the assimilation of human beings and animals, the descent of the commoner from the aristocracy, the conflict in a woman between femininity and humanity, the fickleness of women, the "mastery" of the woman by the man, the woman who regards the man as a god, the small human figure in a large expanse, the pallor of the thinker, the soldier who prefers to be a parson, the character's sense of being no more than a passing thought to others, the precise enumeration of seasons, the isolated and enclosed location, the featureless landscape, the closeness of life to death.[6]

The assimilation of human beings and animals, which has been discussed above, sometimes seems to anticipate D. H. Lawrence: human beings have an animal element in their nature which is not contemptible but on the contrary all the more important if the "cerebral" is not, (and because real animals are), as Lawrence's Ursula says, "quite delicate and sensitive". Something near the Laurentian point is made explicitly when Tess is said not to be an "anomaly" in the "environment" which did not recognise the "social law" requiring children to be legitimate. But in so many cases the treatment is comic, almost frivolous, and at least uncertain.

Feminine fickleness is a major element in the characterisation of Elfride, Bathsheba, Ethelberta, Eustacia, Anne Garland, Paula, Lucetta, Grace Melbury, Arabella and Sue, and, therefore, in the novels of which they are the heroines: two examples, one of a single chapter and the other of a whole novel, must suffice. In Chapter XXII of *The Hand of Ethelberta* the heroine writes to Julian not to come to say farewell, intending the letter to arrive after he's left, is angry with him for not coming, refuses to see him when he does come, but lets him wait and sends her sister to say she will see him if he insists, and does come to see him after he has gone again. In Sue this element bulks much larger than her being an "Ishmaelite" and a "bundle of nerves" justifies. " 'You mustn't love me' " is followed by " 'If you want to love me, you may.' " She promises to meet Jude, and breaks her promise. She treats his marriage as an obstacle to love and accepts Phillotson; then she rehearses this marriage with Jude — a sort of stage marriage to him. Married to Phillotson she tells Jude he must not visit her, and then that he may, and when he does, kisses him but will not let him embrace her, but then does let him embrace her when they are parting. She leaves Phillotson, but returns on a visit; really she is thinking of going back to Phillotson permanently, but " 'as you are

not so ill ... I cannot!' " She refuses to sleep with Jude, and
then does, and then stops doing so: refuses to marry him, then
agrees but doesn't. She remarries Phillotson, but " 'if he had refused ... it might not have been my duty' ".

That the seasons are precisely enumerated in almost all the
novels is of course natural since they are concerned with
country life, but there is a certain rigidity and repetitiveness in
the fact that so many begin and end in autumn or winter:
*Under the Greenwood Tree, Far from the Madding Crowd, The
Return* (only "Aftercourses" ends in summer), *Two on a Tower,
The Mayor*, and *The Woodlanders* (to the death of Giles).

Enclosure and isolation are repeatedly combined in the location of the principal settings. Blackmoor Vale is "engirdled and
secluded", Little Hintock "sequestered" and "wood-environed",
Endelstow Rectory in a "dell" and "enclosed from the wilder-
ness", Swithin's column in "solitude" among "environing trees".
The remoteness of Little Hintock and of Overcombe is described by the same image of a wave: news "exciting and moving
those unimportant natives as a ground-swell moves the weeds in
a cave", "news from the outside world, which entered and ex-
pired at Little Hintock like the exhausted swell of a wave in
some innermost cavern".

A number of motifs, themselves repeated, may be collected
together as all apparently illustrating the idea that "in the midst
of life we are in death", or, as Hardy puts it, "Life and Death
are neighbours nigh." Characters sit on tombs or altars: Alec,
illustrating the contrast made explicitly between live and dead
d'Urbervilles; Anne Garland sits on the vanished altar at
Faringdon Ruin, the ephemeral bloom contrasted with the great
length of time; the young choristers sit on the tomb at
Mellstock waiting for the service to begin. Ethelberta and Neigh
embrace in Cripplegate churchyard. Barrows, which are tombs,
seem to function in the same way: most clearly when they are
compared to the life-giving breasts of Cybele or Diana, and
when a barrow is situated on top of John Power's railway-
tunnel. Tess walking among the "semi-globular tumuli",
Ethelberta on her way to Corvsgate "through a hugh cemetery
of barrows containing human dust from prehistoric times", and

Eustacia on her barrow, seem to repeat the point of Anne
Garland on the altar: the young female figure as the type of life,
the image of Death and the Maiden. The Egdon barrow's bonfire is explicitly called an act of rebellion against death. The
situation of Greenhill Fair, on the remains of an ancient earthwork, and the comparisons between weddings and funerals,
make the same point. After discussing weddings, Timothy
Fairway gives good reasons for preferring "a good hearty
funeral". Miller Loveday promises that his wedding to
Mrs Garland " 'shall be as melancholy as you require – in short,
just like a funeral' "; which Widow Edlin echoes when she says,
in reference to Sue's remarriage to Phillotson, " 'Weddings be
funerals, 'a believe, nowadays.' " The parson marrying Swithin
and Lady Constantine arrives late: " 'he had got it in his mind
that 'twere a funeral' ". Immediately after the remarriage of
Henchard and Susan, Longways thinks of a man who
" 'dropped down dead yesterday' ". Tess, working on her allotment in a white gown and black jacket, gives "the effect . . . of
a wedding and funeral guest in one", which fits the colour and
clothes imagery of the novel and is ironic and appropriate to her
situation as theoretically married and actually soon to die.
Another version of "in the midst of life . . . " is leaving the dead
to bury the dead: " ' Why should a man . . . hurry for lifeless
clay?' " " 'Why should death rob life of fourpence?' " Another
is the deaths of pregnant women – Fanny Robin, Lucetta,
Felice. This collocation of life and death is found as the climax
of stories – Tess and the black flag, Elfride dead on the same
train as her live lovers on St Valentine's Eve, Baptista Heddegan
"in a hideous contiguity to the dead husband and the living" –
and is the main point of many poems, such as "Heiress and
Architect", "During Wind and Rain", "The Six Boards" and
"At the Draper's". Just because the concepts are so big, the
bald simplicity of their repeated confrontation overshadows
variety of treatment and has the effect of monotony in the
oeuvre taken as a whole.

Repetitiousness in the presentation of Wessex which (in his
Preface to *Far from the Madding Crowd*, his titles for collec-
tions of poems and short stories, his overall title "Novels of

Character and Environment'', and the naming of his dog) Hardy stresses as his principal achievement, has the effect of suggesting that the culture is not rich enough to deserve so much attention. The same work processes – cider-making, hiving bees, pig-killing, and tree planting – are repeatedly described, and many are never described at all. The pig-killing, horrific in *Jude*, figures in *A Pair of Blue Eyes* as a cheerful occasion. The descriptions of cider-making in *Desperate Remedies* and *The Woodlanders* are verbally close. Apart from work, the same Wessex ways and qualities are mentioned repeatedly: claiming kin, club-walking, dwindling fairs, consulting ''conjurors'', lifehold and copyhold, outdoor courting, the pulling down of houses, the skimmington, the impact of tourism, the true refinement and delicacy of Wessex. If these are important enough to be stressed by repetition, what of the minor habits such as blacking or oiling boots, calculating by chalk strokes on panels, not applauding artistic performance, looking over Grey's Bridge when miserable, seeing the phantom of the beloved on Midsummer Eve, girls not entering inns with men? Repeatedly we are told of the different varieties of apple and how to sell apple trees, the unreliability of clocks, the worthlessness of smart bought clothes, the continued observance of the Julian Calendar, the impropriety of kissing or holding hands, the serpents and clarionets in the old bands, the popularity of Bishop Ken's hymns. Within a single novel, the hand-holding and kissing (or not) is effective, indicating the difference between the shy and the bold lover, and the progress of the courting. What is inartistic is the repetition of the effect in seven novels, in five of which – *The Return, The Trumpet-Major, The Woodlanders, Tess* and *Jude* – the motif is prominent.[7]

Considering how many and important the rustic characters are, Hardy's dialect vocabulary – about four hundred words – is not large; but this may be explained by his ''hope that the rustics, although quaint, may be made to appear intelligent, and not boorish''. But within that vocabulary, the repetition of expressions and single words, such as ''chips in porridge'', ''quite the dand'', ''dry as a kex'', ''flung over pulpit'', ''Jack Rag or Tom Straw'', ''nailed up in parish boards'', ''het or wet'', ''little small" and "old ancient", "going underground" (for dying), gawkhammer, larry, thirtover, chiel, gallicrow, hagridden, wambling, and perusing ("a real perusing man"), gives again the impression of the thinness of the culture. The very idea that it is shameful to speak in dialect is used again and again. The repetition of certain folk images – the cigar, the Devil, the diamond has the same effect. We all remember that Alec d'Urberville is associated with a cigar: but so are Wildeve, Fitzpiers and Louis Glanville. It has already been shown in Chapter 2 that the diamond is the folk image of wealth and value: to the examples there given should be added the application of "diamond" or "diment" to a person: to Thomasin, Farfrae, Mrs Durbeyfield's new baby, and Tess. Both Tess and Christian Cantle associate the Devil with a three-pronged fork and flames, and both Tess and Giles – or in Giles's case rather Hardy himself – associate that fork with one in domestic use. Apart from this image, too many people are seen as the Devil or in league with him: Fitzpiers, Percomb, Felice's South Carolina gentleman, the Cross-in-Hand murderer, Alec d'Urberville, Bathsheba, Venn, Dare, Baron von Xanten.[8]

I turn now to repetition as a sign of the limitations of Hardy's art, style or rhetoric, as distinct from his subject-matter, ideas and themes; of his *dispositio* and *elocutio* rather than his *inventio*, to use the old terms. Repetitiousness here suggests that the range of self-expression is limited.

He overuses certain favourite words: intramural, metallic, rencounter, reticulated, flexible or flexuous, and whitey-brown. Most of them are rare words, the objection to the re-use of which is, again, the loss of spontaneity. The visitors to Milton's grave in Barbican make an "intramural stir". Jude's and Sue's lodging in Christminster is "little more than an intramural cottage". Shepherds in Durnover "lived . . . in an intramural squeeze". Grace, staying indoors to avoid Winterborne because she can't get a divorce, leads an "intramural existence". "Rencounter" is, and was in Hardy's day, a very rare word, in the sense Hardy uses of a friendly, or not inimical, meeting. The objections to "flexible", generally used of young women, are complex. It is really a synonym for curvaceous and *ondulante*, and these are merely physical characteristics and if stated should be stated plainly. It is not a very good synonym since any articulated animal is flexible. It tends to reduce those of whom it is predicated — Fancy, Charlotte de Stancy, Lucetta, Grace, Tess, and Sue — to a common denominator. Finally the use of the word "whitey-brown", itself admirable, like the Aeolian wind — it "creeps out of the earth over us" as Melbury says: the earth, like the wind, we are constantly aware of — is (like that of the Aeolian wind) simply too frequent. It is the colour of the boots or smocks of James Dewy, Haymoss, Izz and Tess; of John Loveday's regiment, Bathsheba's labourers and the labourers at the Casterbridge hiring fair, Melbury's companions in search of Grace, and two small boys in the furmity tent; of a pony; of the tilts of Aunt Drusilla's cart and Napoleon's baggage-waggons, and of the landscape of the ridge outside Blackmoor Vale.[9]

Repetitiousness is of course only one fault in Hardy's style. Its syntactical awkwardness and officialese were criticised by Heilman. Maugham described the style of Edward Driffield, who is Hardy, as "an uneasy mixture of the classical and the slangy" and Leavis saw a greater number of ingredients: "he takes as they come the romantic-poetical, the prosaic-banal, the stilted literary, the colloquial, the archaistic, the erudite, the technical, the dialect word, the brand-new Hardy coinage". Lord David Cecil and Douglas Brown noticed the "clumsiness" "roughness" and "uncouthness", but stressed good consequences: they "differentiate [his writings] from the leading article" and produce "an accurate affectionate honesty". David Lodge, discussing *Tess*, found that Hardy was unhappy with syntax and vocabulary far removed from her natural idiom. Morton D. Zabel complained of "pretension and straining eloquence". I do not argue these questions here, and the quotations would mostly be unfair to their authors and to Hardy if supposed to summarise their whole views. They are one side of the case: these criticisms are sometimes true, and the evidence which those who made them collected shows that Hardy is limited in the sense that he could write badly, in these various ways, at times.[10]

One figure of speech may be given as an example of stylistic repetition. It might be called Comtian or looped accumulation:

"I like the parson's opinion on law, the lawyer's on doctoring, the doctor's on business, and my business-man's ... on morals."

Hope sinks to misgiving, and faith to hope.

It [the gargoyle] was too human to be called like a dragon, too impish to be like a man, too animal to be like a fiend, and not enough like a bird to be called a griffin.

These are from *Far from the Madding Crowd*. In *The Return* we find:

[In the light of the bonfire] Those whom Nature had depicted as merely quaint became grotesque, the grotesque became preternatural.

The mouth seemed formed less to speak than to quiver, less to quiver than to kiss. Some might have added, less to kiss than to curl.

To pass to courtship without acquaintance, to pass to marriage without courtship, is a skipping of terms.

In *Ethelberta*:

"A woman forms an opinion of her choice before she has seen him, loves him before she has formed an opinion."

[In the snow] Ordinary houses were sublimated to the rank of public buildings, public buildings to palaces.

A touch to other people was a blow to him, a blow to them his deep wound.

[Picotee is to Ethelberta] what the moon is to the sun, a star to the moon.

"There were bailiffs to look after the work-folk, foremen to look after the tradesmen, a building steward to look after the foremen, a land-steward to look after the building-steward, and a dashing grand agent to look after the land-steward."

In *The Mayor*:

Nothing is more insidious than the evolution of wishes from mere fancies, and of wants from mere wishes.

The turn-pike road became a lane, the lane a cart-track, the cart-track a bridle-path, the bridle-path a footway, the footway over-grown.

In *The Woodlanders*, "more meditation than action, and more listlessness than meditation" and " 'a body who has smiled where she has not loved, and loved where she has not married' ". In *A Pair of Blue Eyes*, "It was a time when mere seeing is meditation, and meditation peace."[11]

More generally, Hardy over-uses the language of contrast and parallel. This is a difficult question because, in the first place, contrast is a useful method for the novelist — one has only to think of Fielding and George Eliot. And, secondly, Hardy's verbal contrasts are of course related to his structural ones. Perhaps the trouble is that these structural contrasts — Cytherea between Manston and Springrove, Fancy between Dick and Maybold, Elfride between Smith and Knight, Bathsheba between Troy and Oak, Eustacia between Clym and Wildeve, Anne between the Loveday brothers, Paula between de Stancy and Somerset, Lucetta between Farfrae and Henchard, Grace between Winterborne and Fitzpiers, Tess between Alec and Angel, Sue between Phillotson and Jude, to name only the main ones — have themselves an element of monotony which survives differences of character and situation. At any rate, since the contrasts occur in all the novels, it does not seem right to claim, as Professor Kramer does,[12] that "the arrangement of opposite qualities" is the "organizing principle" of *Far from the Madding*

Crowd. Indeed he himself rather undercuts this by saying that "in a subordinate role ... the pattern of opposition ... re-appears in later novels."

One of Hardy's repeated forms of contrast and parallel consists in the very pointing out of the contrast or parallel. "Never could there be a greater contrast ... than between this graveyard and that of the further village." "[The town] smiled as sunny a smile upon Elfride as it had done between one and two years earlier when she had entered it at precisely the same hour as the bride-elect of Stephen Smith." "There is a loquacity that tells nothing, which was Bathsheba's; and there is a silence which says much: that was Gabriel's." "Troy's deformities lay deep down ... thus contrasting with homely Oak." " 'Here be I, his former master, working for him as man, and he the man standing as master, with my house and my furniture and my what-you-may-call wife all his own.' " "The current affairs of Casterbridge were interrupted by an event ... stirring the depths of its society simultaneously with the preparations for the skimmington." "Henchard formed at this moment much the same picture as he had presented when entering Casterbridge for the first time nearly a quarter of a century before." "Giles ... had been struck with ... the curious parallelism between Mr Fitzpiers's manner and Grace's, as shown by the fact of both of them straying into a subject of discourse ... foreign to him." "Six months before this date a scene almost similar in its mechanical parts, had been enacted at Hintock House" and (referring to the same two scenes four pages later) "He was arrested by the spectacle ... in its character as the counterpart of one that had had its run many months before, in which he had figured as the patient." "Now she knew what he [Angel somnambulating with Tess across the Froom] was dreaming of — that Sunday morning when he had borne her along through the water with the other dairymaids." "Jude had never before in his life gone that road with Sue, though he had with another." "Strange that his first aspiration — towards academical proficiency — had been checked by a woman, and that his second aspiration — towards apostleship — had also been checked by a woman." " 'I was gin-drunk; you were creed-drunk.' "[13]

Another form, which overlaps with this, as in the last example, is where the contrast or parallel is made by the figure of speech, which is obtrusive like the Comtian accumulation. "By the side of the instructive and piquant snubbings she received from Knight, Stephen's general agreeableness seemed watery; by the side of Knight's spare love-making, Stephen's continual outflow seemed lackadaisical." "It appears that ordinary men take wives because possession is not possible without marriage, and that ordinary women accept husbands because marriage is not possible without possession." "When Bathsheba was swayed by an emotion of an earthly sort her lower lip trembled: when by a refined emotion, her upper or heavenward one." " 'Ordinary powers exhibited in a new way effect as much as extraordinary powers exhibited in an old way.' " "Emmeline [was] of that transitional age which causes its exponent to look wistfully at the sitters when romping and at the rompers when sitting." "An environment which would have made a contented woman a poet, a suffering woman a devotee, a pious woman a psalmist, even a giddy woman thoughtful, made a rebellious woman saturnine."[14]

A third kind is where incidents or scenes are made to contrast with or parallel one another and one does not feel that the contrast establishes much. Knight rescues Elfride on the church tower and Elfride rescues Knight on the cliff. She pursues Knight to London, whither she had unwillingly accompanied Stephen. Tess's ride in the spring-waggon with Angel to the railway station balances her ride in the dogcart with Alec to The Slopes. On the break-up of their marriages, Arabella accepts and Sue refuses the furniture. Jude pursues Arabella up the stairs of her parents' cottage and this leads to their marriage: Arabella takes Jude drunk up the stairs of her father's new home and this leads to their remarriage.[15]

Another stylistic or rhetorical repetition may be called the "soon-resolved mystery". "Somebody came towards him along the deserted footway, and rays from the nearest lamp streaked the face of his sister Faith." "A young man knocked softly at the door ... His visitor was Dare." "The door ... was opened by a slight thoughtful young man. ... The postman put into his hands a book packet. Christopher took the package upstairs." "One evening . . . the dark little lane . . . was paced by a solitary man . . . Pierston — for the man in the lane was he — . . ."[16]

Hardy's use of certain expressions such as "could almost be heard (or seen)" and "he went on" is also.somewhat repetitive. By "almost" in these expressions Hardy does not mean almost, but that he wants to introduce a poetical idea — much the same one in each case — but as near fact and as far from fancy as language permits. In *The Return* "the sap [of hollyhocks] almost simmered in the stems"; in *The Woodlanders* "the rush of sap in the veins of the trees could almost be heard"; and in *Tess* "the rush of juices could almost be heard". Elsewhere we are told that "to persons standing alone on a hill during a clear midnight . . . the roll of the world . . . is almost . . . palpable"; that grass's "activity in sucking the moisture from the rich damp sod was almost a process observable by the eye"; that Bathsheba's "breathing could almost be heard" (why not quite?) during her duet with Boldwood, and Retty's "throbbing heart could almost be seen to shake" when about to be carried by Angel; that Anne "could almost see through the gloom" that the Trumpet-Major was glad of her company; that "a rigid reticence that was almost a third personality" came between Ethelberta's and Mountclere's brother; and that an old road and a barrow were "almost crystallised to natural products".[17]

The last words of *Tess* — "As soon as they had strength they arose, joined hands, and went on" — are extremely effective. *They* went on, Tess had stopped. They went on, the way things go on, mechanically, having to go on living. But unfortunately he uses the same effect as the last words of "Old Mrs Chundle": after her death, the curate knelt "down in the dust of the road . . . Thus, he remained some minutes [Angel and Liza-Lu had "remained thus a long time"] . . . : till he rose, brushed the knees of his trousers, and walked on." The chapter, too, in which Knight takes final leave of Elfride, ends "He . . . breathed a low groan, and went on."[18]

Hardy also re-uses a large number of plot devices and motifs. I am not thinking of major matters such as his use of coincidence or things happening too late or Elfride's purity anticipating Tess's, but of comparatively minor ones. Thus the praised opening of the action of *The Return*, the road with the single figure, is also found as the opening of *Under the Greenwood Tree* and *The Woodlanders*. The elderly couple whose romance parallels that of their offsprings are found in *A Pair of Blue Eyes* and *The Trumpet-Major*: both couples live contiguously, are widows and widowers, and re-marry. Both Henchard and Pierston move in circles round their loved ones: Henchard "by the centripetal influence of his love for his stepdaughter", Pierston "at the end of a radius whose pivot was the grave of Avice Caro". Wildeve and Thomasin don't marry because the licence was for Budmouth and they went to Anglebury: Stephen and Elfride because they went to Plymouth and the licence was for London: Troy and Fanny Robin because one went to All Saints and the other to All Souls. The brother-sister poverty of the Julians repeats that of the Owens. Fanny Robin's and Elizabeth-Jane's identities are both established by colour of hair. The legitimation of bastards is a reason for both Captain de Stancy and Henchard to marry, and their wicked sexual acts cause both of them to abstain from drink, one for twenty-one years, the other for eighteen. Both St Cleeve and Mrs Dollop lose money by marriage. Like Henchard and Farfrae, Manston and Springrove are rivals both in love and business. Both Lady Elfride Luxellian and the Honourable Laura elope with singers. Both Fancy and Bob Loveday lose their appetite when unhappy in love. Eustacia, Grace and Arabella all hate their husbands' books. Bathsheba, Paula and Grace are all proud heroines humbling themselves by pursuing the hero to his simple abode and asking to be made love to. Fancy, Elfride, Tess and Jude all conceal the fact that they have been loved before. Both Elfride's and Sue's earlier lovers die of consumption. Bathsheba, Henchard, Tess and Jude are afraid of being despised by those they love. Dick and Fancy, and Angel and Tess, get their fingers mixed in a washbowl. Bob Loveday and Anne, and Jude and Sue, are compared to Paul and Virginia. Melbury and Angel lift girls over floods. Tabitha Lark appears at the end to take Lady Constantine's place, as Liza-Lu does Tess's. Maybold, Wildeve, Farfrae, Fitzpiers, Tim Tangs and Angel take or propose to take their wives far away from Wessex. Bathsheba, Grace, Avice III and Lady Caroline are given superhuman physical strength by the death or sickness of their beloved. A moth is used as a love signal by Wildeve and by a lover in the poem "The Moth Signal" in exactly the same way. Fancy, Eustacia, Anne, Lady Constantine and Sue speak from indoors through windows to their lovers outside. Cytherea, Fancy, Bathsheba, Thomasin, Grace, Tess, Christopher Julian and Jude accept as husbands or wives those they had previously rejected or did not really want.· Fancy, Bathsheba, Elizabeth-Jane and Sue either become, or try to become, or are taken to be, "staid" or "matronly".[19]

Hardy's uses of abroad, letter-writing, and what may be called voyeurs, demand longer treatment. The voyeurs have been noticed by critics, so it is not necessary to discuss the instances; but, however characteristic the motif may be of the Hardy who "ought to have gone as a ghost" to revisit his school, the fact remains that it is used to convey information to the reader or to a character in an unrealistic way: unrealistic because spying and overhearing are not as common in life as in Hardy. "Abroad" has several aspects. First, characters in three novels — *A Pair of Blue Eyes, Ethelberta* and *A Laodicean* — travel in Europe for no good reason and always to Normandy and on the Grand Tour. Secondly, when Hardy wants people really offstage he repeatedly sends them — only for its remoteness — to South America: Angel and Lady Constantine's brother Louis go to Brazil, Dare is threatened with Peru. Thirdly, shorter escapes from Wessex are repeatedly to Bath: this is where the second Mrs Swancourt takes Elfride, where Bathsheba, Lady Constantine, Humphrey Gould, and Lady Caroline go to be married, where Lucetta's "people really belong to", and where "everybody of any note" is to be found. For further afield in Britain we have "the North", often with bad connotations, based no doubt partly on almost the whole of the island being north of Dorchester, and on the Dorset hills rising on the whole abruptly on their northerly sides. This is where the cold wind comes from in "The Voice" and where Farfrae, Alec, the engine-man of Tess's threshing machine and the legitimate widow of "Enter a Dragoon" come from. Even the northern limits of Casterbridge are "mournful" in contrast to its "cheerful . . . south avenues".[20]

Hardy also over-uses letter-writing. The non-arrival, or possible non-arrival of a letter is repeatedly cardinal to the plot, lovers are repeatedly warned by letter of rivals, and love-making itself is repeatedly carried on by letter.[21]

Apart from the way Hardy's characters are classifiable by type, as noticed by critics (especially Guerard), character-motifs tend to be repeated. Thus the unstable or immoral person tends to be or have been an actor or actress — Troy impersonating Dick Turpin, Felice, Matilda Johnson, Mrs Manston. Lucetta, although she is not an actress, comes near to being one by her remarks about her clothes — " 'You are that person' (pointing to one of the arrangements), 'or you are *that* totally different person' (pointing to the other)" - she changes her character with her costume. Then again, a certain type of character — Worm, Leaf, Poorgrass, Christian Cantle — is proud, or at least not ashamed, of afflictions of mind and body. " 'I'm only a poor wambling man," says Worm, frequently. " 'I never had no head,' " says Leaf, "delighted at being called a fool in such a friendly way". Simon Burden the beacon-tender says " 'I be an old man and of no judgement now.' " " 'I'm the man . . . no woman will marry,' " says Christian Cantle. Twisting his smashed arm, which is itself like Worm's frying noise, Tullidge still feels some of the "glory of exhibition". Poorgrass's "shyness, which was so painful as a defect, filled him with a mild complacency now that it was regarded as an interesting study". The maltster prides himself on his decay: " 'Ye be no old man worth naming — yer teeth baint half gone yet,' " he says to Henery Fray. Even the young Coggan is, by his loose tooth or cut finger, "elevated above the common herd of afflictionless humanity". Another repeated character-motif is found in Christian Cantle, Robert Creedle, and Miller Loveday's man David — the bachelor's inefficient man-servant.[22]

Then there is the question of parallel treatments in prose and verse: some of them noted by R. W. King and others. Hardy, as King points out, says in the Preface to *Wessex Poems* that "in some few cases the verses were turned into prose and printed as such, it having been unanticipated at that time that they might see the light". How contemptuous critics have been of Pope for writing his poems out in prose first, and of Dryden for being in doubt whether "to run his thoughts into verse or give them the other harmony or prose": why should they be kinder to Hardy when he does both? Between "Midnight on the Great Western" and a passage in *Jude* "the verbal correspondences", as King says, "are remarkable". Other verse and prose parallels, beside the dozen listed by King, are: "The Moth-Signal", already noted; "The Fiddler" and "The Fiddler of the Reels"; "At Shag's Heath" and "The Duke's Reappearance"; the poem and the novel entitled "The Well-Beloved"; "The Catching Ballet of the Wedding Clothes" and, especially in its original version, "The Romantic Adventures of a Milkmaid". There are probably a lot of minor repetitions between verse and prose, like the following three examples from one novel, *The Well-Beloved*: "the only woman he had never loved of those who had loved him" (Avice II, Pierston) recurs as "She was the woman I did not love" in "In the Moonlight": two passages, in one of which Pierston reflects on "this curse of his heart not ageing while his frame moved naturally onward", and another in which he sees himself in an actual "looking-glass . . . far, chronologically, in advance of the person he felt himself to be", are put together in the poem "I Look into My Glass". and time's "raspings, chisellings, scourgings, bakings, freezings" of Marcia's face are re-called in the "bodings, broodings, beatings, blanchings, bless-ings" of "Lines to a Movement". Where there is verbal corres-pondence as in these and between *Jude* and "Midnight on the Great Western" or between comparisons of the sun to a crimson wound and to an inflamed wound ("The Wound" and *Tess*), the simplicity of Hardy's poems — in which "not having too much style" is often more apparent than "the art of concealing art" — results in a feeling that there is not much difference between the verse and prose treatments, which we do not get from other novelist poets such as Swift, Scott and Lawrence.[23]

We must next consider Hardy's quotations from literature, and, first, the fact that here too he uses the same material re-peatedly[24]. Repetition of the same quotations is justified if the idea and its source are of special importance, for instance, 1 Corinthians 13 on charity, or if repeatability is of the nature of the thing repeated, as in the case of popular songs and dances, though even here one might have preferred Mrs Durbeyfield to sing, while rocking her cradle at the beginning of *Tess*, a song different from the one sung by Farmer Cawtree's quarrelsome couple at the end of Hardy's immediately preceding novel; and one may feel that "The Girl I Left behind Me" is played too often.

Quotation enriches if it is in character or for any reason adds a dimension. Thus it is in character for Liddy to say "The Philistines be upon us." Quotations may place Hardy in relation to the authors quoted: Wordsworth's "Nature's holy plan" and Browning's "all's right with the world" are examples of simple disagreement, albeit showing that Hardy has not fully understood those authors. In general, widespread knowledge of the Bible justifies Hardy's characters' quotations from it. Moreover in many novels, particularly *The Mayor*, the Old Testament contributes to the picture of an immemorially unchanged world, and comparison to biblical, as to other mythical or historical persons, often suggests admirably that qualities associated with such persons are found in Hardy's apparently simple or negligible characters. Obviously quotation from the Old and New Testaments in *Jude* contributes to the distinction in that novel between Hebraism and real Christianity. Allusions in *Tess* to *Genesis* and *Paradise Lost* do add a dimension: most obviously that Tess as Eve is not merely expelled from Paradise but killed, whereas Angel although expelled has in Liza-Lu a second Eve: the woman pays. Still such considerations do not justify all the quotations from the Bible, as when it is said of Elizabeth-Jane that "she was troubled at his [Henchard's] presence, like the brethen at the avowal of Joseph", where the brethren were troubled because they had tried to murder Joseph, to which nothing corresponds in the relation of Elizabeth-Jane and Henchard. This is the characteristic weakness of Hardy's literary quotations: it is simply the memorable phrase he is after, not its context, as when he quotes the phrase "poor wounded name" on the title-page of *Tess* without any reference to its context in

The Two Gentlemen of Verona, where Proteus's is the wounded
name and Julia's the bosom into which she puts the letter she
has torn. It is the frequency of Hardy's literary quotations
which makes them contribute to the impression of uninventive-
ness: he is using other people's words to express what he wants
to say because they do it better than he could.[25]

Some further examples of slight or inappropriate comparison
may be given from *Far from the Madding Crowd* and *The
Return*. Boldwood suffers jealousy, "the injured lover's hell":
the phrase but nothing else is taken from *Paradise Lost*. Oak,
sacked for giving his opinion of Bathsheba's conduct, left her
with "dignity, as Moses left the presence of Pharaoh" — but
Moses had been told not to ask again for the release of Israel
from captivity. Bathsheba "was the Esther to this poor Vashti"
(Fanny Robin), but Fanny did not disobey Ahasuerus (Troy)
or stand on her modesty. After the apparent death of Troy,
Bathsheba "like the mouldering gentlefolk of the poet's story . . .
could sit and ponder what a gift life used to be"; but this was
not because she and Troy, like the Duke and bride in "The
Statue and the Bust" had failed to light lamps and gird loins.
Cooking pots appear "like Shadrach, Meshack and Abednego"
only because they are surrounded by flames. In *The Return*,
Humphrey's leggings are like Goliath's greaves of brass only
because they are stiff. Yeobright's love is "as chaste as that of
Petrarch for his Laura" although he is about to marry Eustacia.
His sight, good enough for furze-cutting but not for school-
teaching, is "like the wings in Rasselas" which do not fly but
do save their inventor from drowning. Mrs Yeobright recognises
him by his gait as the watchman did Ahimaaz, but Yeobright
is not bringing news, let alone news of death. Finally, 'We have
been told what happens when a woman deliberates; and the
epigram is not always terminable with woman, provided that
one be in the case, and that a fair one." "The woman that deliberates is lost"; but Wildeve, the person here deliberating
whether to visit Eustacia, is less, not more, likely to visit her if
he deliberates, and is not at this stage lost by doing so.[26]

In *Tess* and *Jude*, as has been seen, many of the quotations
fit into larger frames of reference. Attempts to construct such

frames for Hardy's other novels have been less successful. For instance, Dr Beatty sees the image of the labyrinth as lying "behind the whole" of *Desperate Remedies* and connecting it with the Gemini myth. The novel "examines the Classical and Judaeo-Christian cultures". The younger Springrove is part of the "presentation of the Judaeo-Christian world", and on the classical side "the story of Aeneas provides a valid term of reference for much of the book". Cytherea Aldclyffe is Manston's mother as Venus was Aeneas's, and he is a love child. But it is not only because Manston is manipulated by his mother as Aeneas was by the gods that he is called Aeneas, says Dr Beatty. An anchor mentioned by Cytherea Graye is the Christian anchor symbol, and it occurs also in *Jude*; Jude Fawley failed to find anchorage, but "Aeneas, that reluctant sailor . . . *did* in the end achieve what destiny had in store for him."[27]

To this it must be objected that the word labyrinth is only used twice in the novel, once of Cytherea and once of Springrove, and that the connection with the Gemini myth apparently depends on the reader knowing that a labyrinth is etymologically a double-headed axe. Moreover, although the story itself is labyrinthine, Cytherea's and Springrove's situations are simple dilemmas. Springrove's presenting Judaeo-Christianity depends (according to Dr Beatty) on his having the name Edward — the only character in the book with a real Christian name — and on his recalling Swinburne's "pale Galilean". Edward is not a particularly Christian name, and "spectre-thin", the epithet which is supposed to recall Swinburne's Christ and which is applied to Springrove when he has just seen his beloved marry Manston, is actually from Keats's "Nightingale" ode. Cytherea's anchor is the stable home she wanted with Edward, and finally got, not the Christian symbol. Manston "achieved what destiny had in store for him" only in a tautological not a Virgilian sense, in that he got what was coming to him, rather than being the founder of anything; and it is not clear what can be meant by calling him a reluctant sailor.[28]

If the story of Aeneas provided a valid term of reference one would expect all references to the *Aeneid* to contribute. Aeneas sailed reluctantly away from Dido, and there is a storm in

Desperate Remedies like the one which leads to Aeneas and
Dido becoming lovers, so Cytherea Graye could have been Dido
and Eunice Creusa — but Dr Beatty doesn't say they are and
one doesn't see what would be gained if they were. He does say
that the burning of the elder Springrove's inn is like the burning
of Troy. He does seek to fit in some of the quotations from the
Aeneid: by Hardy's comparison of the "entrails" of a Dutch
clock to those of Virgil's Harpy, says Dr Beatty, he "manages to
convey . . . the squalor, dirt and stench of a tenement in mid-
Victorian London" and the "cities' . . . inability to understand
or cope with the problems of the new industrial age". Just as
one cannot say that Manston did not achieve what destiny had
in store for him, so one cannot say that the new industrial age is
not part of an examination of Classical and Judaeo-Christian
culture: it is all too wide and vague. But one may feel that Dr
Beatty has not really explained why the Harpy has to be Virgilian
and in Latin.[29]

The "purple light" on the faces of the young lovers rowing in
Budmouth Bay Dr Beatty traces to its source in Gray's "Progress
of Poesy" and calls a "clear reference to the Classical world".
But, he says, it may also be Virgilian, and he tells us to "see"
A Pair of Blue Eyes and Donald Davie's article on "Hardy's
Virgilian purples". It is not clear whether Dr Beatty accepts
Davie's argument — that the purples exist in a metaphysical
not psychological reality, and that in "Poems of 1912 to 1913"
Hardy is Dido, Emma is Sychaeus and Florence is Aeneas — or
whether the function of the *Aeneid* in *A Pair of Blue Eyes*,
where if anything Elfride is Aeneas, Stephen Euryalus and Mrs
Troyton Helen, enriches, or is comparable or reconcilable with,
its function in *Desperate Remedies*, or even whether Virgil's
purple light, which occurs during the visit to the happy dead, is
part of the *Aeneid's* function as a term of reference in *Desperate
Remedies.*[30]

But whether or not, there are three prominent quotations
from the *Aeneid* in *Desperate Remedies* which can't be fitted
into any theory of the *Aeneid* being a valid term of reference,
and which Dr Beatty makes no attempt to fit in. Anne Seaway
is compared, in Latin, to Camilla "not having feminine hands

used to the distaff and baskets of Minerva": but, unlike Camilla, Anne Seaway is neither warlike nor unused to housework — she merely doesn't want to do housework. The two other quotations, although widely separated and unrelated, are both from Virgil's description of the Sicilian games. In one, Manston is Dares, and in the other Cytherea is Dares and Manston is Entellus who fights Dares. Moreover, separate and unrelated as the two quotations are, the end of one of them is like the other in Dryden's translations which Hardy gives, and this is awkward:

> This and that other part again he tries
> And more on industry than force relies . . .

and

> One on her youth and pliant limbs relies
> One on his sinews and superior size.

Manston's attack on Cytherea, in which the latter quotation occurs, is, in any case, oddly described: any rhyming couplet at this point, and particularly this one — so well known from its comic imitation in the *Dunciad* — increases the oddity.[31]

The case of Shelley and *The Well-Beloved* is somewhat similar. Professor Hillis Miller rightly points out that Hardy's work is "steeped in" Shelley, and that *The Well-Beloved* in particular refers to *The Revolt of Islam*, *Prometheus Unbound*, *Epipsychidion* and the fragment "To the Moon": there can be no doubt that Hardy is thinking of this fragment when he makes Pierston reflect that "the sight of the new moon . . . made him feel as if his wraith in a changed sex had suddenly looked over the horizon at him . . . this sisterly divinity". Professor Hillis Miller says that *The Well-Beloved* takes from Shelley the theme of a brother-sister love, or of a narcissistic loving of oneself in the beloved," but that this combines with an interest in the ways of the creative imagination to produce "an interrogation of the relation between erotic fascination and creativity which makes *The Well-Beloved* one of the most important nineteenth-century novels about art".[32]

However, Professor Hillis Miller does also say that the novel "superficially obeys . . . the conventions of nineteenth-century realism" and that "it might be defined as a parody of [Shelley], or as an interpretation of Shelley's work, or as a subterranean battle to combat his influence". Later he speaks clearly of "the narrator's recognition that the well-beloved is an illusion". But if Hardy's object is to criticise Shelley, why should the realism (which is what he uses to do this) be superficial? One cannot just lift off the realism: without it there is no novel, and in spite of the other references to Shelley the idea of narcissism appears only in the one passage. What does appear most clearly is the hero's fancies for a number of different girls throughout life. This is seen first in I.7, "Her Earlier Incarnations" – a flaxen-haired girl of eight, a brown-haired young lady on horseback, a married woman, and nine others unspecified. Then in I.9 we have a short catalogue of those he loved between the ages of twenty-five and thirty-eight: actress, shop-girl, authoress, pianist, violinist and dancing girl: and in II.6 a similar statement that "she has been a woman of every class, from the dignified daughter of some ecclesiastic or peer to a Nubian Almeh". That Pierston's feeling is simply erotic is further confirmed by the three Avices being "well-beloved" only when they are young and pretty. The point is clearly made in relation to Avice II: when he saw her after twenty years she "was alas! but the sorry shadow of Avice the Second"; and also in the development of his interest in Avice III, which illustrates that "there is no fool like an old fool": his walking with her in the evening so that she can't see how old he is, tempting her with a house in town ("'Your expensive education is wasted down here!'"), kidding himself (in a manner which parodies Melbury's feelings about Giles's father) that marrying Avice III would be an act of "reparation" to her grandmother, and, after she runs away with her young man, reflecting on his life that "it was not the flesh" he had sought but that his sentiment had been "loving-kindness".[33]

There are matters which complicate this account, but they don't bring the novel nearer Shelley. There is the explanation of Avice II's parallel pursuit of *her* well-beloved, that it "meant probably that there had been some remote ancestor common to

both families", and the explanation of the similarity between
the three Avices as "the outcome of the immemorial island customs of intermarriage and of prenuptial union, under which
conditions the type of feature was almost uniform from parent
to child through generations". However absurd, these gratuitous
explanations emphasise the realism and make any symbolic
dimension that much more difficult, as does Pierston's *telling*
Avice III that he had loved her mother and grandmother.[34]

At one point Pierston reflects about Avice III that "she was
somewhat like her mother, whom he had loved in the flesh, but
she had the soul of her grandmother, whom he had loved in the
spirit". This merely makes difficulties for any account of the
novel. It is inconsistent with the reflection we have already seen
that he had never "sought . . . the flesh". It is true that Avice II
lacks her mother's culture, but Pierston's solution for that is a
repetition of Melbury's plan for his daughter: "pack her off to
school for two or three years, marry her, enlarge her mind by a
little travel". What really happens in *The Well-Beloved* is
another treatment, less effective because it is grafted on the im-
plausible three-generation structure, of *Jude*'s "war between
flesh and spirit": Avice I's letter, refusing the prenuptial union
which Pierston had not demanded, might have been written by
Sue.[35]

To call the novel "an interrogation of the relation between
erotic fantasy and creativity" seems an overstatement. The relation is the simple conventional one found in Cellini, Ingres and
numerous Hollywood films: "all these dreams he translated into
plaster" — narrowed still further towards popular cliché by the
fact that Pierston's only artistic activity was as a sculptor of female figures. So, when he stopped "dreaming", "the artistic
sense had left him": he didn't, like Beethoven or Titian or
Monet, develop in old age a new manner or new subjects.[36]

We should also consider what it really means to say that
Hardy was "steeped in Shelley". Dr Pinion claims that "Shelley's
influence on Hardy's thought and basic outlook was greater
than that of any other writer", and it is his essay, making the
most detailed claims, that I answer. Certainly Hardy read
Bagehot and Dowden on Shelley, and said he "thought of

going" to find a cottage Shelley had lived in, and liked to think he had once stayed in a room used by Shelley, and wrote a poem, "Shelley's Skylark", near Leghorn; but the contact with Shelley was part of his whole attitude to the past. He liked to be in places where the great were or had been, and to meet anyone who had known them: Garrick, Johnson, Newton, the Burneys, Sir Joshua, Dickens, Admiral Hardy, Napoleon, Byron, Barry Cornwall, Wordsworth, Leigh Hunt, Keats, Lamb, Scott, Milton, Crabbe, Mill, Constable, Gibbon, Browning's Pompilia, Scott's Edie Ochiltree; and to make similar contact with past great events: Monmouth's rising, the Reform League, the Napoleonic Wars, the first mail-coach from Poole to Bristol, the Indian Mutiny, the Phoenix Park murders, the Franco-Prussian War.[37]

It does not seem possible to demonstrate the impact on Hardy of Shelley's attack on the tyrant responsible for the cruelty of nature, or to see *The Revolt of Islam* and the "Ode to the West Wind" as sources of Hardy's winter imagery, or the final stanzas of *Prometheus Unbound* as the source of Hardy's emphasis on charity, or the spirits in that play as sources of the spirits in *The Dynasts* (especially in view of Hardy's debt to Buchanan), as Dr Pinion claims. The ideas in the Notes to *Queen Mab* are too general and familiar for Hardy to need to get them from anywhere: the immensity of the universe, necessity (that is, the laws of nature), God's regret thereat, chance, free will, marriage and when to end it.

Dr Pinion also finds more particular influences of Shelley. On Shelley's denial that God "begat a son upon the body of a Jewish woman" he says "cf. 'Panthera' ", ignoring the specific sources for "Panthera" given by Bailey. He says Hardy's association of the rainbow with love and hope "was reinforced by Shelley", but it is a common association. And he says that *Epipsychidion*'s well of truth (familiar since Aristophanes) and world-as-wilderness "find their place" in Jude's well and the Talbothays garden, although he admits that the latter "harks back" to Eden and *Hamlet*. Jude's well is associated with the one where Christ sat when weary.[38]

Dr Pinion is on firmer ground when he says that "three of his last four novels suggest that Hardy came to realize the hazards of Shelleyanism in practice". The three are *The Well-Beloved*, which I have discussed, *The Woodlanders,* and *Tess.* The main point is the Shelleyan inadequacy of Fitzpiers and Angel Clare. Fitzpiers, as Dr Pinion points out, is explicitly and sarcastically connected with *The Revolt of Islam* and *Epipsychidion*, in dignifying his lust for Grace and justifying his adultery with Felice; but Angel also, as Dr Pinion does not point out, is called "less Byronic than Shelleyan". Because of his "preferring the ideal world to the real" and "passing in a grand solar sweep throughout the zodiac of the intellectual heaven", and quoting Spinoza to Giles and Schleiermacher to Grace, the Shelleyan element in Fitzpiers is associated with nothing but evil. The Shelleyan language in *Jude*, noticed by Dr Pinion and really consisting in his calling Sue ethereal, is a similar but more sympathetic criticism of Jude. But it does not seem to me that "Shelley's Skylark" is really a tribute to Shelley either. Even in the concluding lines the emphasis is that "it inspired" Shelley, and nothing is said of the lark as symbol of visionary imagination: the emphasis is all on the reality and ordinariness of the bird. David Perkins, who made this point, bracketed the poem with "The Darkling Thrush" which is full of Keats's "Nightingale" language but, again, not as a symbol but as something close to man — aged, frail, blast-beruffled, and lacking in magic casements. The "tendency to think in terms of Shelley's imagery" may be conceded to Dr Pinion; but it has been shown that Hardy thought in the imagery of many writers.[39]

I turn now to the evidence of the *Literary Notes.* Dr Björk, in his "Critical Introduction" to them, points out the distinction Hardy himself makes in "The Profitable Reading of Fiction" between "trifles of useful knowledge" and elements of "intellectual and moral profit"; and comments that "a great number of entries [in the *Literary Notes*] have the potential function of providing 'trifles of useful knowledge' ". Björk also rightly points out that, in the "1867 Notebook", "most quotations are stylistic". In fact Hardy read far more for stylistic models and sources of factual information than for ideological influences. In one novel alone, *The Return of the Native*, as Björk points out, references to Sheridan's Begum speech, Frederick the Great making war on Maria Theresa, haughty Fitzalans and De Veres, the planet Mercury, the impeachment of Strafford, Lavinia Fenton, Raphael and Perugino, the tiger-beetle, the behaviour of ants, the Black Hole of Calcutta, Socrates asking what wisdom is, the *coup-de-Jarnac*, Egdon's vegetation (uniform, carboniferous, monotonous, warm, vaporous, with few forms of plants and no flowers or birds), Dr Kitto, beautiful Greek youths, Hellenic joyousness, the Pitt Diamond, the Dodo, Albertus Magnus's animated statue, Homer's fame, and Gray's "fearful joy", are derived from extracts from books found in the *Literary Notes*.[40]

Since so many of Hardy's notebooks have been destroyed, and much of the remainder is still unpublished, it is not significant that stylistic and factual borrowing for any other novel cannot be demonstrated to the same degree as for *The Return*, which Hardy was writing at the time he was making the earlier extracts. However something similar can be demonstrated in the cases of *A Laodicean* and *Tess*. The case of *A Laodicean* is not very significant since much of it was written when Hardy was ill: its borrowings are like those in *The Return*, only less frequent — some of Balthasar Gracian's maxims, the expressions "the Wertherism of the uncultivated" and "prédilection d'artiste", a phrase from Keat's "Nightingale".[41] In the case of *Tess* there is not that verbal identity which makes borrowing certain, but there is similarity enough. It is particularly interesting to find that Hardy had just been reading Zola – *Germinal* and *Abbe Mouret's Transgressions* – in English. The heroes of *Tess* and *Mouret* are both lacking in passion: Angel had "less fire than radiance", while in Zola's Serge "a flame was lacking". Zola's "sun . . . gazing inward on his soul" may have suggested Hardy's sun's "curious sentient, personal look"; Zola's "trees [which] are no longer trees", Tess's " 'trees [with] inquisitive eyes' "; Zola's "room [with its] hothouse atmosphere", Hardy's "air of the sleeping-chamber [which] seemed to palpitate with the hopeless passion"; Zola's dust from the dancing-floor, Hardy's "cloud of dust" at the Chaseborough dance. "A tide of impassioned emotion stirred the garden to its depths", writes Zola of his le Paradou, and this may have suggested not only the uncultivated garden in Chapter XIX of *Tess* through which the heroine walks, but the connection between heat, external nature, and passion which is made at the beginnings of Chapters XXIII and XXIV.[42] Also, as Björk points out, there is some similarity in the story: both heroes desert their girls and for not very dissimilar reasons: Angel because he has not sufficiently liberated himself from conventional "Christian" morality, Serge to serve the church — a motive Angel had considered and rejected: both lead to the girls' ruin. In comparing Hardy and Zola one would expect to find Hardy's treatmen subtler, less emphatic and less outspoken. But there is a vein of bluntness or coarseness in Hardy which becomes much more obvious in *Tess* and *Jude*, and this may be the effect of Zola and not only of a late recklessness or determination to be understood.[43] Apart from Zola, *Tess* derives from Mahaffy the idea that it was no dishonour to be a Greek concubine, and from the *Fortnightly* Thermidorean heat and the Wintoncester hospice.[44]

Beautiful Greek youths appear in *A Laodicean* and *Two on a Tower* and Gray's "fearful joy" in *Far from the Madding Crowd*, as well as in *The Return*, and Mahaffy also supplies to *Two on a Tower* the notion that love in Homer is mere desire. A maxim of Balthasar Gracian also turns up in *The Mayor*, and *The Mayor* derives its Canadian woodsmen walking in circles from a book Hardy read, and the expression "she well knew how it came there" (referring to Elizabeth-Jane's gloom) from something that Arnold said about Goethe. *The Saturday Review*'s Hellenic joyousness is used again in *Jude*, where we also find that Jude is, like Antigone with whom he has nothing else in common either in character or situation, "neither a dweller among men nor ghosts". The question to the Prince Regent ("Where's your wife?") in *The Dynasts* was noted from Greville's Memoirs.[45]

The notes in the New Wessex edition, and Dr Björk's edition of the *Literary Notes*, must not encourage the notion that Hardy is particularly learned or intellectual. Dr Björk's commentary seeks to collect all the references in Hardy's work to anyone from whose writing he has transcribed an extract, and refers us to discussions by earlier critics of Hardy's debt to them.

This leads to questionable judgements such as that Liddy's
" 'The Philistines be upon us' " is "a possible echo" of *Culture
and Anarchy*, and that the "[Shakespearean] Jaques of this
forest and stream" (the Baron von Xanten) is an "allusion to
Rousseau". It is not necessary to call Fourier "a conspicuous
background" (whatever that is) to "the deadly war waged between flesh and spirit" in *Jude*: Hardy gets the war from
St Matthew's Gospel, if from anywhere. Similarly Hardy's statement in "The Profitable Reading of Fiction" that "the best fiction ... is more true ... than history" doesn't (as we saw in
Chapter 3) have to come from Leslie Stephen: Hardy could
have got it from Fielding or, as Fielding did, from Aristotle.
That Jude thinks of a sentence of Newman which Hardy had extracted about theological probability does not, as Björk says, go
to show that "much nineteenth century thought [is] reflected
in the Literary Notes". The rather obvious sentiments of
Hardy's "The Science of Fiction" and "The Profitable Reading of Fiction" do not show the influence of Arnold's distinction between the naturalistic and moral interpretations of life
nor his demand that poetry should be "the application of ideas
to life". Björk's long note on Hardy's "many-faceted response"
to Carlyle obscures the facts. Hardy did not regard him as "a
thinker", praises only his style, and owes to him only a phrase
quoted in his essay on Goethe and applied by Hardy to
Henchard, who "quitted the ways of vulgar men". In fact,
critics have never claimed much more than this influence of
Carlyle on Hardy. Stewart said that, like Carlyle, Hardy "has a
fancy for great men"; Southerington thought that an idea which
a *Spectator* article claimed that we owe to Carlyle — that being
born "requires of us the kind of life which defies necessity" —
was Hardy's view. Wright quotes two short notes which Hardy
extracted from Carlyle's *French Revolution* as showing interest
in French history. And that is all.[46]

Hardy's stylistic and factual use of other writers is apparent
of course from other sources as well as from the *Literary Notes*.
Of the relation between the storm in *Far from the Madding
Crowd* and Harrison Ainsworth's *Rookwood* we may choose
between Weber's conclusion that Hardy "proceeded to make

free use of Ainsworth's description" and Pinion's that "his youthful imagination was impressed by such scenes". Of Robert Buchanan's *Drama of Kings* the evidence forces us to accept Fairchild's conclusion that it "exerted so strong an influence on Hardy's *Dynasts* that it deserves to be regarded as the immediate source of the work", and reject Wright's more qualified judgements that "he could have obtained little or no philosophic stimulation" from Buchanan, that he could not have "had much respect for most of Buchanan's verse" and that he "knew . . . others who had employed supernatural personages". Hardy, after all, indisputably shares with Buchanan Napoleon, a chorus of supernatural spectators sometimes divided into semi-choruses, sometimes with solo voices, and sometimes called "intelligences", the dynasts themselves and the common people suffering under them, the idea of a Prelude or Fore-Scene in (as Buchanan puts it) "the Heavenly Theatre" and an Epilude or After Scene, and a final melioristic chorus; and at one time Hardy thought of taking from Buchanan the idea of a Familiar, or "Famulus" as Buchanan called him, for Napoleon, and indeed the very title of his work.[47]

Weber also revived the charge, made soon after publication, of plagiarism of 275 words in the drilling scene in Chapter XXIII of *The Trumpet-Major*. The New Wessex Notes, referring to four separate books — Longstreet's *Georgia Scenes*, Gifford's *History*, Lambert's *Travels*, and a work by O. H. Prince — though accurate, are confusing. Hardy's defence, in his Preface, was that the scene "received some additions" from Gifford's book which he, Hardy, "was mistaken in supposing . . . to be . . . authentic, or to refer to rural England". Since the scene is comic, rustic and conversational, and Gifford had explicitly stated he had borrowed it from Lambert (who liked Longstreet had reprinted it from Prince), and since Gifford called it a "satire upon American discipline", it is difficult to believe Hardy; but even if he had merely been extremely careless, the fact remains that until the charge of plagiarism was made Hardy offered the passage as his own writing. What matters is not the question of good or bad faith but the simple fact that Hardy felt he needed to use a passage of this kind by another author.[48]

There are other such cases. Millgate merely says, of the account of the performance of *Love's Labour's Lost* in *A Laodicean,* that it "functions along the lines . . . of the *Lovers Vows* episode in *Mansfield Park*", adding that Hardy "intended to suggest a correspondence between the King of Navarre's vow to avoid the company of women and the similar vow taken by de Stancy" and "perceived a similarity . . . between the Princess's tactics of discouragement and postponement and the behaviour of his own heroine". But Hardy is simply using Jane Austen and Shakespeare as quarries, and the fact that *Love's Labour's Lost* exists explicitly in the novel doesn't lessen the impropriety. Nor does this exhaust the debt either to Jane Austen or to *Love's Labour's Lost.* The statement that Somerset might be "favoured by Paula as her lover. . . . But not to be chosen as architect now was to be rejected in both kinds" is surely derived from Emma's conviction that "a poet in love must be encouraged in both capacities or neither". And the central situation in *Love's Labour's Lost* — the conflict between astronomy and love — is, as pointed out by J. I. M. Stewart, the central situation of *Two on a Tower*: even Shakespeare's most frequent image of it — stars versus eyes — appears when Hardy says of Swithin: "His heaven at present was truly in the skies, and not in . . . the eyes of some daughter of Eve."[49]

Granted all this, one becomes suspicious in other cases. Hardy's rustic humour is sometimes taken from literature and not from life. " 'The Lord only concerns himself with born gentlemen. It isn't to be supposed that a strange fiery lantern like that would be lighted up for folks with ten or a dozen shillings a week' ": this seems to combine the conversation between Shepherd and Clown in *The Winter's Tale* about being "gentlemen born" with Calpurnia's "when beggars die there are no comets seen". And on the next page in *Two on a Tower* we have " 'she's . . . meaning to commit flat matrimony' ", which is from Dogberry's "Flat burglary as ever was committed". Just as *Love's Labour's Lost* carries on from *A Laodicean* to *Two on a Tower,* and "The Spotted Cow" from the end of *The Woodlanders* to the beginning of *Tess,* so Dogberry reappears in the next novel after *Two on a Tower, The Mayor,* both in his mala-

propism and in letting the skimmity "steal out of his company".
And the maltster ("as a young man . . . I was . . . liked' ") is
from Aguecheeek ("I was adored once too"). After all, as he
wrote to Chew, "it was Shakespeare's delineation of his
Warwickshire clowns . . . that influenced Hardy most", and, as he
said in the *Life*, he "regarded real country humour as rather of
the Shakespeare and Fielding sort".[50]

Hardy said this while expressing surprise that *Far from the
Madding Crowd* should have been supposed to be by George
Eliot. It is rather extraordinary that the only detailed exploration of the relationship between George Eliot and Hardy was
published in 1917. This book, Miss Lina Wright Berle's *George
Eliot and Thomas Hardy: a Contrast*, although it contains some
throught-provoking criticisms of Hardy, is so moralistic, over-
drawn and inaccurate as to be of very little use. The argument
is simply that Hardy is decadent whereas George Eliot is a
scientific realist and humanist, and, apart from the inaccuracies,
the treatment is too selective to justify the conclusion, since it
deals almost exclusively with fallen women, women in general,
weak men, love, and old age. Wildeve and Tess are given as an
example of Hardy studying "degenerates". Sue Bridehead is a
study of a single "humour" with no concern for maternity.
None of Hardy's characters, says Miss Berle, has a sense of relation to society. Hetty Sorrel is better than Tess because she always knows the fruit is forbidden. That Angel leaves Tess shows
that Hardy's lovers have no sense of duty; and they also lack
common interests. Even when praising Hardy for his rich
pictures of old age, Miss Berle does not see that Hardy himself
criticises Mrs Yeobright, Henchard, and Mr Melbury.[51]

Nevertheless, comparison with George Eliot was the starting
point of Hardy criticism. Contemporary reviews refer to her far
more often than to any other writer, and the summary by the
editor of *Thomas Hardy: the Critical Heritage* seems entirely
just:

As Hardy developed his characteristic rural themes, George
Eliot increasingly appeared the obvious comparison, and . . .
a standard by which to judge him. . . . As George Eliot's repu-

tation declined ... critics even began to blame her influence
for the pedantic element in Hardy's style.

The commonest points of contact noticed were rural life,
peasant characters and speech, tragedy of circumstance and
authorial comment. As with Miss Berle, the approach is more
often to compare than to allege influence, but *Adam Bede* is the
novel by George Eliot most often cited. One review of *Far from
the Madding Crowd*, while explicitly denying that Hardy
imitates or plagiarises *Adam Bede*, does point out that both
novels have a harvest (or shearing) supper, a military seduction,
a reprieve, an outstanding workman as hero, and a vain girl with
a looking-glass. Another review says that *Tess* and *Adam Bede*
have "much in common ...", yet how superficial were the
points of resemblance"; dairies in both, both girls seduced in a
"Chase". James, on *Far from the Madding Crowd* in 1874, goes
further in speaking of Hardy's "imitation" of both George
Eliot's "humourous" and her "serious" manner, but the *Times*
also said Hardy was "consciously or unconsciously imitating
[her] phraseology and style".[52]

Comparisons by modern critics, in whichever writer's favour,
have been brief and particular, although they may all be seen in
a rather general way as saying that one or the other is more, or
more importantly, realistic. Following Havelock Ellis, for whom
Hardy lacked George Eliot's "larger issues ... massive quality,
and serious sustained power", J. I. M. Stewart has compared
The Mayor adversely with *Middlemarch*: Mixen Lane is not felt
as a real social force, Henchard's story is merely set against a
background of, not enveloped in, a complex moral atmosphere.
For Howe, George Eliot's ethical dilemmas and analysis of female characters are beyond Hardy, and he lacks her concrete-
ness of observed detail. Hillis Miller distinguishes Hardy's idea
of causality from George Eliot's: his is "concatenations of
phenomena" in individual lives, hers either the single act with
its "irremediable" chain of effects or the complex web. Many
modern critics compare Tess with Hetty Sorrel. Where Hardy is
seen as the more realistic writer, it is really because he lacks
George Eliot's insistence on making events illustrate her ideas.

Thus he "avoids a set *Weltanschauung*" whereas she has a " 'philosophy' ", according to L. St J. Butler; his agnosticism is "more logical" than hers and he is more tolerant according to Morrell. It is interesting that Webster, who likewise praises Hardy because his reading of life lacks the "speciousness" of George Eliot's, also *complains* that the fates of Hardy's characters, unlike George Eliot's, are only partly explicable in terms of moral or natural laws – and even says that Henchard is pursued by a "George Eliot-like Nemesis", that is, Hardy *has* (at least in this one case) that very "speciousness".[53] Surely Hardy does make events illustrate *his* ideas as much as George Eliot made them illustrate *hers*.

Little has been said since the first reviews of *Far from the Madding Crowd* of Hardy's *debt* to George Eliot: in general, only that her example encouraged him to introduce rustic humour, and that he learned from her to avoid excessive localism. The particular debts pointed out are the reference to Dutch painting in *Under the Greenwood Tree*, the image of drifting in *Desperate Remedies* and *Tess*, the image of converging streams in *Tess*, the debt of Talbothays and Flintcomb-Ash to Loamshire and Stonyshire, Novalis's "Character is Fate" in *The Mayor*, and a "possible germ of the story" of *Two on a Tower*. Tom Tulliver's sword exercise, I would add, with Tom fainting and Maggie the only spectator, may have suggested Troy's, however differently handled in other respects.[54]

An examination of one novel alone, *Adam Bede*, the one most frequently mentioned by Hardy's critics, shows how much more he owed her than has been realised. It is here that we find the Dutch painting of *Under the Greenwood Tree*; the harvest supper, military seduction, superior craftsman hero, girl-with mirror and reprieve which Hardy used in *Far from the Madding Crowd*, and the Loamshire and Stonyshire, dairy and Chase which he used in *Tess*. There is also the sense of the community, laboriously presented by George Eliot mainly through chapters devoted to its constituent parts, The Workshop, Home, The Rector, The Hall Farm, The Games, The Dance; more slightly presented by Hardy, either through similar scenes, or by focusing on one important element such as Weatherbury or Casterbridge, or through the rustic chorus. Then there is retrospection, characteristic, as has been shown in Chapter 1, of Hardy; and nostalgia, and a sense of change. The changes are similar. For instance, the differences between Irwine and Ryde are more detailed and more seriously treated than those between Grinham and Maybold in *Under the Greenwood Tree*, but contain their source. Ryde "visited his flock a great deal in their homes" whereas Grinham " 'never troubled us wi' a visit from year's end to year's end' ". Ryde "put a stop . . . to the Christmas rounds of the church singers", and although Maybold didn't do this, there *are* Christmas rounds in *Under the Greenwood Tree* and Maybold does oust the singers from the church. Particularly *The Mayor* seems to illustrate George Eliot's often-quoted contrast between "dear, old, brown, crumbling, picturesque inefficiency" and "spick-and-span, new-painted, new-varnished efficiency."[55]

In many of the points in which Hardy seems to follow *Adam Bede* it could be said, of each individual motif, that both writers are merely giving true pictures of the society they describe. Hetty nearly, Eustacia quite, drowns herself in a pool, but wronged village maidens usually did. Women had on occasion to make long lonely journeys on foot, as Hetty, Fanny Robin and Tess do. Hetty's and Troy's incorrect amours are betrayed by the colour of hair in a locket: lockets were common. So were hovels of the kind in which Hetty and Winterborne take refuge. It was normal to pick the pall-bearers for your own funeral as old Martin Poyser and Hardy's Julie-Jane did. If Bishop Ken's Evening Hymn was sung in Hayslope Church as well as in most of Hardy's churches, that is because it always was. Hieroglyphic pictures, whether of Napoleon or of a French cock and Nelsonian anchor, were part of the folk art of the period. A peasant, as George Eliot herself says, cannot help believing in traditional superstitions; such as a willow wand or a phantom coach presaging death. Great occasions such as the Squire's coming-of-age or a "national event" would be celebrated by outdoor sports, and these would naturally include, as Arthur's and Henchard's do, greasy poles and sack and donkey races. Half-wits such as Tom Tholer and Thomas Leaf were all too common, and the village really did react to them, as best it

could, with laughter. To walk beside a girl, but at a distance and
without arming or holding hands, was the normal way of showing respect. Manor-houses commonly decayed into farmhouses
as Hayslope Hall and Oxwell Hall did. Performances such as a
hornpipe or a mumming really were "unsmiling" and "phleg-
matic". If there is a similarity between Mrs Poyser's wit and
that of many of Hardy's peasants, such wit was a fact, and if the
wit is comically exagerated that only draws attention to its
source and value.[56]

The first difficulty of this defence is that the similarities are
too many: so many that one would want to feel that they are
deliberate, that Hardy is saying "this is how it is and not as in
George Eliot". This probably was his intention in creating Tess
without Hetty Sorrel's faults, but with the other things,
although one can see that this or that is better done, or done for
a different purpose, in Hardy, and although one can see that
Hardy with his pessimism and restricted canvas and without
George Eliot's feminism and belief in the redemptive power of
suffering (to go no further) will have different purposes, one
cannot explain all these points of contact in terms of such overall
differences of outlook. The other difficulty is that the similarities are not confined to social observation, but include similarities of style and approach. The reality of both Hayslope and
Marlott is stressed by saying that they were unvisited by artists.
The contrast of Adam at the end with what he was at the beginning of the novel is repeated with Henchard: Adam is now *without* his basket of tools, and walking without his old erectness:
Henchard *has* his basket, but walks now with "a perceptible
bend". And the more important similarities are harder to
demonstrate because more general and less verbal. One is the
obtrusive authorial comment pointing out a contrast: in Hardy
this is discussed above; in *Adam Bede* a simple example is
"What a strange contrast the two figures made!" at the end of a
chapter called "The Two Bedchambers" in which Hetty has
looked at herself in a mirror and Dinah has looked out of a window and then closed her eyes, and so on. This approach in
George Eliot has been criticised but it is integral to her art and
view of society and reaches its climax in *Middlemarch*: it is not

integral to Hardy. Another such similarity is the crediting of peasants with uncharacteristic depths of sententiousness. An example in George Eliot is Adam Bede himself: " 'It 'ud be a poor look-out if folks didn't remember what they did and said when they were lads. We should think no more about old friends than we do about new ones, then.' " Any example is likely to be disputed, but at any rate this profundity is necessary to George Eliot in order that Adam may fit the theory of irremediable evil and redemptive suffering, and she insists that he is not ordinary or average. For Hardy, the reader had best be referred to W. J. Hyde's article "Hardy's View of Realism: a Key to the Rustic Characters": Hyde reconciles the characteristic that I am noticing with Hardy's accuracy but shows it was also noticed by the contemporary reviewers: thus R. H. Hutton complained of Poorgrass's " 'Your next world is your next world, and not to be squandered lightly' " and Coggan's " 'He's found me in tracts for years and I've consumed a good many in the course of a long and rather shady life.' "[57]

The *Life* to some extent confirms the feeling that Hardy's attitude to other writers was stylistic rather than ideological. He tells us there that *The Poor Man and the Lady*'s style had "the affected simplicity of Defoe's", that he "read again" a number of authors, mostly of the eighteenth century, "in a study of style" and that he discussed style with Matthew Arnold who said that "the best man to read for style — narrative style — was Swift". In itself this proves nothing except that one does not feel that a man with something to say should consciously imitate another author unless for pastiche, burlesque, satire or some other kind of contrast, especially not an author writing 150 years earlier. But the references to style do not exist by themselves, but alongside a large number of lists of his reading and meagre comments on particular authors. That Hardy lists his reading at all seems odd: one may suppose that he was stressing the fact that he was self-educated, and acknowledging that he had become a great man about whom books had been and would be written and therefore that any detail was important, but it is still odd: his poems and prose fiction were themselves the necessary evidence of his reading, and he continued to give lists up to when he was fifty and the author of *Tess*. He makes no comment on his response to most of the books listed. The comments that he does make are commonly that he became "familiar" with the work or knew it "by heart" (the *Aeneid*, Horace, Ovid, the *Iliad*, Mill's *On Liberty*), that it "impressed him" (*Essays and Reviews*, Bagehot's *Literary Studies, Hedda Gabler*), that it was a "cure for despair" ("Resolution and Independence", *Liberty*, Carlyle, J. P. Richter) and that it and its author were "considered to be" good (Thackeray, *Vanity Fair, Barchester Towers*, though here he is writing to his sister from London and may be really or ironically seeing himself as purveying metropolitan wisdom to a provincial). The reader feels that much of Hardy's reading made little or no ideological impression on him.[58]

This chapter has been concerned with the details of Hardy's repetitions and his use of other writers. What Professor Millgate has called his "exploitation of autobiography" could be demonstrated in equal volume, and carries an equally important suggestion of limited invention. The detail is not given here only because it is familiar from the work of most Hardy critics and, in particular, Professor Millgate and Dr Gittings. Of course a writer must use his own experience. But too many of Hardy's protagonists are architects, masons, poets and novelists like himself; and when they are, they pursue with thematic irrelevance Hardy's own course of entry into an architect's office and first job (Owen), or write Hardy's own kind of poetry and like him can't get it published (Somerset). They follow his itineraries round the Continent (Knight, Ethelberta, Somerset) or to the Boat Race (Ethelberta). Like him, they play for dancing (Julian) and think of going to university and entering the Church (Angel, Jude) and looks at the sun through straw hats (Jude). Like his wife, they play the harmonium in church (Fancy) and read as they walk along (Henchard). The technical terms of architecture — jambs, fillets, string-courses, arch-labels, laps, rolls — abound.

5 The Good

Probably the various conclusions I have drawn do not greatly affect the common view of Hardy. The most obvious inference from limited inventiveness is that he wrote too much; and, after all, his short stories, half his novels and *The Dynasts* remain commonly unread, and critics have largely ignored the minor novels and advised us not to read more than twenty, or fifteen, or a dozen of his poems.[1] And if he is uninventive he is also, obviously, highly inventive. Furthermore it is commonly agreed that realism, the standpoint from which his limitations as a social critic and Victorian thinker must be discussed, is not the whole story. And the common reader does not concern himself with the influence of Schopenhauer or Comte. However, some criticism of Hardy uses ideas which might be held to render my conclusions entirely beside the mark: the ideas of development, form, myth, ballad, poetic structure and "substance not manners".

A sophisticated idea of development is found in Professor Gregor's article "What Kind of Fiction Did Hardy Write?" and in his book, *The Great Web*. The article sees in Hardy an increasing ability to "bring [his] various responses – as tragic philosopher, as creator of character, as social historian – into effective relationship with one another", and these, with the substitution of story-teller for character-creator, are also the elements in the book, which seeks to "relate the novels to one another as a coherent imaginative journey". The same sort of judgements are made in both works, such as that the heath is not in "effective dramatic relationship" with the characters in *The Return*, whereas *The Mayor* is "an integrated tragic structure"; that there is a "sense of interrelatedness . . . in sexual relationships" in *The Woodlanders* and *Tess*, but not in *The Mayor*; and that Grace suffers a worse "dissociation" than Bathsheba or Eustacia.[2]

Such judgements are highly general, and require more proof than they receive. *The Great Web* is not exclusively concerned with development as a feature of Hardy's art, and it is not always clear whether or not its particular judgements are directed towards isolating the characteristics of individual novels and so placing them in Hardy's development. Some of them seem to me to be true of , but not to define, particular novels; others simply false. It is true of, but does not define, *The Woodlanders* that in it "nature, work and sex [are] shown as interconnected". It is true of, but does not define, *Tess* that it "recognizes the continuities . . . between the . . . self . . . and the . . . conditions of the age". It is false that Grace's "dissociation" is worse than Bathsheba's or Eustacia's, that "moral interest was remote from Hardy's purpose" in *Far from the Madding Crowd*, that "the role of 'place' in *The Return*, of character in *The Mayor*, is . . . occupied by time in *The Woodlanders*", that Marty and Giles are to be blamed for "the sterility of self-abnegation", and that Henchard "becomes aware of his place in the universe". If one cannot agree with the statements on which the conclusion is based, one cannot agree with the conclusion; and since in the article Gregor discusses only four novels and in the book only six, any development that he traces cannot give us an overall view.[3]

Of course Hardy's art and content develop. There is, generally speaking, in *The Mayor, The Woodlanders, Tess* and *Jude* a closer texture, a fuller and more effective use of images and symbols, of contrasts of character and situation, and so on, and fewer blemishes and slack and irrelevant passages, than there are in most of the earlier novels. Yet, for what they are trying to do, the texture of the writing in *Under the Greenwood Tree* and *Far from the Madding Crowd* and even, with all its fundamental faults, *The Return,* is as close as in the later novels; whereas novels without this closeness of texture continued to be written right up to *The Well-Beloved*. Moreover even in the greatest novels there are serious faults of narrative and motivation, as we shall see, as well as the occasional lapse of tone, such as Willie Dunbleeze and Maitland Macfreeze in *The Mayor*. In his content, Hardy shows more intellectual response in the later novels, but his views did not change and were never much influenced by Victorian thinkers, and we do have references to Mill in *Ethelberta* and Arnold in *A Laodicean*. My whole argument makes it impossible to see development in social concern: his interests were selective, he sees them as timeless problems rather than as social questions, and his fundamental impulse is to record. Nevertheless the overriding feeling is always regret for, or fear of, the loss of the old ways, and in no novel is this more emphatic than in the early *Far from the Madding Crowd*.

Perhaps a book could be written showing that some idea of development was the key to understanding Hardy. It would not have to be concerned with questions of form. But Gregor does claim to have found, in "the great web of human doings then weaving in both hemispheres from the White Sea to Cape Horn" which, Hardy says, "Marty's and Giles' lonely courses were part of the pattern" of, "the form of Hardy's major fiction"; and cites in support a sentence in the *Life* noted at the time Hardy was writing *The Woodlanders*: "The human race to be shown as one great network or tissue which quivers in every part when one point is shaken like a spider's web if touched." So, says Gregor, in *The Return* "for the first time the web of human doings becomes visible. . . . In the next three of Hardy's major novels, the web is to be drawn into a finer and finer mesh. . . . In *The Woodlanders* the whole web becomes fully defined." In *Tess*, Hardy "returns to that web, but watches now more intently the strange process of its spinning". In *Jude* the web is "threatening to become a grid". In the plethora of his judgements, indeed, this development of the web is the only form to emerge. But neither Hardy's fiction nor Gregor's book shows us human doings from the White Sea to Cape Horn or the human race as one great network. Gregor discusses the characters we find in Hardy, or rather their "consciousnesses" — their relations with and isolation from one another and dissociation within themselves — and he uses the word "web" in the same sense as the words "interaction" or "interlocked" when he says that we have "interaction of people with nature" in *The Woodlanders* or that "the recording consciousness . . . [is] interlocked with the different levels of consciousness in nature itself".[4]

Hardy said that he carried out the idea of the human race as one great network in *The Dynasts* (not *The Woodlanders*). It reminds us of stage directions in *The Dynasts*:

> The scene becomes anatomized, and the living masses of humanity transparent. The controlling Immanent Will appears thereon as a brain-like network of currents and ejections, twitching, interpenetrating, entangling and thrusting hither and thither the human forms.

> The unnatural light ... [brings] into view ... the films or brain-tissues of the Immanent Will, that pervades all things, ramifying through the whole army.

> The ubiquitous urging of the Immanent Will becomes visualised. The web connecting all the apparently separate shapes includes Wellington in the tissue with the rest.

It is precisely because Hardy cannot, and doesn't want to, deal (either in *The Dynasts* or the novels) with a whole army, the living masses of humanity, or the web of human doings from the White Sea to Cape Horn, that he has to bring in the Immanent Will as a metaphysical assertion of universality and to tell us in a stage direction that what cannot be seen let alone described "becomes visualised". In the novels, Hardy has a very small cast of similar characters, and, as we have seen, does not even study the whole society of South Wessex. Images of interconnectedness – water, tissue, the labyrinth, the key, the scratched pier glass, and, at least once, the web – are common in George Eliot, and "the great web" is more appropriate as a title for a book about her, or Scott, Dickens, Balzac, Zola or Jules Romains, than about Hardy. If it means anything in *The Woodlanders* (the only place it occurs outside *The Dynasts*) it means the Immanent Will.[5]

Professor Kramer also discusses Hardy in terms of form: his novels are "the forms of tragedy":

> Hardy in each novel uses a dominant aesthetic feature, or

organizing principle, that informs the entire work and creates the peculiar quality of tragedy that distinguishes it: the arrangement of opposite qualities in *Far from the Madding Crowd*; the conflict of value systems in *The Return of the Native*; the incorporation of a view of history that shapes plot and characterisation in *The Mayor of Casterbridge*; the indirect expression of tragic significance through a conflation of characterisation in *The Woodlanders*; the intensity that directs the characters' behaviour in much the same way that it guides the readers' reaction in *Tess of the d'Urbervilles*; and the manipulation of perspective that evaluates the protagonist in *Jude the Obscure*.

Already one feels that these features do not distinguish their particular novels. Characters have opposite qualities in themselves in most of Hardy's novels, most obviously in *Jude*, but what about Grace's modern nerves and primitive feelings, or Eustacia as Queen of Night and simple passionate woman? The qualities of Clym and Eustacia, Winterborne and Fitzpiers, Henchard and Farfrae, Alec and Angel, are opposed to one another. And if we may speak of the "value systems" not only of intellectuals like Clym but of Mrs Yeobright, Thomasin and Eustacia, as we must if they are in conflict in *The Return*, what is this but opposite qualities under another name? Indeed Professor Kramer reduces the distinctiveness by adding that, although "Hardy never repeated a dominant organizing technique he might use the technique again in a subordinate role". Discussing *Far from the Madding Crowd* in terms of "schematism" and "dichotomy" he says "Hardy continued to use the schematic method. . . . *The Return of the Native*, for instance, is permeated with this sense of dichotomy." "The uniqueness of *The Return of the Native* . . . is that . . . Clym and Eustasia . . . inhabit different psychic worlds . . . [This] repeats, but in quite different terms, the contrast between the values of . . . Troy and . . . Oak." Professor Kramer does not always express himself so simply. He says, for instance, that Clym's adequacy as tragic hero depends, not on whether he has learned anything of use to anyone except himself, but on "whether his knowledge evokes

an expanse of meaning beyond the applicability of the knowledge to his own individual condition". Nevertheless one can
discover at the base of his theories some simple errors of judgement. From Clym's ineffectuality at the end he infers that "in
the absence of conflicting . . . forces, life has become mediocre
rather than noble"; but the conflicts with Eustacia and his
mother did not make Clym noble, and it is not the absence of
conflict but their deaths and the vagueness Hardy has created
about Clym's aims and our response to them which make him
ineffectual. The "organizing principle" in *The Mayor* resolves
itself into two: "One . . . the presentation of an individual
struggle as but one occurrence of timeless rhythm, the cycle of
change within the organisation of society; the other compresses
the entire action into a single portion of the novel's plot
[namely the Royal visit]"; "the repetitive action . . . shows
[that] human history is not linear but cyclic". This action is the
"creation of an authority; the consolidation of its power; its
weakening; and its collapse. . . . Both Henchard and Farfrae
follow this pattern." They do not: Farfrae does not weaken or
collapse, and we see nothing of the creation or consolidation of
Henchard's power.[6]

To some extent Professor Bayley is also concerned with form.
"Form in the novels . . . is apt to be strongly influenced, if not
actually determined, by Hardy's relation to the heroine."
" 'Form' is the atmosphere of the text in a dominant but imponderable sense, connected with contrivance, but not determined by it." "*Jude the Obscure* has no form, in the sense I
have been using the term, because the appearance of such form
is not compatible with the mechanical intentions about 'contrast' in Hardy's 'original conception'." It is significant that
Bayley's idea of form in Hardy is of something imponderable,
and that he does not regard as valuable much that would confer
form in a simpler sense. He finds "an unnatural uniformity of
tone" in *Tess*, and dislikes Tess's "representative" quality and
the "representational significance" of *The Return*. In fact there
is a general approval of unrelatedness in Bayley which dis-
courages my present search for unifying factors. Hardy's
"physical perceptions are always his own . . . his opinions and

ideas . . . seldom". The "rich absentness of the narrative" in
Tess and the "lack of placing" of the heroine are praised. It is
bad when "Hardy's apprehensions of Tess do seem uneasily
aware of each other": the opposite, which is good, is "the style
of separation". The short stories are inferior to the novels and
poems because they lack "the distinction of non-effect".[7]

But of course there are numerous formal elements in Hardy:
the "uniformity of tone" in *Tess*, the contrasts in *Jude*, the contrast between Henchard at the beginning and Henchard at the
end of the action. It is only form as a cardinal principle, as the
key to Hardy's goodness, whether of Bayley's imponderable
kind or the kinds claimed by Gregor and Kramer, which is
lacking.

All agree that Hardy is a poetic novelist. He himself said that
his Wessex was a "partly real, partly dream country" and that
"he took no interest in manners, but in the substance of life
only". As we have seen, in one critic's view he treated the collapse of agriculture "in imaginative form", and in another's his
characterisation was "imaginative recreation".[8] There is a
danger of vagueness here, and it is increased by the fact that his
poetry has a prosaic and narrative element, for instance the
"Satires of Circumstance", "A Sunday Morning Tragedy" and
the blank verse of *The Dynasts*. One attempt to make more precise what is meant by calling Hardy's fiction poetic is to combine the idea of poetry with what we have just examined, the
idea of form — as Mrs Brooks does in her *Thomas Hardy: the
Poetic Structure*. But for several reasons, no such structure
emerges from her work: like Gregor, she makes so many
particular judgements that one cannot tell what is subordinate
to what; she uses the word "poetic" too frequently and
variously;[9] her commonest concept, "poetic underpattern",[10] is
unsatisfactory in itself; and she makes particular errors of judgement. Her "poetic underpattern" is only to be found in the
"Big Six" novels: in "the rest of his fiction . . . the lacking
quality is a consistent poetic 'underpattern' ": so much for
Virgil in *Desperate Remedies* or Shelley in *The Well-Beloved*.
However, a single "scene [in *A Pair of Blue Eyes*] does yield
elements of a poetic underpattern . . .: the recurring skeletons,

real and metaphorical, which warn of the dangers of indecision";
and, in *Under the Greenwood Tree*, "Nature . . . contributes . . .
to a poetic underpattern of resonances." In *Far from the
Madding Crowd* there is "interplay between surface narrative
and poetic underpattern" and in *Tess* we are to distinguish "the
surface story" from "the poetic underpattern": in both these
novels the underpattern, and, in *The Mayor*, the plot, is "archetypal". "The poetic underpattern of *The Woodlanders* is . . . a
close network of interrelated images." In *The Dynasts* we have
"a poetic underpattern . . . of assent and dissent to traditional
epic".

　　If Hardy's novels, or some of them, have a poetic structure or
structures, one must be able to describe this underpattern in
such a way that it is clearly visible. Again, the example of
Middlemarch helps: there we are constantly aware of design,
themes and structure, because of the natural interrelation of the
characters (as squire, banker, parson, doctor, mayor, workman
and possible spouse) and because of the varied application of
images of light, water and complexity, and the indications of
varied applicability of the book-titles. Mrs Brooks does not succeed in showing that Hardy's novels have poetic structures, and
indeed could not do so except through the ideas of archetype,
myth and ballad which she uses: a single scene cannot yield an
underpattern for a whole novel, and the interrelated images in
The Woodlanders are variations of the woods image and do not
confer structure. Nature does provide a pattern in *Under the
Greenwood Tree*, and also in *The Woodlanders* and many other
Hardy novels, but it is not an underpattern, but the seasonal un-
folding of the action. What Mrs Brooks really does is to pile up,
in her discussions of individual novels, every effect of art that
has ever been noticed, adding some of her own (some of them
erroneous), and to call it poetic structure. Some examples must
be given of her mistaken judgements. We do not in fact notice
any reference in the scarlet throne at Greenhill Fair to Troy's
red jacket, or, in the wind that stops Bathsheba's breath at the
end of the sword-exercise, to the breeze that deterred Oak from
suicide. We do not relate Henchard to "the pre-human world"
when he is compared to animals and to a "great tree", or think

of John Durbeyfield prostrate among the daisies when we see the effigies in the d'Urberville vault. Winterborne, climbing South's elm, does not "dramatise the destructive power of modern thoughts and codes". Deceiving the bull by playing the Nativity Hymn does not "caricature Angel's attempts to impose his superhuman vision on the living physical world". The children's deaths in *Jude* are not "poetic foreshortening of the reality that comes to all".[11]

The question of Hardy's narrative skill is relevant to the attempt to determine how far he was realistic and in what sense poetic. In Mrs Brooks's account, the opposite of "poetic underpattern" in *Tess* and *Far from the Madding Crowd* is "surface narrative". Brown almost equates Hardy as novelist with his narrative art: "The agricultural tragedy is the substance of his narrative art": "He is not generally profound or exploratory in his analysis of human character or motive. His narrative art calls rather for a strong and simple delineation." Hardy encourages this by at the same time equating novel-writing with story-telling and saying he is really a poet and not a novelist. In 1874 "He did not care much for a reputation as a novelist in lieu of being able to follow the pursuit of poetry . . . 'but . . . for the present . . . I wish merely to be considered a good hand at a serial' "; and he found George Eliot "not a born storyteller". In 1926 he asked Virginia Woolf whether *The Mayor* "held her interest".[12]

Can we say that Hardy's narrative skill shows that he is a novelist rather than a poet, and in particular a realistic novelist, or that his lack of skill shows that his genius is naturally poetic and lyric? Critics have often pointed out narrative faults. "The total structures [of the novels] do not draw out . . . the [tragic] suggestion." "The plot [of *The Well-Beloved*] is ridiculous." "No mature mind is likely, after the opening chapters, to pay serious attention to the plot" of *The Woodlanders*; which includes the "lengthy and tiresome process of reuniting Grace and Fitzpiers and the "absurd punctiliousness" of Winterborne's sacrifice. "Nonsense could not farther go" than making Fitzpiers break with Felice because the hair he had stroked was transplanted. In *Desperate Remedies, Ethelberta, A Laodicean* and

Two on a Tower "a displeasing artificiality spoils the narrative". "Whatever rude effigy of [Henchard] the rabble had constructed . . . could scarcely retain so recognizable an identity after its immersion." Hardy himself said he had "damaged" *The Mayor* in order "to get an incident into almost every week's part". "We cannot believe that Mr Swancourt . . . should be unaware that his parishioners the Smiths . . . have a clever son who has gone to be an architect in London." In *Tess*, not only are Angel's repudiation of Tess and Alec's conversion hard to believe, but so is the implication of Tess's asking "Will you forgive my sin against you, now I have killed him?" after Angel had said "If he were dead it might be different": Hardy is not prepared either to suggest clearly the preposterous idea that Tess killed Alec because of a hint from Angel, or to remove the implication altogether. Clym could never have supposed Eustacia would be willing to remain in Egdon and help him teach. Jude and Sue's happy private life together should have been described, since it is the positive value of the novel.[13]

These are some of the faults found with Hardy's narrative art. Yet obviously there is magnificent narrative, forward movement, in *Tess, The Mayor* and *Far from the Madding Crowd*. But also many of his poems, including many bad ones, are narrative. Indeed Hardy himself did not always associate narrative with the novel: "It was not as if he had been a writer of novels proper. . . . He had mostly aimed at keeping his narratives close to natural life and as near poetry in their subject as the conditions would allow."[14] So we cannot conclude that Hardy's talent is or isn't narrative, or infer that he is either more or less a poet than a novelist.

Mrs Brooks and Professor Carpenter make much of myth in Hardy, a matter we touched on in discussing folk-culture and possible influences on Hardy's attitude to Christianity and Hellenism. I said that "the comparison of Wessex characters to persons famous in history or legend only involves a single point of contact". Carpenter, following the definition of myth as "the dramatisation of powers that are assumed to have universal authority over the actions of men", finds in Hardy "a basic mythic structure" and, in particular, the myths of the dying

god, rebirth, the scapegoat (Henchard and Tess), and the Prome-
thean benefactor hero (Clym), and sees in *The Woodlanders* "a
mythic connection between the life of man and that of trees"
and "a most pointed mythic scene" in the "ancient fertility rite
on Midsummer Eve". "The mythic dimension" in *The Woodlanders* is, he says, fortified by references to Norse mythology
and, in contrast to these, "Classical references, which are related to the more sophisticated characters".[15]

Part of Carpenter's definition of myth ("universal authority
over the actions of men") if it applied to Hardy would require
him to be completely deterministic, which in practice he is not.
But if one substitutes a dictionary definition – "a fictitious
supernatural narrative embodying a popular idea" – it is going
to be hard to distinguish a mythical reference from the poetic,
imaginative treatment of popular, or folk, ideas which we do
find in Hardy. To make such a distinction, to make myth important enough in Hardy to save him from charges treating him
as a realist, there must be what Carpenter himself calls a mythic
dimension, as there is when Euripides uses the story of Ion to
criticise contemporary Greek religious and social practice, or
when Dryden uses the stories of Adam and Eve and Absalom to
indicate his views about the English political scene in 1681, or
when Hardy himself uses the Paradise myth in *Tess*. There is no
such dimension in *The Woodlanders*. There are four Norse references, connected with Marty, Giles and Grace but also with
things – darkness, mist, a wood. Felice is connected with
Olympus and Tempe, Fitzpiers with Prometheus, and a
gentleman-farmer with Actaeon. But also Giles is Socratic and
makes cider on Pomona's plain, and Giles and Grace are
Arcadian, while Grace, *after* she has lapsed back to nature
unadorned, is compared to Daphne, Artemis and Aphrodite. And
the references which are neither Norse nor classical – Fitzpiers
seen by Marty as a chapbook Faustus and by Felice as
St Veronica, Felice seen as Isis, Hintock's Hapsburgian inter-
marriages – further prevent any pattern of contrast between
Norse and classical from emerging. The characteristic Hardyan
use of such references is seen when Grace's case is compared in
the same sentence to those of characters from Greek myth, the

Old Testament and English history: Ariadne, Vashti, Amy Robsart.[16]

The "mythic connection between the life of man and that of trees" is only made by Marty's father, and Hardy presents it as a mistaken but natural idea which the outsider, Fitzpiers, doesn't understand. The "ancient fertility rite on Midsummer Eve" is called a "performance": no one any longer believes it leads to discovering your fated husband, but some girls and men take part for their own reasons.

In *The Return*, Carpenter sees "allusions" rather than myth. They aim at grandeur, he says, but fail. Since Eustacia, to name but one character, is compared to so many different figures of classical myth and classical and modern history, there cannot be a "mythic dimension" there. But the same is true of other Hardy characters, for instance Henchard, who is Achilles, Faust, Bellerophon, Saul, Cain, Napoleon, and perhaps Oedipus and Lear, at different times, as Hardy pleases. Even when, for instance in *Jude*, the references are controlled by a single scheme, what we have is not underlying myth but a perfectly conscious system of allusions – to Jerusalem, Cyprus, St Stephen and so on – to suggest that people are not truly Christian and that the Greek tradition is more valuable than the Hebraic-Christian one. This may be seen even in Little Father Time, the most obvious scapegoat in Hardy but not, and not claimed by Carpenter to be, part of a scapegoat myth. "For the rashness of those parents he had groaned ... and for the misfortunes of these he had died," recalling specifically the supposed prophecy of Christ in *Isaiah*. Henchard and Tess are not scapegoats: Tess is the victim of the social law and of nature, and it is absurd to speak as Carpenter does of "ritual combat" and "the king must die" in *The Mayor*: Farfrae is, as Carpenter himself says, merely "more able to provide for the agricultural well-being of the society".[17]

Like Carpenter, Mrs Brooks finds the Prometheus myth in *The Return* and *Tess*. But also, to her, *The Mayor* is "a myth of responsibility and rebellion against the human condition"; *The Woodlanders*, because "human relationships are interwoven with the seasonal movements", has "the resonance of myth",

Car and her friends are "vegetation gods"; Jude is a Jewish myth-hero, but also Everyman; and Tess is Everywoman. Jude's "quest is the basic myth of twentieth-century man", though he and Sue fail "to stand alone as human beings without myth". Mrs Brooks is quite happy to have Henchard "compared with Achilles, Ajax, Oedipus, Orestes . . . , Cain, Saul, Samson . . . , Job, Coriolanus, King Lear, and Faust", and Jude to St Jude, Samson, Tantalus, Sisyphus, Faust and Job. So far, the arguments against Carpenter apply against Mrs Brooks.[18]

But the ballad is also part of her "archetypal pattern": the betrayed maiden, the faithful lover, the inconstant soldier, the rags-to-riches rise and the crime of passion are, she rightly says, ballad elements in *Far from the Madding Crowd*. Of course the ballad is a strong influence on and element in Hardy, but it will not provide that key to the good that we are looking for. One feature of the ballad is that it deals with simple elemental types, motives and situations, and it is precisely characteristic of Hardy at his worst that he repeats these too often. The following extracts from "The Contretemps" illustrate this:

> . . . Her lover rose . . .
> And then her husband entered . . .
> "Take her and welcome, man!" he cried . . .
>
> And next the lover: "Little I knew,
>   Madam, you had a third! . . ."
> — Husband and lover then withdrew.
> I let them . . .
> And there was the Jersey boat . . .
>   "One pairing is as good as another . . ."

This difficulty is not overcome in Beckman's sophisticated idea of character typology, of which the following is an example:

> Farfrae's vernal opportunism provides only a practical and not especially admirable adjustment to Hardy's ironic universe. Henchard like summer is luxuriantly energetic, but his passions cannot prevail. . . . Lucetta, exotic and autumnal, lan-

guishes, pathetically beautiful in decay. Winter, personified in Elizabeth-Jane's neutral esthetic and purified temperament, remains Hardy's norm.

Here, and throughout Beckman's article, one is left to find one's own evidence: he never quotes from the text. Yes, we say, Lucetta is ageing and such ladies are often called autumnal, but isn't Elizabeth-Jane with her "somewhat richer complexion" and "incipient matronly dignity" becoming autumnal too? And Hardy gives Farfrae "energy" as well as Henchard. When Hardy wants to connect a character with winter he does, by calling him Winterborne; and what is opportunist about the spring? And when we read of "an analogy . . . between the cycles of evolutionary development and seasonal change as Hardy interpreted them", we wonder why evolutionary development should be called cyclical, and whether Hardy "interpreted" or only presented seasonal change. And when we read of an "archetypal pattern of Nescience — Consciousness — Nescience" or a "quasi-seasonal pattern of pessimism — sensationalism — pessimism", we are lost.[19]

The trouble with the ballad is also the trouble with substance, the universe, the cosmos, the eternal. Critics have accepted these too easily. "His theme is man's predicament in the universe." "The rise and fall of Henchard is the tracing out in a moment of time the movement of the cosmos." "Tess was not only beset by society but also by the very nature of the universe." Clym "mistakenly emphasizes *his* guilt instead of the guilt of the universe". "The symmetry and intensity of Hardy's plots . . . join with his poetic vision . . . to bring out the pattern of the larger forces driving the cosmos and its creatures. Sensational events [etc.] . . . present a universe where every action is a hostage to . . . fate." Hardy encourages this way of writing about him when he says he is not interested in manners but in the substance of life and that in fiction "things unusual" should be "adjusted" to "things eternal and universal", and by his references in his fiction to an "infuriated universe", a "soul, conterminous with the universe", and so on. The trouble is that we can have knowledge of sense-data and of long times and great

spaces, but not of substance, eternity or the universe; and this
is not just a technical point, answered by saying that the words
are used popularly and not philosophically. It probably is all
right to say that Tess was beset by the universe: certainly by
frost, snow, rain and hard labour. But it is not always all right,
and in fact Hardy doesn't generally do it. He says, for instance:

> The hints that perishing historical remnants afforded her of the
> attenuating effects of time even upon great struggles cor-
> rected the apparent scale of her own.

> The heath ... having defied the cataclysmal onsets of cen-
> turies, reduced to insignificance by its seamed and antique
> features the wildest turmoil of a single man.

> Tess stood still upon the expanse of verdant flatness like a
> fly on a billiard-table.

Time, the heath, centuries, antique, a billiard-table; not eternity or the universe. The danger of writing not about manners
but substance and the universe is, as with the ballad element,
that you do not particularise, and are left with concepts such as
life, and death, and infidelity, and ageing, and the Immanent
Will, which impress the first time by their grandeur, but, as we
saw in the case of life and death in Chapter 4, when often repeated become monotonous in the manner of the old heroic
plays because of their generality.[20]

Hardy's use of the supernatural is also a possible departure
from realism, a possible poetic element. Where the supernatural
is presented as believed by a character, it is part of the presentation of Wessex, and not unrealistic: it is superstition, which we
have briefly discussed,[21] and in fact something which the peasant is generally trying not to believe in. But sometimes, particularly in the short stories and poems, the supernatural is an unrealistic element of art, sometimes well-used and sometimes not,
for making something or other (generally feeling) public and effective. Thus the withering of "The Withered Arm" represents
the hatred of one woman and guilt of the other, and the death

of the guilty one may be seen as realistically due to shock, without accepting the superstition of "turning of blood"; and Mop Ollamoor's magic simply combines the powers of music and sex. In the poems the supernatural is generally a ghost, and the ghost generally a means of saying and doing what you couldn't really say or do. Thus the Trampwoman is able to reassure the ghost of her fancy-man that "I had kept me from all men" and Hardy is able to rewrite, without contradiction, the story of his marriage in "Poems of 1912–13". The ghosts in "Wessex Heights" are simply a way of saying particular places revive unhappy memories. "The Romantic Adventures of a Milkmaid" combines both kinds of supernatural. If one could see it simply as a criticism, in terms of reality, of the milkmaid's fantasies of Cinderella and her demon-lover, it would belong to the first kind – realistic treatment of superstition; and the fact that actual attributions to the supernatural are only made by the characters in that story (" 'Twas a stroke of the black art' "; " 'He was like a magician to me. I think he was one.' ") supports this. But the events are not presented only through Margery's consciousness, and the element of fantasy is realised as much as it is criticised. There are in Hardy strange occurrences which are significantly if not plausibly given natural and not supernatural causes, such as the resemblance of Marchmill's son to Trewe "by a known but inexplicable trick of Nature". There is then a duality in Hardy's use of the supernatural, and it does not always take us away from realism.[22]

All these ideas – development, form, story-telling, myth, ballad, the universal, the supernatural – have to be used in discussing Hardy, but none of them can be taken very far, and he doesn't use any of them consistently well. All sorts of dualities and dualisms have been found in Hardy: his "double vision", according to Harold Child ("If he sees the littleness, he sees also the greatness"); Lodge's "second Hardy dealing with aspects of things" which "demand a quality of distance"; Hillis Miller's "engaged" and "detached" Hardy; Holloway's "two quite different roles ... chronicling a ghastly world of planless and ironic Fate, and ... recording all the interest and variety and even charm of rustic life"; Morton Zabel's "ambivalence" between "acquiescence and protest"; Goldberg's two worlds of science and poetry.[23] Perhaps we have discovered some more: he is inventive and uninventive; he develops, and he does not; he is formal, and formless; his prose is like poetry, but then his poetry is like his prose; his narratives are either powerful or absurd; he is mythic but lacks, except in *Tess*, mythic dimension, is realistic and unrealistic. This last duality can be explored in his critical remarks in the *Life*.

These remarks suggest that behind the duality between realism and unrealism there is a tension between desire for freedom and unwillingness to stray far from ordinary reality, and as a result some confusion. It is not true, for instance, that "he took no interest in manners". He was interested in but not good at describing what he calls "ordinary social and fashionable life", and he was good at describing the manners of country life. He says one should "strike the balance between the uncommon and the ordinary ... [but] the uncommonness must be in the events not in the characters", and this is impossible since people are what they do, so perhaps Hardy was not thinking of what he was saying but of his own love of the uncommon: yet Tess *was* "almost a standard woman", while Anne Seaway watching Miss Aldclyffe watch Raunham's detective watch Manston carrying his dead wife in a sack *was* certainly an uncommon event.

The demand for freedom appears most simply when he says that "he carried on into his verse ... the Gothic art-principle ... the principle of spontaneity" and that "the whole secret of a living style [in prose] ... lies in ... being a little careless, or rather seeming to be": he seeks freedom from critical canons. It also appears in his use of what we have discovered to be a favourite work, "idiosyncrasy":

The seer should watch that pattern among general things which his idiosyncrasy moves him to observe.

Art is a changing of the actual proportions and order of things, so as to bring out ... that feature in them which appeals most strongly to the idiosyncrasy of the artist ... the kind [of changing] which increases the sense of vraisemblance ... is high art. ... Art is a disproportioning ... of realities to shew more clearly the features that matter. ... Hence "realism" is not art.

The use of the word "idiosyncrasy" expresses more than the commonplace about the personality of the artist. It almost asks for freedom to be eccentric, to express rather than communicate. But there is at the same time the unwillingness to stray far from reality: even in an argument leading to the conclusion that " 'realism' [in quotes] is not art" the right kind of art increases "vraisemblance", which is a synonym for realism. Similarly when talking about impressions and objects, Hardy writes: "In getting at the truth, we get only at the true nature of the impression that an object, etc., produces on us, the true thing in itself being still, as Kant shows, beyond our knowledge." Behind the antithesis between truth and impression we sense the Hardy whose tentativeness and "impressions" we have discussed who wanted to be free to record "mere impressions" untrammelled by a "consistent philosophy" − the thing in itself couldn't be known, so one was free to combine and create − yet this contrast is spoiled by speaking of the impression itself as if it could be false and ought to be true, so one is brought back to reality again. And, as we have seen, when denying he was "a writer of novels proper" he did not simply say his novels were poetic but that he kept them "as close to natural life and as near to poetry" as he could − having it both ways. Again, when Hardy writes: "Romanticism will exist in human nature as long as human nature itself exists. The point is (in imaginative literature) to adopt that form of romanticism which is the mood of the age" − he is offering himself as a Victorian thinker, "adopting" romanticism only to write about it; but one surely feels also that he is thinking of his own romanticism, his personal preference of the past to the present, the ghost to the person, and the dream to the reality: Victorian only in its (in Hardy's case very slight) hope for the future.

Most telling of all perhaps is the following:

If Nature's defects must be ... transcribed, whence arises the art in poetry and novel-writing? . . . The art lies in making these defects the basic of a hitherto unperceived beauty, by irradiating them with "the light that never was".

"Irradiate" is the word used of Angel's love of Tess, most significantly at the moment when he saw her *"without* irradiation". In the light imagery which is discussed in Chapter 3, light is the condition of seeing, and to see Tess without irradiation is not to see her at all. The word is constantly used of Angel's seeing Tess, and its use of a mist, of gnats, and of the party returning from the Trantridge dance, generalises the point in accordance with Tess's representative character; and it is a favourite word of Hardy's. It is the perfect word for creative imagination, functioning as in *A Midsummer Night's Dream* in the lover and the poet. But it is characteristic of Hardy that, though he explains it by the Wordsworthian "light that never was" he in fact insists on the reality of the result — not simply a new beauty but one "hitherto unperceived".[24]

Hardy was not a man to thrive on tension, and his best novels are those in which the dream is closest to the reality. In *The Woodlanders*, which Stewart strangely calls "the least poetic of Hardy's major productions", the trees provide all the work and all the poetry — South's elm, the night-hawk, the great green vase in which Fitzpiers and Grace seem to move, the deeper recesses, the house of death. In *Tess*, the heroine's quest for love, security and truth produces the imagery of appearance and movement. In *The Mayor* the contrasts between old and new and between wealth and poverty are as much matters of feeling and folk-images as of fact. In *Far from the Madding Crowd* the real threat to the farm appears in the poetry of fire and storm and ballad-soldier as well as in the plot. In *Jude*, as well as the symbolic indictment of Christianity, there is the *Revelation* image of a city of light to relate to the old Jerusalem and to Christminster and to stand apart from "modern unrest".

The most general truth about Hardy is his desire for freedom, with which we must connect idiosyncrasy, wilfulness and indiscipline. We see it in his personal life (in his dislike of being touched or weighed and in his poor performance as a husband)

and in his literary career: he gave up novel-writing not because of the outcries, which he provoked and enjoyed, but because he could afford to please himself. His desire for freedom made him want freedom for others, "a system based on individual spontaneity". It is however the subject of hostile criticism by Graham Greene, that "he wrote as he pleased", and by Eliot, that he was "uncurbed by any institutional attachment or by submission to any objective beliefs; unhampered by any ideas, or even by . . . the desire to please a large public". It is true that he was uncurbed by attachment to Christianity or marriage, that he did not simply believe in the old rural values but also saw their faults, and that he was unhampered by ideas — not without ideas, but unhampered by them, using those he fancied but only as they contributed to his tentative impressionism, and equally selective in his social interests. His concentration on what he was interested in may be illuminated by his note in 1878: "Felt that I had not enough staying power to hold my own in the world." So he could not afford too great an effort. So, where he is not interested (or cannot do better) he uses the words and ideas of others, turns from the hard work of "manners" to a "substance" which can become monotonous, and doesn't trouble to avoid absurd errors of narrative and motivation. The same selectivity or concentration is seen in the narrow range of his characters, of which "flexible", easy-to-be-interested-in women, and men like himself, form so large a section: and in his repetition of his favourite, idiosyncratic ideas and favourite quotations. Self-indulgence is the explanation of failures such as *The Well-Beloved* and *The Dynasts*.[26]

More important than his repetition of idiosyncratic ideas is the fact that he had them. Cecil says that "instinctively his eye gravitated towards the queer" but the result doesn't have to be queer, like Troy's gargoyle. It can be accurate, like Bayley's example of Margery's jacket "rolled and compressed . . . till it was about as large as an apple-dumpling", or poetical, as when, on the eve of Ethelberta's marriage, "the music of songs mingled with the stroke of the wind across the iron railings, and swept on in the general tide of the gale, and the noise of the rolling sea, till not the echo of a tone remained"; and it can be irrelevant, as when, on the Isle of Slingers, "the raw rain flies level as the missiles of the ancient inhabitants". It can be, and in the better work is, relevant, part of a larger whole; but it is in such atomic perceptions that we meet the essential Hardy.

Short Titles

The following works are referred to by the short titles indicated here in capitals:

I.   Works by Hardy

BJORK: *The Literary Notes of Thomas Hardy* Volume I ed. Lennart A. Björk, Göteborg, 1974.

CP: *The Complete Poems*, ed. Gibson, 1976.

D: *The Dynasts*, Pocket edition.

DR: *Desperate Remedies.*

FMC: *Far from the Madding Crowd.*

HE: *The Hand of Ethelberta.*

ILH: *An Indiscretion in the Life of an Heiress.*

JO: *Jude the Obscure.*

L: *A Laodicean.*

LIFE: F. E. Hardy, *The Life of Thomas Hardy 1840–1928* 1962, comprising *The Early LIfe,* 1928, and *The Later Years,* 1930.

LLE: *Late Lyrics and Earlier* (included in CP)

LLI/CM: *Life's Little Ironies* and *A Changed Man and Other Tales.* New Wessex hardback edition.

MC: *The Mayor of Casterbridge.*

OMC: *Old Mrs Chundle and Other Stories with The Queen of Cornwall,* New Wessex hardback edition.

PBE: *A Pair of Blue Eyes.*

PW: *Thomas Hardy's Personal Writings,* ed. Orel, 1966.

RN: *The Return of the Native.*

TD: *Tess of the d'Urbervilles.*

TM: *The Trumpet-Major.*

TT: *Two on a Tower.*

UGT: *Under the Greenwood Tree.*

W: *The Woodlanders.*

WB: *The Well-Beloved.*

WT/GND: *Wessex Tales* and *A Group of Noble Dames*, New Wessex hardback edition.

References are to page numbers, and, in the case of novels, book or part (where so divided) and chapter numbers; of the New Wessex paperback edition where not otherwise stated: in the case of D. to Part, Act, Scene and page.

II.   Other Works

ANNAN: Noel Annan, *Leslie Stephen*, 1951

BAILEY, MELIORISM: J. O. Bailey, "Evolutionary Meliorism in the Poetry of Thomas Hardy", SP 60, 1963.

BARZIN: I. de R. Barzin, *Le Pessimisme de Thomas Hardy*, 1932.

BAYLEY: John Bayley, *An Essay on Hardy*, 1978.

BEACH: J. W. Beach, *The Technique of Thomas Hardy*, Chicago, 1922; New York, 1962.

BECKMAN: Richard Beckman, "A Character Typology for Hardy's Novels", ELH 30, 1963.

BLUNDEN: Edmund Blunden, *Thomas Hardy*, 1941.

BRAYBROOKE: P. Braybrooke, *Thomas Hardy and his Philosophy*, 1928.

BRENNECKE: Ernest Brennecke, *Thomas Hardy's Universe*, 1924.

BROOKS: Jean R. Brooks, *Thomas Hardy, The Poetic Structure*, 1971.

BROWN: Douglas Brown, *Thomas Hardy*, 1954.

CARPENTER: Richard Carpenter, *Thomas Hardy*, 1964/1976.

CECIL: Lord David Cecil, *Hardy the Novelist*, 1943.

CHEW: Samuel C. Chew, *Thomas Hardy, Poet and Novelist*, 1921.

COX: R. G. Cox, ed., *Thomas Hardy, the Critical Heritage*, 1970.

DE LAURA: D. J. de Laura, " 'The Ache of Modernism' in Hardy's Later Novels", ELH 34, 1968.

FIROR: Ruth Firor, *Folkways in Thomas Hardy*, Philadelphia, 1931; New York, 1962.

GARWOOD: Helen Garwood, *Thomas Hardy: an Illustration of the Philosophy of Schopenhauer,* 1911.

GITTINGS, YOUNG: Robert Gittings, *Young Thomas Hardy,* 1975.

GITTINGS, OLDER: Robert Gittings, *The Older Hardy,* 1978.

GOLDBERG: M. A. Goldberg, "Hardy's Double-Visioned Universe", EC 7, 1957.

GREGOR, MORAL: I. Gregor and B. Nicholas, "The Novel as Moral Protest" in *The Moral and the Story,* 1962.

GREGOR, WEB: I. Gregor, *The Great Web: the Form of Hardy's Major Fiction,* 1974.

GREGOR, WHAT KIND: I. Gregor, "What Kind of Fiction Did Hardy Write?" EC 16, 1966.

GRIMSDITCH: Herbert B. Grimsditch, *Character and Environment in the Novels of Thomas Hardy,* 1925.

GUERARD: A. J. Guerard, *Thomas Hardy, the Novels and Stories,* 1949.

EVELYN HARDY: Evelyn Hardy, *Thomas Hardy, a Critical Biography,* 1954.

HEILMAN: R. B. Heilman, "Hardy's Mayor: Notes on Style", NCF 19, 1964.

HOLLAND: N. Holland, *"Jude the Obscure:* Hardy's Symbolic Indictment of Christianity", NCF 9, 1954.

HOWE: Irving Howe, *Thomas Hardy,* 1966.

HYDE, JUDE: W. J. Hyde, "Theoretic and Practical Unconventionality in *Jude the Obscure",* NCF 20, 1965.

HYDE, REALISM: W. J. Hyde, "Hardy's View of Realism", VS 2, 1958–9.

HYMAN: Virginia R. Hyman, *Ethical Perspective in the Novels of Thomas Hardy,* Kennikat Press, New York, 1975.

HYNES: Samuel Hynes, *The Pattern of Hardy's Poetry,* 1956.

LIONEL JOHNSON: Lionel Johnson, *The Art of Thomas Hardy,* 1894/1923.

S. F. JOHNSON: S. F. Johnson, "Hardy and Burke's Sublime", *English Institute Essays,* 1958.

KETTLE: Arnold Kettle, *An Introduction to the English Novel,* 1953, vol. II: "Thomas Hardy: *Tess of the d'Urbervilles".*

KRAMER: Dale Kramer, *Thomas Hardy, the Forms of Tragedy,* Michigan, 1975.

LERNER: Laurence Lerner, *Thomas Hardy's The Mayor of Casterbridge: Tragedy of Social History?,* 1975.

LODGE: David Lodge, "Tess, Nature and the Voices of Hardy" in *The Language of Fiction,* 1966.

MAXWELL: J. C. Maxwell, "The 'Sociological' Approach to *The Mayor of Casterbridge*", in I. Gregor and M. Mack eds., *Imagined Worlds,* 1968.

MILLER: J. Hillis Miller, *Thomas Hardy, Distance and Desire,* Cambridge, Mass., 1970.

MILLGATE: Michael Millgate, *Thomas Hardy: His Career as a Novelist,* 1971.

OREL: Harold Orel, *Thomas Hardy's Epic-Drama,* Lawrence, Kansas, 1963.

PARIS: B. J. Paris, " 'A Confusion of Many Standards': Conflicting Value Systems in *Tess of the D'Urbervilles*", NCF 24, 1969–70.

PECKHAM: Morse Peckham, 'Darwinism and Darwinisticism", VS 3, 1959–60.

PINION, ART: F. B. Pinion, *Thomas Hardy: Art and Thought,* 1977.

PINION, COMPANION: F. B. Pinion, *A Hardy Companion,* 1968.

RUTLAND: W. R. Rutland, *Thomas Hardy, a Study of His Writings and Their Background,* New York, 1938/1962.

SOUTHERINGTON: F. R. Southerington, *Hardy's Vision of Man,* 1971.

STEVENSON: Lionel Stevenson, *Darwin Among the Poets,* 1932.

STEWART: J. I. M. Stewart, *Thomas Hardy,* 1971.

TANNER: Tony Tanner, "Colour and Movement in Hardy's *Tess of the D'Urbervilles*", CQ 10, 1968.

THURLEY: Geoffrey Thurley, *The Psychology of Hardy's Novels,* Queensland, 1975.

VAN GHENT: Dorothy Van Ghent, "On *Tess of the D'Urbervilles*" in *The English Novel: Form and Function,* New York, 1953.

WEBER: C. J. Weber, *Hardy of Wessex,* 1940/1965.

WEBSTER: H. C. Webster, *On a Darkling Plain, the Art and Thought of Thomas Hardy,* 1947/1964.

MERRYN WILLIAMS: Merryn Williams, *Thomas Hardy and Rural England,* 1972.

RAYMOND WILLIAMS: Raymond Williams, "Wessex and the Border" *in The Country and the City,* 1973.

WRIGHT: Walter F. Wright, *The Shaping of the Dynasts,* Lincoln, USA, 1967.

ZABEL, Morton D. Zabel, "Hardy in Defense of his Art: The Aesthetic of Incongruity" in *Craft and Character in Modern Fiction,* 1957.

III.   Periodicals

CQ: *Critical Quarterly.*

EC: *Essays in Criticism.*

ELH: *ELH, A Journal of English Literary History.*

MLR: *Modern Language Review.*

NCF: *Nineteenth-Century Fiction.*

PMLA: *Publications of the Modern Language Association of America.*

RES: *The Review of English Studies.*

SP: *Studies in Philology.*

VS: *Victorian Studies.*

Notes

CHAPTER 1. MODERNITY

1. UGT Preface 27; RN Preface 29; TM XXXIV, XXXV (Trafalgar); MC XXII. 182 (the Museum "in a back street" to which moved in 1851), XXXVII (the Royal visit naturally taken to be Prince Albert's to Portland in 1849); W XXXVII.298 ("the new law ... last year 20 and 21 Vic."), XXI.183 (the South Carolina gentleman left the US on "the failure of the Southern cause"); WT 13, 40, 72, 82, 11, 127; LLI 15, 47, 57, 92, 128, 142, 193; CM 207, 214, 290, 302.

2. JO IV.i.224 (Sue refers to Cowper's *Apocryphal Gospels*), *Life* 433; TD III.50 (Tess educated under the Revised Code), 1912 Pref. 30; FMC XXXIX.291 (the Union workhouse).

3. PBE II.48: in the serial and later editions the date is "18—": the fact that the text was "basically little altered" (New Wessex, p. 420) further suggests the precise date didn't matter; HE XVII.138; TT Introduction 25.

4. RN 29; TM IV.63, XXVI.221, XL.343, Xii.126; MC XXXVI.282, IV.57, IX.91; W I.35; FMC XXII.177. Cf. Cecil, p. 148: "Hardy was a man born after his time ... into the alien world of the later nineteenth century"; and Guerard, p. 40: "The facts of Hardy's life are very nearly as irrelevant to an understanding of his novels as the literary tendencies of the age."

5. *Life* 320, 221 432; D Preface ix; HE Preface 31–2; RN III.ii.196; JO VI.i.345, iii.372, x.419, V.iv.305.

6. FMC 37 (Hardy actually says that press and public "joined me in the anachronism of imagining" such a place: it is hard to see what he meant by anachronism — perhaps "going back in time"); RN I.ix.104; TD XXX.227; JO III.i.153; L I.ii.52; TT III.50; WB I.4.40; FMC XXII.176; JO IV.i.221; LI.xi.119, I.ii.46; DR VIII.4.161 (New Wessex ed. says Manet or Courbet). It is not clear that Hardy knew or understood French Impressionism. Considering the numerous artists he does name, it is remarkable that he never names an Impressionist. He once uses the expression "impression-picture" (W II.41) which is explained by the New Wessex editor as "an allusion to the French Impressionist school". He visited the Society of British Artists in 1886, where, he said, "The impressionist school is strong. ... Their principle is, as I understand it, that what you carry away with you from a scene is the true feature to grasp; or in other words, *what appeals to your own individual eye and heart in particular* [his italics] amid much that does not so appeal, and which you therefore omit to record." This, although a fair description of one aspect of Impres-

sionism, seems to have been picked out by Hardy because it agrees with his own "impressionism", which I discuss briefly at the end of this chapter; his insistence that his work is only his impressions, not a consistent philosophy. What this means I discuss further in Chapter 5 in terms of freedom, idiosyncrasy and fancy. It is a question whether the freedom of the artist to speak the truth that he sees, or the freedom to imagine, is meant. The "impression-picture" in W is of Marty at night by firelight: "the girl's hair alone, as the focus of observation, was depicted with intensity and distinctness, while her face, shoulders, hands, and figure in general were a blurred mass of unimportant detail lost in haze and obscurity". Distinctness suggests pre-Raphaelite, the background is consistent with Impressionism, but the whole rather suggests Rembrandt or the Dutch candlelight school. The MS has "post-Raffaelite picture" for "impression-picture" which agrees with this. "Impression-picture" is not "Impressionist-picture" but Hardy's own coinage, perhaps to describe what is sometimes called a "tete d'expression". I am indebted to Professor Ronald Pickvance of Glasgow University for help with this note.

7. L II.iv.230; WB III.3.164; W III.47, XL.325; TD XLI.323; JO II.ii.104.

8. RN I.i.34-6; TD XLV.357; RN II.vi.162, III.i.191.

9 M. A. Goldberg, "Hardy's Double-Visioned Universe" EC 7, 1957, 374–82; RN III.v.224, III.ii.201, 199, 196 and note *ad loc. Spectator* no. 117.

10. WB II.1.78, III.8.201, III.1.146.

11. TD XLIII.332; RN III.i.191; TD IV.59; W 33; TD XLIX.390; JO I.iv.50.

12. FMC XXXVIII.287; RN V.iv.353; TT XXXVIII.265; MC XLI.318 XLIV.339, XV.128; TD XXXV.276, XXXVI.282, XXXIV.264; JO I.xi.91, FMC LIII.401; JO I.xi.91 VI.ii.355; W XLIII.353; FMC XXXVIII.287; RN V.i.328; TT IX.92; MC XX.163; TD XXIII.187, LII.414, LVIII 447; JO VI.ii:352; WB I.1.31, III.3.165; RN III.iv.219; TD XII.111, XXX.231; JO I.iv.50, V.iv.305, VI.xi.423–4, VI.i.351, 353; TM xxi.183, TD XIII.120; JO I.ii.36; TD XXXVI.287; JO VI.ii.356; TD III.51; JO I ii 38

13. TD XIX.163; I discuss de Laura on "the ache of modernism" in ch 3.

14. RN V.vii.337; MC XXV.201; PBE XV.176; FMC XXXIX.288; W XVII.153; XIV.132.

15. W XVI.144, 147; Fielding, *Tom Jones* III.iii; TD XXXVI.284, XXXVII.294, XXIV.192, XLIX.390, XXXVI.287, XXXII.245, XXXIII 254, XXXI.237, LV.429.

16. JO I.ix.78, II.iv.118, VI.ix.412, V.iii.296; RN IV.vi.302.

17. PBE XXII.243, XIII.162; FMC XLII.318; TT IX.92; W XXXVIII 305, XXV.208; JO VI.iii.362–4

18. Dorothy Van Ghent, "On *Tess of the D'Urbervilles*" in *The English Novel: Form and Function,* 1953; L III.vi.246; FMC II.52; DR IX.3.179; MC XIX.154, XXII.176; RN IV.iii.279.

19. MC IX.94, XXIV.267, XLI.320; W XXXV.284, XLVII.383; FMC XV.141; RN II.iii.144; TD XI.107, LI.406; JO III.x.216; MC XIV.117.

20. Pinion, *Art,* "Chance, Choice and Charity", RN IV.viii.317; W XIX. 169, XXVI.219; JO VI.ii.358; W XV.140; TD XLII.327, V.72, VI.77; W XXV.204; TD XXXII.244; FMC VIII.97; TD XLII.328; UGT I.vi.66.

21. Crickett says it about being his wife's third husband, DR VIII.3.157; Mr Penny about the death of his grandchildren, UGT I.ii.39; Enoch and Mrs Penny about marriage, UGT II.vi.116, V.i.195; Henery Fray about his failure to beome bailiff, FMC XV.138; Tess's "own people" about her seduction, TD XI.108. Similarly Arabella says "what's done can't be un-done" about her marriage, which was entirely the result of her simulated pregnancy, and could be and was undone by divorce, JO I.ix.82.

22. TD LVIII.442.

23. TM Vi.75; RN I.i.35; MC I.36; W XXVIII.236, XXXIX.318; PBE XIV.168; TM XVI.154.

24. Gregor, *Moral,* pp. 143–4; TD III.51, XIV. 131, XXIII.187, X.98, XII.117, XVIII.158, XIII.120–1, XLI.324, XIV.128.

25. MC XLIV.339; JO VI.ii.358; TD XI.108, XII.117, XIV.127, XV.135, XVIII.154, XXIII.187, XXXVI.286, XL.314, 315, XLIV.347, XLVI.362, 370, JO I.ii.37, V.vi.327, I.ix.82, II.iv.118, III.i.148, III.ii.158, IV.i.226. IV.ii.235, IV.iii.238, V.viii.338, VI.i.346, VI.ii.353, 356, VI.iv.379.

26. See my "Hardy's 'Pedantry' ", NCF 28, 1973; MC XI.100; FMC XLVII.349, TD II.40; W XIII.123; MC XVII.143, XXVI.211, XVII.144; RN II.iii.142; TD XIV.131; W I.37; RN I.iii.53; W V.69; TD III.48; MC VIII.83.

27. W XXX.249, XLV.361; *Life* 258. He adds "It is doubtful if this Utopian scheme possessed Hardy's fancy for any long time." W XVII.153 XXIII.194, XXV.209, XXXVIII.308, XXIV.201, V.68; TM V.68; MC X.97. "Sophisticated": MC IV.56, XIV.117; W XXIX.244, XXXVIII.311; TD XXVI.206, XXX.228, XXXII.245, XXXVI.286, XLI.320; JO I.ix.79, IV v.262.

28. JO IV.219; MC XXXI.242; JO Preface 25; MC XLIV.339, XLI.317, XVII.141, XLIV.339.

29. RN III.i.192; W IX.103; TD XXX.276; JO VI.iii.364; TM XI.113, XIX.169; W XLIII.354, XLVIII.389; TD XVI.140; JO V.vii.331; TD XLV.357; MC VIII.86; TD XXIX.221.

30. *Life* vii, 155; CP 84; PW 48–9; *Life* 377; TD Preface to the Fifth and Later Editions 29; JO 23; CP.66; JO VI.iii.362; TD XXIII.183, XXII. 180; MC XLV.354; W XXX.246; TD V.72, LVIII.446; *Life* 247–8; CP 485, 67.

CHAPTER 2. THE SOCIAL CRITIC

1. Cecil, pp. 14–5.

2. Chew, p. 126; Gregor, *Moral,* p. 128.

3. TD V.72; JO VI.i.346, IV.v.262.

4. Brown, pp. 42, 32.

5. Lerner, pp. 77–97; MC XLIV.345, XLV.350, XXIV.195, XLV.351, XXXIV.265, XXVI.278–9; DR X.6.212; W II, V, XXIII–XIV; TD IX.88.

6. FMC XXII.177; W XIX.166; MC XXIV.193; JO IV.i.220; TD XXXI.235.

7. Lerner, p. 92; Brown, pp. 142, 55, 63; Merryn Williams, pp. 197–200; FMC Preface 38.

8. TD V.66; Merryn Williams, pp. 159, 171; W XX.189. "Claiming kin" is economic not social. Elizabeth-Jane does it to Henchard as well as Tess to Alec.

9. TD XLII.329, XLIII.336, XLVII.374, XLVIII.382; PW 187; Merryn Williams, p. 13 table 3.

10. W 394, note on p. 45; PW 172–3; MC XXIII.187–8; PW 181; TD LI.400–401. Pulling down: FMC XLII.311; HE XXXVII.303; TT XI.99; MC 1.37, IV.60 n., VI.72, IX.91 n., XXII.186; W XV.138; TD LI.401; JO I.i.30, IV.i.220. The pulling down of Mixen Lane, MC XXXVI.278, is a social improvement.

11. UGT I.ii.39, I.vii.69, II.vi.117, III.ii.136, IV.vi.182–3, V.ii.206; FMC XXXII.252, XXXIV.258; PBE XII.156, XIII.158; W II.42–4; TD XII.116; JO VI.i.345.

12. MC XXI.170, XXVII.217, VIII.83, XVIII.148, XXIII.188, I.43, XI.103, XXX.241, XXXVII.290–1.

13. MC XXXII.253, X.98, XII.109, XX.163; W XII.119.

14. PBE XII.152–8, XIV; RN IV.viii.318–21; W IV.57, V.71, VI.79; TT II.44; RN V.ii.339; PBE XXXVII.372; HE XXXII.269; L IV.i to V.x; TD XXXIX.305; TT XVI.133.

15. MC V.65; TD VI.75, XXIV.262; RN II.i.132; JO I.iii.41–2.

16. MC XXI.167; L VI.5.436; W VIII.91, HE XLVI, XLVII, Sequel; TD V.66, IX.88.

17. UGT I.ii.39; TD XIV.128; FMC VIII.91; MC XIII.114; W XLIII.353, FMC XLII.312, XXXIX.290, V.73; RN I.ix.105, I.iii.52; W IV.56.

18. PW 185.

19. Mrs Margaret Oliphant, "The Anti-Marriage League", *Blackwoods* 159, 1896, in Cox; Hardy to Edmund Gosse, 10. Nov. 1895; JO V.v.315, I.ix.78, II.iv.118, III.vii.192, IV.iii.239, V.i.278, V.iii.290; WB II.7.108.

20. JO I.ix.78, VI.v.383, III.vi.187; FMC XLIII.327; W XXIII.195; FMC LVII.423; *Life* 376.

21. JO V.ii.289; W XXXIX.321.

22. JO IV.219; FMC VIII.97; MC I.36; W XXXV.288; JO VI.viii.404; RN I.vii.96, V.iii.348, IV.iii.284; W XXIX.239.

23. JO VI.ii.357; TD XL.311; JO VI.iii.362; TD XXV.200, 198, XXVI.208, XLIV.348, XII.114–16, XIV.133; JO V.vi.323, vii.332; UGT II.ii.91; PBE IV.59; RN I.x.113, I.iii.48; PBE XXIII.253; TM XXIII.205; JO II.iv.117, IV.i.221; TD X.97; TM XXIII.206, XXVIII.248; RN I.iii.55, I.v.74; TD XXIII.182; DR X.5.211; "The Distracted Preacher" WT 159;

TM XXII.206; W XLIII.350; TD XXXV.276; FMC XXII.176; DR X.5.210; TT XI.101; TD I.34; TT I.40.

24. FMC XLII.314; TD XIV.132–3; CP 446; TD XXXVI.284; JO VI.iv.381; TD XLVI.368; DR XII.1.240; FMC XXXIII.250; RN VI.iii.410, VI.iv.422; cf. "Surview", CP 698.

25. MC XV.126; W XXX.251, XLVI.371; MC XXIV.195 (" 'Then the romance of the sower is gone for good' observed Elizabeth-Jane"), XXV.204 ("one of the 'meaner beaties of the night' ", from Wotton "On His Mistress the Queen of Bohemia"), XXX.239, XLV.350, XIV.116, 119–20, XVIII.147; W XXX.252; TD XLVII.377, XXXIX.308.

26. PBE VIII.107, VII.82–4.

27. JO VI.i.346, IV.iii.239, II.i.99–102, VI.ix.412. On Arnold's neo-Christianity see de Laura.

28. TD XVIII.153–4, XXV.198.

29. JO II.vi.134–7.

30. JO VI.i.346.

31. JO I.iii.45, II.vi.132, V.vii.332.

32. JO II.ii.104.

33. JO I.ii.37, I.v.53, VI.i.346, V.v.308, V.vii.332; RN III.ii.196 and on Clym see my Chapter 1, p. 5.

34. Sir Llewellyn Woodward, *The Age of Reform 1815–70* 2nd ed., 1962; Asa Briggs, *The Age of Improvement 1783–1867,* 1959; Burke, *Thoughts on Scarcity,* 1775. Hardy does mention the Penny Post, as we have seen, in the Preface to FMC. His poorer characters write frequently but without authorial comment about the cheapness. He mentions Arch, founder of the National Union, in "The Dorsetshire Labourer" but not in the novels. The point that Hardy disregards the Agrarian Revolution is made by Lerner, p. 97. Hardy does briefly mention the enclosure of a plantation of trees in Egdon, RN III.vi.231. And see RN III.ii.198, quoted below, p. 61, and my comment there.

35. CP 446, 491, 877, TD XLI.323; JO I.x.85, IV.ii.234, VI.i.346; FMC XL; PBE XXIII.251; HE XXXI.251; TT XIX.153 and Introduction 16.

36. George Eliot, *Middlemarch,* chs. II, III (*bis*), IV, XIII, XV, XVI, LVI. And Bayley, p. 179, is in effect making the same point by contrasting *Tess* with *Esther Waters.*

37. FMC VI; CP 198; LLI/CM "A Changed Man", MC XXXVII.287; TD XXX.227; JO I.iii.39, III.ii.157; RN I.ix.104. Cf. TM XI.120 for Hardy's feeling for the life of the road.

38. W XLVII.377; TD XLVII.373; MC Preface 33 ("The incidents narrated arise mainly out of three events . . . one of them the uncertain harvests which immediately preceded the repeal of the Corn Laws."); RN I.iii.55, v.74; TD X.97; JO IV.i.221; W XXVI.217.

39. Hardy is not always accurate even about country matters. He describes the shearing of a sheep in 23½ minutes as "done quickly" (FMC XXII.179) when in fact it would have taken no more than four (A. R. B.

Haldane, letter in *Times Literary Supplement*, 27. Oct.1978), and confuses house-martins with swifts and swallows, and omits from Egdon the truly local black grouse and dartford warbler Desmond Hawkins, "Hardy as a Countryman", *Country Life*, Vol. CLXI. no.4149, 6.Jan.1977, p.28).

40. See Hyde, "Realism".

CHAPTER 3. IDEAS

1. This distinction is made by Björk.

2. Ch. 1, pp. 24—5.

3. Letter to Helen Garwood, quoted by Weber, p. 246. For Hume, see below, p. 92.

4. *Life* 128.

5. *Life* 33. "But few people were not" (Stewart, p. 10).

6. *Life* 315.

7. CP 307; TD XLIII.332; W VII.83; TD XXV.198; CP 502; JO II.vi. 135; W XVI.147.

8. J.O. Bailey, "Evolutionary Meliorism in the Poetry of Thomas Hardy", SP 60, 1963; *Life* 149.

9. F. A. Hedgcock, *Thomas Hardy Penseur et Artiste*, 1911, p. 499.

10. Rutland, pp. 89—90; TD XIX.165; JO VI.ii.356.

11. TD XXXVI.284; W XXIX.239; *Life* 258; TD V.72; JO VI.iii.372; RN III.ii.196; W XIV.133; DR XIII.2.264. On the hangings in *Jude*, see below, p. 66.

12. TD XIX.163; D III.vi.ii.461; TD XIV.126, XLI.323.

13. "German pessimistic philosophy, whether Schopenhauer's or Von Hartmann's, cannot have affected him at any radically formative stage of his career" (Stewart, p. 32). For *The Dynasts*, see my Appendix.

14. See J. W. Burrow, *Evolution and Society*, 1966, p. 20.

15. If Lerner were right about a "single cultural upheaval" Hardy could not be Darwinistic.

16. *Life* 153, 259, 321, 349, 111; Darwin, *Origin of Species*, 1859, Penguin ed., ch. 14, p. 455; CP 907.

17. Björk, Entry No. 895; *Origin of Species*, Penguin ed., ch. 11, p. 345.

18. J. O. Bailey, "Heredity: Hardy's 'President of the Immortals' ", *Thomas Hardy Annual Review*, 1977, p. 94, claims that he had.

19. CP 561.

20. "Possibly no other single book made a greater immediate impact on Hardy than *The Origin of Species*. . . . In *The Woodlanders* . . . the Darwinian view of Nature is . . . indivisible from the principal theme. [That the insects enjoyed the heat which was too much for Mrs Yeobright showed that] cruelty to one species . . . may be ideal for another." (Pinion, *Art*, p. 35). "Perhaps the most powerful influence of all . . . was that of Darwin. . . . [*The Woodlanders*] is the most overtly Darwinian of Hardy's books." (Southerington, pp. 217, 120). "Darwin . . . destroyed his faith. . . . According to Darwin . . . chance . . . seems to be the deciding factor in survival.

... As a result of his own thinking about the consequence of Darwinism, Hardy early realised that the struggle for existence applies to society. ... No intellectual influence as important as that of Darwin affected the form of Hardy's thought." (Webster, pp. 44, 64, 92, 132.) Webster also refers to the passages discussed below from *The Woodlanders* as showing that life is "a struggle in accordance with natural laws" and discusses its characters in terms of "sexual selection" and "the struggle for existence", pp. 167–9; and sees Darwinian elements in *A Pair of Blue Eyes, Far from the Madding Crowd*, and *The Mayor*, pp. 104, 109, 126, 148; but he also says: "When we look over Hardy's early novels, it often seems that ... unaccountable accident is more important than natural or sexual selection. Here, certainly, Hardy diverges from Darwinism in his emphasis" (p. 127). David Lodge, in reference to the same passages from *The Woodlanders* as Webster, comments: "this view of Nature comes from ... Darwin"; and speaks of "the evolutionary struggle in nature" (W Introduction 22–3). Dr Pinion's claim is made at the beginning of an essay entitled "Chance, Choice and Charity" which discusses the extent to which Hardy leaves room for human choice, without further reference to Darwin. For Bailey and Stevenson see pp. 64–9 below.

Peckham distinguishes between the worlds of *The Return, Under the Greenwood Tree* and *Far from the Madding Crowd*: they are ruled respectively by accident, providence, and causality: *The Return* is therefore post Darwinian. But he gives no evidence: chance and natural or causal events, are found in all three, providence in none. And accident without variation is not Darwinian.

Since it is mentioned by Björk, I should explain briefly why I do not answer in detail the arguments in Jean R. Brooks's *Darwinism in Thomas Hardy's Major Novels* (unpublished thesis for University of London M.A Degree, 1961). Mrs Brooks claims that Hardy used Darwinism as his "underlying pattern of the ordering of experience" (p. 7). In the six major novels "the pattern is integrated into an ethic of evolution". Mrs Brooks transfers to human and social relations what Darwin intends as biological, for instance his statement that for creatures "placed in a new country among new competitors, the conditions for life will generally be changed", which for her is illustrated by Bathsheba's change to the new occupation of tenant farmer (p.11). She also quotes out of context remarks by Darwin which are not in themselves in the least Darwinian, such as that "great lawgivers ... philosophers and discoverers in science aid the progress of mankind in a far higher degree by their works than by leaving a numerous progeny" – which Clym is supposed to exemplify (p. 60). Mrs Brooks continually drags in the words "struggle", "survival" and "fit" with absurd results: "Mother and child pay the penalty of Fanny's unfitness to increase in numbers" (p. 9). Troy's "success" in the struggle for survival (which ends with his childless death) means that he will "increase in numbers" (p. 13).

21. RN IV.vi.308.

22. MC I.40–41, 44–45, VI.72, FMC XXII.178, V.74; TD VIII.85, XXXI.235, XLI.321, LVIII.447, XVI.142; W I.37, XXXV.285; TD XVI. 147; XIX.160, XXVII.209, XLV.352; JO I.vi.59, II.iii.III.

23. RN I.i.35–6, III.ii.198, I.ii.40, III.iii.213, v.227, VI.i.397, I.x.113, II.i.131, III.v.227, vi.233, viii.253–4, IV.ii.273, v.297, vi.308, vii.312, 314, V.ii.336, iii.343, vi. 361; *Origin of Species*, Penguin ed., ch. 4, p. 136. Hardy in most of his work, and not only *The Return*, uses precise or scientific terms, sometimes contrasted with something simpler or more poetic or human, to express pathos or show that the culture of Wessex is more complex than its vocabulary. Reins form a "catenary curve" and Grace's kiss is contrasted with Fitzpiers's "febrifuge" (W I.37, XLIII.346, XLIV.356). "Heart-hydromels" (CP 607) combines the opposites. Henchard was "emolliated" (MC XLIV.44). The tracks of animals, are a "geological record" (TM VI.74).

24. W XLII.339.

25. By Webster and Lodge, 11.c., no. 20.

26. W IV.54; *Origin of Species* Penguin ed, ch.3, p. 126: Webster (p. 41) and Lodge misquote Darwin, and Lodge prints the passage as if it were continuous with another (p. 116) beginning "We behold the face of nature," which also mentions birds and beasts preying on insects, seeds and other birds; W VII.83; *Origin of Species*, Penguin ed., ch. 3, p. 115; W XII.116; RN III.vi.231, IV.v.298; W III.47; TD XLIV.344; CP 111, 829.

27. W VI.78, XXVII.229, XLVIII.393. The Darwinian interpretation of Fitzpiers and Marty is in Webster, l.c., n. 20.

28. See n. 18.

29. TD XI.108, XXIII.188, XVI.140, XXX.229, XXXII.244, XXXIII. 254.

30. JO I.xi.90–1, V.iv.301, III.vi.188, IV.ii.230, V.i.278.

31. TD XIX.166; TM II.47; W XXII.189, XXIII.190; L III.iii.216; PBE III.52, XII.152; HE XXIV.185.

32. Bailey, "Meliorism", p. 570, claims that from 1862 to 1886 Hardy's views "echo his reading in Darwin, Huxley, Spencer and J. S. Mill", but his only Darwinian examples are (p. 572) "Heiress and Architect" in which, he says, we find "the Darwinian idea that 'winters freeze' " and (p. 576) "In a Wood" which, he says, "rests upon Darwin's thought, but it is dated 1887; it is consistent with Schopenhauer's theory of the selfish Will in all life". "In a Wood" bears the superscription "See *The Woodlanders*" and like *The Woodlanders* lacks the ideas of natural selection, variation and inheritance of variation. The trees are Malthusian, "to men akin – Combatants all". That the same poem has been thought to be both Darwinian and Schopenhauerian is, like the doubt whether the hangings in *Jude* are Lamarckian or Schopenhauerian, a sign that Hardy's thought is only evolutionary in a vague and general way.

33. Stevenson, p. 259.

34. pp. 54–5 above; Stevenson, p. 266.

35. *Life* 218.

36. Stevenson, p. 270.

37. Stevenson, p. 283.

38. JO V.v.316; TD XXV.199; Björk, Entry No. 1176; JO I.v.53, II.iii. 112, 113, III.vi.187, II.v.126, V.iv.302.

39. TD XIV.122, XVI.141, XLV.352, XXV.199, XXVII.213, LVIII. 445, XXIX.222, XXXIII.256, XLVIII.384, XXXIX.304; RN IV.iii.281; L I.i.39. It is still "pagan customs" which linger on the Isle of Slingers, WB I.2.36; cf. II.9.121.

40. As Pinion argues, *Art and Thought*, pp. 103, 107–10. I cannot accept his argument that Greek mythology "functions" in RN, on the basis of Eustacia being compared to Greek goddesses, the occasional reference to Prometheus and Hades and the idea that sensuousness is Greek because Pater and Arnold said it was: Greek and Norse myth coexist with Leland, Albertus Magnus, William the Conqueror, Strafford, Napoleon, Heloise, Cain, Ahasuerus, Scheherazade, etc., etc.

41. RN VI.i.401; MC XI.100, TD XLIX.389.

42. TD XIV.129, XVII.148, L.393, IV.55, XXI.172, XXXII.248, XXXIII.255–6, LI.402, VI.73, XVIII.153–4, XXV.201, XXVI.208, XLVII.377, XIV.133, L.397, XLVII.377, LIII.417, XL.311, XLIV.348, XLV.356, XLVI.368, XLIV.343, XLV.357, 359.

43. Hyde, *Jude*, p. 155, argues that Sue in returning to Phillotson accepts Arnold's "Hebraism aiming at self-conquest and rescue from the thrall of vile affections". In the "Apology" to *Late Lyrics and Earlier* Hardy quotes John; 8:32: "The truth shall make you free", as Arnold does in *Culture and Anarchy*, in the chapter "Hebraism and Hellenism".

44. See de Laura, p. 386.

45. Rutland, p. 50; Webster, p. 44.

46. PBE XXII.240, TD XVII.146, XXXI.235.

47. JO III.iv.172.

48. TD XLVI.364, XLVII.378, XLVI.370.

49. TD L 397; HE VII.80 (the New Wessex edition does not notice the quotation from Hood), XXXV.282.

50. Paris, p. 65.

51. HE XXIII.181; FMC XLIII.327; MC XXIV.198; JO VI.iii.363.

52. RN I.iii.45; TD XVI.141; JO IV.v.262; FMC XLIII.327; JO V.vi. 327, VI.xi.423, MC XII.108; RN V.i.327.

53. Hyde, *Jude*, p. 155; J. S. Mill, *On Liberty* Everyman *Utilitarianism, On Liberty, Representative Government)* ch. 3, p. 120.

54. JO IV.iii.245; TD XIX.165; JO I.ii.37, VI.iii.362, II.iii.112, I.v.53.

55. TD XVI.141; JO III.iv.171; MC II.49; RN I.vi.81; DR XIII.3.269; Björk, Entry Nos. 641, 642, 647, 669.

56. Björk, Entry Nos. 647, 663, 664, 669; TD XXVII.213; JO I.v.53; TD XII.115; RN IV.iii.281, VI.i.401; L I.i.39, TD XVI.141, XXV.199,

XXXIX.304, XLV.352.

57. *Life* 146. On the looped orbits, see no. 61 below.

58. *Life* 98; FMC XLIII.321; MC VII.75; RN III.ii.196; TD II.43; TT 29, XXXV.244–5, XXXVII.257, XLI.281; RN I.x.120, TD XVIII.154.

59. PBE XXII.244; Hyman 43, 106–7, 76, 100, 57; RN IV.viii.317; Hyman 71–2, 103, 118; TD LI.406; Hyman 113–4, 119, 138; TD LVIII.437.

60. Hyman 160, 171, 162; Auguste Comte, *A General View of Positivism*, trans. J. H. Bridges, 2nd ed. 1880, ch. II, p. 70.

61. Björk Entry nos. 668, 670, 724–5, 728, 730, 749, 751; RN III.v.228. Mention should be made of Comtian influence claimed by Kramer and Pinion. Kramer (pp. 22, 71, 75) sees in *The Mayor* "Comte's idea of cyclic change" —the looped orbits. But Kramer's view, that *The Mayor* is cyclical, seems to depend on the unjustified assumption (p. 84) that Farfrae will be overthrown like Henchard, and on Henchard's fall itself which is only cyclic in the sense in which the Wheel of Fortune is. Kramer sees no other Comtian influence in Hardy. Pinion, *Art*, p. 114, says "Hardy's own philosophy was rooted in Comte's Positivism." Pinion seems to think that all Hardy's approval of altruistic or unselfish behaviour is Comtian; but the only passages he cites are two in *Tess* in which he sees "the merging of the human narrative and the mythology which Hardy constructed on the basis of scientific humanism". One is about Mrs d'Urberville's birds, and the other the scene at the threshing-machine ending " 'Once victim, always victim.' " Pinion gives a mythic explanation of the birds, Mrs d'Urberville's house and garden, and Alec's intrusion, which is in fact independent of Comte, and comments on the second passage: "To the Positivist in Hardy here was Tess, her one life ruined." Why to the Positivist? Apparently because the machine is Tess's *primum mobile*, and the *primum mobile* is the First Cause in Frederic Harrison's positivism. But so it is for anyone who uses the term.

62. De Laura, pp. 393, 394–5, 397, 391, 383; L VI.v.437; CP 558; RN III.ii.196. If the *Literary Notes* (Bjork Entry Nos. 101–4) are any guide, Hardy stopped reading *Literature and Dogma* at ch. 1, § 2.

63. HE XXXVI.295–7; JO IV.iii.244; Mill's *On Liberty* (Everyman ed. pp. 117, 118); Mill, *The Nature and Utility of Religion*, New York, 1958, p.53. Björk, Entry No. 1; JO IV.vi.268; Hyde, *Jude*, pp. 157–60. Pinion, *Companion*, p. 107, suggests that Mill's *Three Essays on Religion* may have suggested to Hardy the idea of consciousness developing in the Will, which, as I quote above (p. 54), Hardy said was his own idea.

64. *Life* 100, 128, 109, 308; Björk, Entry Nos. 980–3, 1190–5, 1217.

65. Gittings, *Older*, p. 9; Evelyn Hardy, p. 139. Webster, pp. 91–2; Pinion, *Companion*, p. 120. Rutland's discussion of Stephen's influence (pp. 78–83) is confined to agnosticism.

66. Björk, Entry Nos. 980 n., 1217 n.; PW 117, *Life* 386.

67. Southerington, ch. XIV, "Conclusion". Southerington's view is that

Hardy wanted to believe people could to some extent change the world, and he therefore needed to impose some order on – that is, make some sense of – his own experience: the novels show he made his own philosophy out of his own experience, but he was influenced by contemporary thinkers in seeing man as part of a whole, "belonging to a single organism". He believed that man could change the world when it was in a state of equilibrium, which he saw as a hypnotic state in which impulses can be implanted into it: but he concentrated, in a note reproduced in the *Life* (*Life* 146) which divided "the organism, Society" into periods, in the "Apology" to *Late Lyrics and Earlier* and in the novels and *The Dynasts*, on intellect as the source of change; in the novels the tragedy is often caused by the individual's failure to adapt to the environment, but in *The Mayor*, *Tess* and *Jude* Hardy because of his own experience is more sympathetic to the aspirations of the individual.

Divested of the influence of contemporary thinkers this becomes a very common and not at all nineteenth-century pattern of tragedy, and if one cannot regard the later novels as aberrations they reduce the importance of adapting to the environment: instead, the world should be changed so that Tess's, Sue's and Jude's aspirations are fulfilled.

It is not only Stephen's influence that Southerington detects. He quotes an extract from Symonds's *The Greek Poets* in the *Literary Notes* and says it is about "Hellenic consciousness", thus seeking to make it an influence on Hardy's distinction between conscious man and the unconscious Will: but Symonds says nothing about consciousness. Another extract by Hardy, from D. G. Ritchie's *Philosophical Studies* (1905), is quoted as contributing to Hardy's idea of equilibrium, but it describes a stable equilibrium coming at the end of the evolutionary process. Southerington supports the idea that Hardy's equilibrium was a hypnotic state of society by his extract from an article by F. W. H. Myers and his comment on it, but the organism which Myers and Hardy are talking about there is the individual, and in any case Southerington appears to argue that Hardy dropped the idea.

68. Apology, LLE, CP 558.

69. See Annan, especially ch. VII for a discussion of evolutionary ethics and chs. VII–IX for Stephen's shortcomings as a critic: his preoccupation with masculinity and morbidity, confusion between the moral and the aesthetic, insensibility to language.

70. I have tried to separate Stephen from Comte and discuss Dr Hyman's views when discussing Comte. She generally represents Stephen as following Comte and Mill, but claims that in saying in *The Science of Ethics* that "the path of duty does not coincide with the path of happiness" he is disagreeing with Mill, and that Hardy is following Stephen in dramatising in his novels the conflict between happiness and altruism. I do not believe that any such source can be found for Hardy's deep-seated and lifelong pessimism.

71. *Life* 304.

72. F. W. Maitland, *The Life and Letters of Leslie Stephen*, 1906, p. 272.

73. Evelyn Hardy, p. 140 points out the similarities and differences between them.

74. "A Bad Five Minutes in the Alps" in Stephen's *Essays on Freethinking and Plainspeaking*, 1873; PBE XXII; Björk, Entry No. 981; TD L.395.

75. Björk, Entry No. 1217; L V.iv.333. T. Paulin, *Thomas Hardy: the Poetry of Perception*, 1975, uses the phrase as the title of a chapter, but I cannot understand his argument here or anywhere else in his book, beyond the commonplaces that Hardy was a visualiser and that there is an intellectual element in perception.

76. Cf. Cecil, p. 19; "He sees human beings less as individuals than as representatives of a species and in relation to the ultimate conditioning forces of their existence. His subject is not men, but man. His theme is mankind's predicament in the universe."

77. Annan, p. 265:"Stephen echoed Johnson's dictum that the greatest writers examined not the individual but the species, disregarded contemporary laws by rising to general and transcendental truths, and wrote as the interpreters of nature and the legislators of mankind."

78. E.g. Pinion, *Art*, p. 36.

79. *Life* 7, 15, 16, 59, 61, 98, 105, 120, 134, 230; 9, 37, 42; HE XIII.117, XVI.132; R. B. Heilman, "Hardy's Sue Bridehead", NCF 20, 1965–6. For Shelley, see my ch. 4. For Wordsworth, TD III.51, LI.406; "The Impercipient" ('an inland company' etc.), CP 67; *Life* 306.

80. Leslie Stephen, *Hours in a Library* III.338, quoted by Annan, p. 284; JO III.iv.172, II.i.101, II.iii.115; CP 159. For the reference to Hume, see n.3 above. It is as the author of the essay on miracles that Hume appears in "Drinking Song", CP 906.

81. Much of the material for this view of *Tess* is in Tanner, particularly Hardy's reference, in the General Preface, to Spencer's view that the universe may be incomprehensible. But Tanner's "colour" is predominantly red, which he says "dogs, disturbs and destroys" Tess, whereas there are other significant colours and much mention of colour; he does not discuss fog, mist and atmosphere; and his sun is merely one of the things Tess is the victim of. TD XV.134; *Life* 176; TD XLIX.390, XXV.198; MC XLIV. 339; Arnold "had a manner of having made up his mind upon everything years ago", *Life* 134.

82. TD XIX.163, XXVII.211, XXXV.270.

83. TD XVIII.156; W II.41; JO II.i.96. On actresses, cf. *Life* 227: "the morality of actresses, dancers, etc. cannot be judged by the same standard as that of people who lead slower lives". On Thackeray, cf. *Life* 40.

84. HE VII.75; UGT IV.iv.175; *The Letters of Philip Dormer Stanhope, 4th Earl of Chesterfield*, ed. B. Dobree 1932, vol. III, p. 1115; Fielding,

Tom Jones XIII.xi. XV.iii, XVI.ii, XVIII.ii. viii, xii; cf. *Spectator* nos. 181, 189.

85. PBE XXI.231, XXII.240; RN I.vi.82, IV.ii.273; *Life* 21; R. F. Jones, *Ancients and Moderns*, 1961, pp. 33, 39, 187, 193, 201, 239, 247, 252; *Tatler* no. 119. *Tom Jones* XVIII.xii; UGT IV.iv.175.

86. *Letters of John Gay*, ed. C. F. Burgess, 1966, p. 34; *Tatler* no. 248, *Spectator* nos. 37, 92; X XLVI.371.

87. *Life* 150, 239, 252, 362; *Tom Jones* VIII.i; TT XXVI; *Tom Jones* V.v, XIV.ii. XV.7; HE XXXV.

88. Lionel Johnson, p. 234; Gittings, *Young*, p. 155.

89. UGT I.viii.78; PBE VII.92; D II.vii.i.290; JO VI.vi.394. *Gulliver's Travels* IV.ix, "some tincture of reason"; "Letter to My Cousin Sympson", "some tincture of common sense"; D After Scene 522; W X.109; FMC XL. 295; Boswell, *Life of Johnson*, ed. Hill/Powell, IV.387, n. 1; L II.ii.162; *Phèdre* I.iii ("Vénus toute entière à sa proie attachée"); W X.104 (and cf. VII.83); MC XIII.113; TD V.66; FMC XLII.309, 315; MC V.63; JO VI.i.347; W II.41; HE I.35.

90. PBE XXVIII.295: Desmond Hawkins, *Hardy, Novelist and Poet*, 1976, p. 48, points this out.

91. TT XXXI. Norman Page, *Thomas Hardy*, 1977, p. 113, points this out.

92. HE XXXI.244; *Persuasion* II.vi.

93. Justi, *Diego Velasquez and his Times*, 1888, tr. 1889. R. A. M. Stevenson's *Art of Velasquez*, 1895, confirms that Justi started a vogue.

94. TT IX.92, XII.104, XV.122 and notes *ad loc.*, and Introduction 25; Millgate, p. 390, n. 18.

95. TT X.96, XI.102, XXXII.225 and notes *ad loc.* But also the whole business of Burton, Speke and Stanley, cf. III.51: "a mania for lion-hunting, which he dignified by calling it a scheme of geographical disco-very". And see PBE XIX.213 and note *ad loc.*

96. X XXI.183; RN II.v.160; TD XLI.320; WB I.6.53; the note *ad loc.* says Pierston is not so referring; but what else can he be referring to? Lysias 14.29?

97. See R. C. K. Ensor, *England 1870–1914*, 1936, pp. 183, 339.

CHAPTER 4. INVENTION

1. Miller, p. 166. Hynes, p. 129, calls him "repetitious".

2. DR V.1.93, VI.3.125, VIII.2.147, 151, VIII.3.154, 155, IX.5.186, XIII.2.267, XIII.5.280, XVII.1.339.

MC: dead leaves: I.37, III.53, IX.88, XLV.351. Respectability: I.38, VI.71, VII.74, VIII.81, 87, X.98, XIII.114, XXIV.196, XXX.239, XXXVI.279. Mechanical: XIII.lll, XVI.132, XXII.176, XLI.315, XLII.323, XLIII.333, XLIV.340: not only Henchard but Susan, Elizabeth-Jane, Farfrae and Newson act mechanically, and the last reference is to "the ingenious machinery contrived by the Gods for reducing human possibilities to a minimum". Old-fashioned: IV.59, IX.90, XVI.132, XXI.167.

3. More than I can bear: RN IV.vi.307; TM XXXV.302; MC XLIII. 334; TD XXXVII.297, XLI.323, LVII.436; "The Supplanter", "A Sunday Morning Tragedy", CP 180, 205. Fear of the future: RN III.iv.221 (Eustacia); TD XIX.163 (Tess); JO III.iv.171 (Jude). Misremembering history: MC VIII.83 (Monmouth's rebellion), XXXVI.277 (Peter's Finger); TD III.47 (Cubit), 48 (Oliver Grumble), IV.55 (King Norman), XXX.228 (ambassadors and centurions). Homelessness: FMC XXII.181; RN I.iii.51; TD LI.403; MC I.37; JO I.ii.33. Evil ceasing when it has done its work: TT XVI.129 (the wind); MC XXXIX.302 (the skimmington). The peasant no stereotype: PBE X.119; TD XVIII.156. Heroism of sexual confession: UGT IV.iii.189 (Fanny advised to, doesn't); TD XXXI.233 (Tess, advised not to, does); JO III.i.151 (Jude does); MC XIX.153 (Susan does, but only after her death). The individual and time: TM XIII.128 (Anne's superfluity in the stream of recorded history); TD XIX.165 (Tess one of a long row only); JO IV.i.223 (Sue crushed by the weight of previous lives). Dead leaves: HE XXXIX.323; W.I.38; TD XXXIV.261. Harlican: JO I.i.30. Maphrotight: RN I.iii.53. Projick: W VI.79; TD IV.54. Randyvoo: W IX.102, and as "randy" often. "Projick" is surely from "project" as the *Tess* New Wessex editor says, or even "projector" in the seventeenth-century sense – it is applied to Fitzpiers – not from "prodigy", as *The Woodlanders* note says.

4. DR XII.1.239, TM XXII.199, Weber, p. 166; DR XII.6.252, RN III.v.228, Pinion, *Companion*, p. 18; WB II.ii.84, *Life* 232, Pinion, *Companion*, p. 50; "Dorsetshire Labourer", PW 170–1, 175, 177–8, TD XVIII.156, LII.408–9, MC XXIII.187, Pinion, *Companion*, p. 138; "The Queen of Cornwall" Scene XVI, OMC, PBE XXXIV–XXXV, Reginald Snell, "A Self-Plagiarism by Thomas Hardy", EC 2, 1952; PW 94, TD 11.39, Millgate, p. 129; DR XXI.2.408 and n.; "An Indiscretion", OMC 112. D I.ii.v.48, I.ii.iv.47, III.ii.i.367; TM XXVI.221–2, LLI/CM 354, 197–8. Advice on marriage: UGT II.viii.124; WB II.10.124. Birds: RN I.x.113; TD XLIII.334. Two endings: WB III.6.189–90 and 244–5. It is absurd to write as the New Wessex editor does of the "superimposition of the two endings" and, comparing *The French Lieutenant's Woman*, to say that "the multiple endings ... undermine any belief in necessary ends" They are not superimposed: one replaces the other, and since the description was not integral to the theme and he was providing "something light", Hardy saw no reason why he should re-write it. They are not, strictly speaking, endings, since in both cases the novel ends with the reunion of Pierston and Marcia: in book form this is better done, and connected with Pierston's loss of "artistic sense". Leyden jar:DR V.3.106; W XVI.146. Outer chamber: DR XVI.4.335; MC XLII.328. "Cliff without a Name": PBE XXI.236; "It never looks like summer": CP 507, DR XV.3.317: "a wild hill that had no name, beside a barren down where it never looked

like summer". Geographical degrees: MC IV.57; TD XV.136. Diana Multi-Mammia: MC XLV.350; TD XLII.326; CP 262.

5. "Idiosyncratic": *Life* 153, 225, 228. Flames flap: DR XI.6.236, XIII.2.265; PBE XXX.326; TD XLVIII.380; JO IV.iv.247. Drops rap: FMC XLII.310; MC XXXIV.263. Hedges (or trees) as strainers: FMC VI.80; RN I.ix.105, 110; TT I.31; W III.48, IX.99, XXXV.285; TD XLIII. 335, L.396; "The Voice", CP 346. Embers like desert: FMC VIII.95; W X,109. Ponds like eyes: FMC XIX.157; TM XXII.189. Footpath meridians: TM XXIII.201; W I.35. Ivy-leaves as neighbours: W XII.116; TD XLIV.344; JO II.i.99, II.vii.144. Sad Germans: TM IV.61; "The Melancholy Hussar of the German Legion", WT. Skies darkened: FMC XI.119; TD LVIII.444. Blue gowns: UGT IV.v.177; TM XXX.254; WB II.i.75; "Destiny and a Blue Cloak", OMC: "The Voice", and cf. L I.iv.66 (Paula's canopy). Haloes: TD III.50, X.102, XIV.127, XVI.140, XXXI.236; UGT I.viii.75; PBE III.54, XXXVIII.379; FMC XL.292; HE VIII.87; RN III.iv.223, IV.iii.278; L. I.x.108; MC XXVI.207; CP 62, 495; JO I.iii.42; D II.ii.1, 149. Shadows cast upward: FMC VIII.89, XIV.133; W VI.75; TD XXXIV.268. Eye-sockets: TM VI.76; L I.v.74; TD XLI.323. Inside of mouths: RN I.x.116; TD XXVII.210. Duchess of Richmond's Ball: L V.ix.360; D III.vi.ii.454n. Adam, sunset: DR II.4.65 and n. *ad loc.*; WB I.vii.55. Soil and Time: TM X.107; TD XXXI.235. Drawings, outlines, profile: FMC XXXVII.277; W V.66; JO III.ix.205; TD LIX.449; HE XLVI.389; TT II.41; UGT I.i.33—4; PBE III.54; RN I.vi.82, IV.iii.283; L I.iii.57; MC 1.35; W I.37; TD XVI. 142, XXIV.190. Speech unnecessary: UGT I.vi.61, II.vi.113; TM III.57; MC IX.91; W XV.138; TD XXV.199; PBE XIV.167. Aeolian: TM XXII. 193; MC XI.102; XVI.134; W XIII.123; FMC II.46; RN I.iii.44, 58, I.v.70, I.vi.81; L V.ii.319; TT IV.54, XIX.152; TD IV.60, LVIII.444; HE XLIV. 359; MC XXXIX.304; W I.36, III.47, VIII.94; CP 271, 111,298; LLI/CM 319; L I.ii.50; CP 306; TD XIX.162; JO V.iii.297. Hardy extracted into a notebook Arnold's statement that "the poet . . . aspires to be a sort of human Aeolian harp", Björk, Entry no. 1172.

6. Humans and animals, aristocratic origins: see ch. 3, pp. 59—60 and 67. Femininity and humanity: HE VIII.86; MC XV.126; W XLVIII.393. Woman is fickle: HE XXII.168—74; JO III.v.176, vi.185, 187, vii.190, 192, ix.211, x.217, IV.ii.236, iii,237, v,259, vi.269—72, V.i.278, ii.286, iii.290, iv.306, vi.320, VI.iii.366, v.385, 389. Mastery by man: FMC XXIV,196; W XX.178; TD VIII.85, XII.113, XVI.140, XLVII.379. God-like men: TM XI.120; TT XVI.134; W XXXVIII.305; TD XXIX.222. Small human, large expanse: RN IV.ii.273; TT Preface 29; MC XLIII.331; TD XVI.142. Pallor of thinker: PBE XIII.159; RN II.vi.162; L I.i.38; TD XVI.140, XXXVI.285. Soldier parsons: L II.iv.175—6; "A Changed Man", LLI/CM. To others, only a passing thought: DR XIII.4.273; MC XLIII.330; TD XIV.127; "Wessex Heights", CP 320. Seen from the thinker's point of view, this is the idea of the "Well-Beloved", e.g. WB I.34 "she was a sub-jective phenomenon". Enclosed and isolated: TD II.39; W I.38; PBE IV.58;

TT I.33; TM XII.122; W XXIV.201. Featureless landscape: FMC II.46, XI.118; TD XLIII.331. "In the midst of life . . .": "Nature's Questioning", CP 67. Altars, tombs: TD LII.413; TM XXXVIII.322; UGT I.vi.62; HE XXVII.213. Barrows: TD XLII.326; MC XLV.350; L I.xii.121; HE XXXI. 246; RN I.ii.41, iii.45; FMC L.361. For the frequent mention of barrows as reminders of death, see HE XLIV.361; TM XII.123, XXXIII.280; MC II.48, XIII.111. Weddings and funerals: RN I.iii.50; TM XX.181; JO VI.ix.417; TT XIX.148; MC XIII.115; TD L.396. Dead to bury dead: FMC XLII.315; MC XIX.149. Deaths of pregnant women: FMC XLII.318; MC XXXIX.302; W XLV.361. Ends of stories: TD LIX; PBE XXXIX; "A Mere Interlude" v, LLI/CM 399. Life and death in poems: CP 75, 421, 495, 820.

7. Cider: DR VIII.3.154; W XXV.205, XXVIII.235. Bees: UGT V.i; FMC XXVII. Pig-killing: PBE XXIII.251; JO I.x.83–6: cf. HE XXXI.251 for another cheerful, and D III.vii.v.499 for another horrid reference. Tree-planting: PBE VIII; W VIII. Claiming kin: HE XIV.124; MC III.52, XI.103; TD V.64. Club-walking: UGT II.viii.125, V.i.200; FMC XXXIII.252; RN I.v.75; TM XXIII.206; TT II.45; TD II. Dwindling fairs: MC III.52; JO V.vii.329. "Conjurors": UGT IV.iii; MC XXVI; TD XXI.172; WT/GND 68 ("The Withered Arm" ch. V). Lifehold: DR X.6.212; MC XXXVI.279; W V.66, XIII.122, XIV.130; TD IX.88, L.399. Outdoor courting: UGT IV.v.176; TD XXXI.235; JO I.vii.65, II.iv.119: and cf. W XXVII.226 (Felice and Fitzpiers): "the window curtains were closed and a red-shaded lamp and candles burning, though out of doors it was broad daylight"; and W XLIV.358 (Marty about Giles): " 'In all our outdoor days and years together . . . the one thing he never spoke of to me was love.' " Pulling down: see ch. 2, n. 10 above. Skimmington: RN I.v.73; MC XXXIX; CP 74 ("The Bride Night Fire", last stanza). Tourism, strangers: UGT I.vi.63 (stranger in church); PBE XXXI.337 (Knight's interest in the tower); FMC XLII.311; RN I.i.34; MC XXXVI.283 (Newson's attitude to the skimmington); TD II.39; JO V.v.309. Delicacy: FMC XLIII.321 (Bathsheba troubled by Troy's infidelity); W XXV.210, XXIX.244, XXX.250 (Melbury's provision of a separate entrance for the newly-weds, lack of suspicion of Fitzpier's infidelity, and refusal to enquire into it); TM V.68 (Stanner's omission of the dubious verse); MC X.97; TD II.39. Boots: UGT I.vi.61; RN III.i.194; MC XXXVII.286; W XXIV.202. Chalk strokes: TM II.48; MC XVI.136. No applause: FMC XXIII.186; RN II.vi.163. Grey's Bridge: UGT IV.vii.187; MC XXXII.248. Phantom of beloved: UGT I.viii.76; W XX; JO III.viii.196. Girls in pubs: UGT III.ii.138; W XXXVIII.311. Apples: DR VIII.3.158; UGT I.ii.38; RN II.ii.136, IV.v.299; TM II.48, XVI.150; W VI.72, X.109, XXV.205. Selling apple trees: MC XXII.180; W V.67. Wessex clocks: PBE XXIII.252; FMC I.42; RN II.v.154; TM VI.75; L I.iv.64; MC IV.61; TD III.52. Bought clothes: MC XXIV.192; W V.69, XXIV.201; TD XXXII.248; JO III.ii.156. Julian Calendar: DR XII.8.259; UGT I.viii.76; RN VI.iv.416; W XIX.169, XX.175; TD XLII.329; XLIX.391; JO III.viii.196. Holding hands and kissing: DR XII.6.252; PBE

VI.78, VII.90, XXV.268, XXVII.287; FMC III.59, IV.65, XX.165, XXXIII.249, LVII.423; RN I.vi.91, I.xi.127, II.iv.151, III.iv.222, III.v.228, IV.iii.286, IV.viii, 322, V.i.333, V.iii.348, V.iv.352; TM IX.97, XI.117, XXI.186, XXII.196, XXV.217, XXVIII.241, 247, XXX.256, XXXVII.312, 314, XXXVIII.316, 323, XXXIX.327, 330, 332, XLI.343; L I.xi.115, 117; MC I.36, III.51, XLI.316; W VI.73, XXIII.193, XXXVIII. 308, 311, XXXIX.320, XLV.365, XLVI.370, XLVII.384; TD XI.104, XXIX.221–2, XXXI.235, XL.316, XLVI.365, XLVII.378, LI.404, LVII.437, LIX.448–9; JO I.vii.65, 67, II.v.127–9, III.i.152–3, III.vi. 186–7, III.vii.192, III.ix.206, IV.i.222–3, IV.ii.231, 235–6, IV.v.261, IV.vi.271, V.i.277, V.iv.302, 306, V.v.314, VI.vi.395, VI.xi.426. Serpents and clarionets: UGT I.iv.51; FMC LVII.423–4; RN I.v.75, II.v.155; TM IX.98; MC XXXIX.302. Bishop Ken: DR XII.8.256; TM XVI.152; TT II.41, XLI.284; TD XIII.119; JO II.i.100, 102; *Life* 10.

8. *Life* 97. Chips in porridge: UGT II.iv.99; RN III.vii.249. Dand: DR Sequel 417; PBE X.122; FMC XLIX.357; MC XXVII.217; TD VII.78. Cf. "dandy", W XII.117, XIV.132, XXXVII.298. Dry as a kex: RN I.iii.55; W XLVIII.389; TD XVII.145: cf. Farmer Kex UGT V.i.200. Flung over pulpit: FMC XX.165, "The Bride-Night Fire", CP 71. Jack Rag or Tom Straw: HE XII.109; TT XXII.167; MC I.41. Nailed up in parish boards: FMC XLII.312; W XLIII.353. Het or wet: UGT V.i.198; FMC LVII.421; "The Three Strangers", WT/GND 22. Little small, old ancient: UGT I.viii.77; MC I.37; W I.36; TD XVII.145; "Andrey Satchel and the Parson and Clerk", LLI/CM 169. Underground: UGT I.iii.47; HE XI.107; JO I.ix.78, III.viii.200; "The Colonel's Soliloquy", CP 88; and cf. TD XIV.126 ("grassed down"); "Rain on a Grave", "I found her out there", "Voices from Things Growing in a Churchyard", "Friends Beyond" and "Drummer Hodge", CP 341, 342, 623, 59, 91. Gawkhammer: UGT I.ii.89; FMC X.114; MC XXVII.216. Wambling: PBE II.46, XXIII.256; TM XXVII.234; TT XVI.129; MC XXVIII.225, XLV 352; W XI.112; "Andrey Satchel and the Parson and Clerk", LLI/CM 164, Perusing: RN II.i.132; MC XLIII.329; W IV.60, XXIII.190. I have not collected the other words I mention. Shameful to use dialect: UGT I.vii.69, V.ii.204; HE XVIII.150; TM I.40; MC XX.157; JO IV.iv.250; "The Ruined Maid", CP 159. Cigar: RN IV.iv.290; TT XXXVIII.265; W XLVI.372; TD VII.80, X.97. Diamonds: RN I.v.75; MC XV.130; TD III.47, LII.414; and see ch. 2 n. 15. Satan: RN III.vii.249; TD XIV.129; W IX.101, I.38, II.43, XXI.181; TD XLV.359, L.397; FMC XLIII.327; RN I.ix.104; L II.v.181, 188; "The Romantic Adventures of a Milkmaid", LLI/CM 479. See J. O. Bailey, "Hardy's Mephistophelian Visitants", PMLA 61, 1946, and Pinion, *Companion*, 156–8. My simple argument that there is too much of it is unaffected by Bailey's conclusion that Hardy is saying "that the spiritual forces formerly symbolised as Vices, Satan and Mephistopheles are still operative". I do not follow Bailey in regarding Newson and Farfrae as Satanic.

9. Intramural: HE XXVII.211; JO Vi.ii.352; MC XIV.121; W XL.322. Metallic (of glare): RN IV.v.296, 299; TD XXXI.236. Rencounter: DR XII.1.239; PBE VI.77; RN IV.i (title); W XXXI.253; TD XLV.352; JO V.v.312. Reticulated: MC XIII.113; W VII.83; TD V.66. Flexuous, flexible: UGT I.vii.71; L I.iii.57; MC XX.161, XXII.178; W V.67; TD XIII.120, XIV.124, XXXVI.285; JO V.v.311. Whitey-brown: UGT I.iii.44; FMC IX.111; TM I.45; TT I.39 ("the ... match between his clothes and the clods"); MC III.53, XXIII.187; W IV.63, XLVIII.388; TD XLII.326, XLIV.343, XLVII.372; JO I.v.51; WB III.1.146; "Andrey Satchel and the Parson and Clerk", LLI/CM 166; "No Buyers", CP 737; D II.ii.i.181; and cf. TD XLVIII.380 (Tess's "white bonnet embrowned" by the corn-dust) and XLIII.331 (sky and land at Flintcomb-Ash, "The white face looking down on the brown face").

10. Maugham is quoted in Hynes, p. 56; Cecil, p. 138; Brown, p. 106; F. R. Leavis, "Hardy the Poet", *Southern Review* vol. 6, 1940, p. 88.

11. FMC LI.380, XI.118, XLVI.340; RN I.iii.45, I.vii.94, II.v.156; HE XIX.155, XX.156, XXII.174, XLV.380, Sequel 406; MC XV.125, XXVI.210; W I.38, XXXI.257; PBE X.124.

12. Kramer, p. 21.

13. PBE XXV.271, XXIX.320; FMC XXII.178, XXIX.220; MC XXXII.253, XXXVII.285, XLIII.333; W XVI.147, XLII.342, XLIII.346; TD XXXVII.291; JO III.ix.208, IV.iii.238, VI.viii.409.

14. PBE XXVII.279; FMC XX.163, 168; HE XIII.117, XV.127; RN 1.vii.97.

15. PBE XVIII, XXII, XI, XXXV; TD VIII, XXX; JO I.viii.76, VI.vi.396.

16. HE IV.59; L V.xi.372; HE II.46; WB II.13.141. For other examples see L I.x.111 to xi.113; TD I.34; FMC XI.119–20, XLIV.330, and the whole of Fanny Robin's journey in XXXIX–XL where she is never named. My impression is that it is very common.

17. RN IV.v.299; W XIX.165; TD XXIV.189; FMC II.47, XIX.157, XXIII.188; TD XXIII.184; TM XI.116; HE XLIV.360; RN I.i.36; WB I.2.36.

18. TD LIX.449; OMC 18; PBE XXXIV.360.

19. Elderly romance: PBE XI.132, TM X. Centripetal love: MC XLIV.339; WB II.3.92. Mistaken marriage places: FMC XVI; RN I.v; PBE XI. Colour of hair: FMC XLI.301; MC XIV.118. Legitimation by marriage: L II.v.186; in MC this follows from the iteration of "respectable", see n. 2 above, and the actual marriages. Vow to abstain: L II.v.184; MC II.49. Losing money by marriage: TT XVIII.142; TD XXIX.220. Eloping with singer: PBE XXVI.277; WT/GND 351ff. Loss of appetite: UGT IV.iv; TM XXII.189. Hatred of books: RN IV.i.262; W XLVI.371; JO I.ix.79. Humbled heroines: FMC LVI.416ff; L VI.iii.422; W XL.327–XLI.337. Concealment of earlier love: UGT V.ii.208; PBE XXVII, XXVIII, XXIX; developing as TD XXVIII, XXXIV. Consumption: PBE VIII.108; JO

III.iv.168. Fear of being despised: FMC IV.67; MC XLIII 333; TD XXXV. 275, XXXVI.286, XLVI.370, LVIII.442, 447; JO II.vii.143. Fingers mixed: UGT II.vii.121; TD XXXIV.260. Paul and Virginia: TM XXV 218; JO IV.iv.252. Lifting over flood: W XXI.187; TD XXIII. Tabitha and Liza-lu; TT XLI.292; TD LVIII.445. Taking wives out of Wessex: UGT IV.vi.183; RN IV.viii, V.v., MC XXXIV.266; W XLV.364, XLVIII.388; TD XXXI. 236. Female strength: FMC LIV.405; W XLH.341; WB III.6.186; WT/GND 280. Moth-signal: RN IV.iv.290; CP 392. Girls at windows: UGT IV.vi.180; RN IV.ii.272; TM XXVII.237; TT XXXVI.252; JO IV.i.225, IV.ii.235. Matronly: UGT V.ii.205; FMC IX.110; MC XLV.350; JO VI.xi.428.

20. Voyeurs: PBE XXV.265; FMC II.51; HE XVIII.149, XXXV.284; DR XIX.v–vi.381– 92; RN IV.viii.322; TM XXVIII.247; L II.i.154, II.vii. 196; MC VII.76, IX.88, XXVII.219, XXXV.271, XLII.327–8, XLIII.331; W III.49; TD LVI.431; JO IV.iv.252; WB I.2.35; II.6.100, III.1.147. Travel in Europe: PBE XXXVII.372; HE XXXIII.269; L IV.i–V.x. South America L V.xi.376; TT XVI.133; TD XXXIX.305. Bath: PBE XII.157; FMC XXX–XXXIV, XXXVII; TT XVII.135; "The Melancholy Hussar", "The Marchioness of Stonehenge", "Lady Mottisfont", WT/GND 42, 53, 282, 297; MC XXII.178. The North: CP 346; MC XXIV.195; TD V.68, XLVII. 373; LLI/CM 316; MC XIX.155. Cf "a no'thern simpleton", MC XXVII. 222. Troy's circus is in "a Northern town", FMC L.365.

21. Delivery of letters: RN V.vii.368, 370; TM XXIV.209–10; W XXXIV.276, XLIII.354; TD XXXIII.251, 253. Warning lovers: TM XXXVIII.324; TD LII.414. Love-letters; HE Sequel 410; W XLV.362; "On the Western Circuit", LLI/CM 85.

22. Actors: FMC L.365; W XXXI.257; TM XVI.154; DR IX.6.189; MC XXIV.192. Proud of afflictions: PBE II.46, FMC VII.93, IX.109, XXII.182; UGT II.iii.95; TM I.43, IV.63; RN I.iii.52.

23. R. W. King, "Verse and Prose Parallels in the Works of Thomas Hardy", RES NS 13, 1962, King's parallels are: "Beyond the Last Lamp" iii, CP 314, and TD XXXV.275; "In Time of 'The Breaking of Nations' " ii.1–2, CP 543, and DR X.2.198; "The Temporary the All", 1–8, CP 7, and PBE XIII.162; "Valenciennes" 25–36, CP 20, and TM IV.63; "Friends Beyond" 19–21, CP 60, and MC XVIII.149; "In a Wood" CP 64, and W VII.83; "The Pine Planters", CP 271, and W VIII.94–5; "In a Eweleaze near Weatherbury" 9–16, CP 70 and TT II.45, W IV.61; "Tess's Lament", CP 175; "We Field Women", CP 881, and TD XLIII; "The Oxen", CP 468, and TD XVIII.148; "A Young Man's Epigram on Existence", CP 299, and TD XV.134; "The Wound", CP 465, and TD XXI.174; "Midnight on the Great Western", CP 514, and JO V.iii.294. King's concern is with the question which version was written first, which is not material to my argument. Some of his parallels are slight or general. He does not relate "Tess's Lament" to any specific passage in TD, but the poem does have the following motifs which are found in the novel: the wish to die and be for-

gotten; the chimney-seat and favourite cow at Talbothays; and Tess blaming herself. Other verse/prose repetitions: WB II.3.86, II.xii.140, III.4.170, III.8.201; CP 423, 81, 458. *Life* 105, 301.

24. The fullest list of quotations is in Pinion *Companion*, pp. 200–24. With the notes in the New Wessex edition, the reader can identify almost all Hardy's quotations for himself. I append a list of repeated quotations.

The Bible
Acts 17.23, Athenians, unknown God: L IV.iii.291, Αγνωστωι Θεωι CP 186, LLE Apology CP 558.

   1 Cor.13, Charity etc.: HE XXXI.256; TT XLI.291; W XXXIV.275; TD XXXVI.284; JO VI.iv.381, VI.vi.395; "Wessex Heights", "The Blinded Bird", "Surview", "There Seemed a Strangeness", CP 319, 446, 698, 725.

   2 Cor. 5:1–4, fleshly tabernacle: TD XLV.357; WB I.2.34; "New Year's Eve", CP 278.

   Daniel 2:4, Nebuchadnezzar: RN II.iii.142; "The Three Strangers", WT/GND 13. *Ch. 3*, the fiery furnace: FMC LII.382; L VI.ii.408; JO I.iii.42; "The Burghers", "The Interloper", CP 24, 489. *Ch. 5*, Belshazzar: RN I.vi.84; W XXV.212; "The Three Strangers", WT/GND 23; D II. vii.321. *6:10*, captive in Babylon: FMC XIII.130; "The Bird-Catcher's Boy", CP 826.

   Ecclesiastes 1.14, all is vanity: FMC IV.69; HE XXXI.258; TD XLI.323. *3:4*, to everything a season, a time to, etc.: RN III.vii.239; L I.xv.146; TD XXIII.184; "Andrey Satchel and the Parson and Clerk", LLI/CM 168. *5:4–5*, pay what thou hast vowed: ILH II.5 OMC 104; TT III.52.

   Exodus 1:8, knew not Joseph: TT XLI.286; WB III.8.202, *10:22*, the Ninth Plague, darkness: FMC XXIV.192; HE III.58. *13.21*, the pillar of cloud: TD L.395; "The Sheep Boy", CP 790. *34:29*, Moses's shining face on return from Mount Sinai: W IX.97: "I Met a Man", "She Who Saw Not", CP 549, 662.

   Genesis 7:9, two by two, Noah: UGT II.vi.111; FMC XLII.316. Abraham's prosperity, MC XXIX.230: TD XIX.164. *16:12*, Ishmaelite: RN I.i.35; JO III.ii.159. *19:25*, Sodom and Gomorrah: TT XVI.130; "Absent-mindedness in a Parish Choir", LLI/CM 174. *Ch. 29*, serving fourteen years for Rachel: FMC XLIX, 360, TD XXIII.185. *30:35*, ring-straked and spotted: MC XVII.143; TD XIX.164. *Ch. 40*, Pharaoh and the baker: DR V.1.95; TM XVII.159.

   Hebrews 12:27, removing of things shaken: TD XVIII.154; Apology, LLE, CP 561.

   Hosea 2:7, return to first husband: HE XXXV.282; TD XLVII.378.

   Jeremiah 7:31, Tophet, smoky or Satanic: FMC XXVI.203; TD XLVII. 372; "Fellow Townsmen" iii, WT/GND 93; "The Flirt's Tragedy", CP 212.

   Job 1:7, Satan going to and fro: HE XXIV.185; L II.v.181. *3:2*, "let the day perish wherein I was born": MC XII.108, XL.308; JO V.iii.294,

VI.xi.423. *3:20* "Wherefore is light given, etc.": RN V.i.327 (title); JO VI.xi.424.

John 5:2–13, first in Pool of Bethesda: PBE XXX.329; MC X.96. *8:32*, truth makes free: Apology, LLE, "He Resolves to Say No More", CP 561, 930.

Jonah 4:6–10, Jonah's gourd: FMC XXXVIII.287; TD LV.426.

Joshua 6:20, fall of Jericho: L V.xii.386; TT VII.79. *10:12*, sun standing still on Gibeon: L V.iv.333; "Zermatt: to the Matterhorn", CP 106.

Judges 4:21, Jael's tent-nail: DR XIX.4.378; PBE XI.131. *Ch. 16*, shorn Samson: MC XLIV.343; JO VI.vii.398.

1 Kings 12:10, little finger, father's loins: HE Sequel 409; TD LII.413. *18:44*, cloud like hand: DR XII.4.245; "A Tragedy of Two Ambitions" iii, LLI 73. *19*, Elijah, the Lord not in the wind, etc.: DR XII.5.249; PBE XIX.208; "Quid Hic Agis?", CP 441.

2 Kings 18–19, Sennacherib: HE XXIV.190; RN V.vii.371; "The Melancholy Hussar of the German Legion" iv, WT 52.

Luke 9:62, hand to plough, turn not back: HE XXIV.186; TD XLVII.377.

Matthew 4:13, Capharnaum: MC XLV.353; JO VI.vii.401. *Ch. 5*, Sermon on the Mount: DR XII.1.240; FMC XXXIII.250; RN VI.iv.422; TD XLVI.368; "Compassion", CP 822.

Numbers 22–24, Balaam: RN II.iv.147; TD XL.315.

2 Peter 2:19–22, corruption, washed pig returns to wallowing: TD XLVI.370; JO VI.iii.373.

Philippians 4:8, "Whatsoever things are true ... honest" etc.: TD XXI.237; "The To-Be-Forgotten", "Surview", CP 145, 698.

Psalms 107:23–24, down to the sea in ships, wonders of the deep: HE XXXI.259; TM XXXIV.292; "A Night of Questionings", CP 726. *Ps. 137* by the rivers of Babylon etc: PBE XXXIII.346, XXXIV.353; RN VI.i.398; "God's Funeral", CP 327.

Revelation 3:14–15, Laodicean, neither hot nor cold: DR XII.3.243; UGT II.iv.102; FMC I.41; L Title and II.48. *6:8*, death's pale horse: W XXXV.285; "He Resolves to Say No More", CP 929. *10: 3–4*, seven thunders: TD XLVII.375; D I.ii.v.54. *Ch. 17*, Whore of Babylon: TD XLIV.370; JO VI.vii.401.

Romans 8:22, creation groaning: RN III.ii.199; JO VI.ii.357; "Freed the Fret of Thinking", CP 754.

Ruth 2:13, daughter-in-law of Naomi: PBE XXX.321; HE X.101.

1 Samuel 28, Endor: UGT IV.iii; RN I.vi.91; MC XXVI: "Apostrophe to an Old Psalm Tune", Apology, LLE, CP 431, 561.

2 Samuel 12:3–15, one ewe-lamb, Nathan: FMC XXVI.206; RN I.ix.107; TM XXXVI.306; MC XXX.240. *Ch. 18*, Absalom, Ahimaaz: DR X.5.210; RN IV.v.298; TT XIV.120; W XXIX.242.

Song of Solomon 8:6, jealousy cruel as the grave: PBE XXXVIII.377; "The Face at the Casement", CP 317.

The Spotted Cow: W XLVII.390; TD III.46.

Brighton Camp ("The Girl I Left behind Me"): FMC X.116; TM VI.83; TT XXXVII.255; "A Changed Man" iv LLI/CM 206; D III.vi.iv.468; "The Colonel's Soliloquy", CP 87.

Songs

Marcus Aurelius, be not perturbed: L IV.i.285; TD XXXIX.304.

Browning, The Statue and the Bust, " 'The world and its ways have a certain worth' ": DR XIII.4.277; JO VI.iv.380; ILH I.8 OMC 80; "The Waiting Supper", iv. LLI/CM 232.

Bunyan, Pilgrim's Progress, Valley of Humiliation: W XXXVII.298; TD XIX.163.

Thomas Campbell, "How delicious is the winning", the knot there's no untying: UGT V.i.193 (Title); FMC XXIV.195; JO V.iii.291.

Dryden, Aeneid v.587, "tries ... more on industry ... relies": DR XII.5.249; ILH II.1 OMC 85: cf. DR XX.2.397; Pope, *Dunciad in Four Books* II.169.

R. S. Hawker, The Quest of the Sangraal, throned along the sea: PBE XXI.233; WB III.4.167.

Keats, Ode to a Nightingale various phrases: DR III.2.84, X.4.207; PBE II.47; FMC XXIII.190; L I.ii.52, II.viii.196; JO Preface 23.

Milton, "Lycidas", last infirmity of noble mind: DR II.4.63; HE XXXVI.297.

J. H. Newman, "Lead, kindly light", garish day: DR I.3.43; FMC LVI.413; W XXVII.228; TD XXVII.209.

Scott, "The Maid of Neidpath" faltering welcome: PBE XVII.183; L V.v.337. "Glenfinlas", the Spirit in: PBE XXVII.281; TT XX.155.

Shakespeare, Hamlet, out-Herod Herod: PBE XXXVII.374; MC XLIV. 345; soliloquys, various phrases: UGT III.iii.143; PBE XIII.159; TM XXXVI.307; W IV.59; TD XXXVI.286; JO VI.xi.428; "A Mere Interlude" iii, III/CM 387. *Julius Caesar,* the current when it serves: TM XXXVI.307; L III.iii.222. *Macbeth* a tale told by an idiot, full of sound and fury: FMC IV.61; TD LIV.422; cabined, cribbed, confined: L I.ix.103; TT VI.73; TD II.43. *Measure for Measure* heaven has my empty words, my invention hears not my tongue: TT VI.73, ILH I.1 OMC 53. *Twelfth Night,* worm i' the bud: PBE XXXI.331; MC XXXIV.268; time's revenges: TT XLI.282; WB III.vii.195. *Sonnets-* 111, hand subdued to what it works in: W II.40; JO III.i.152; PW 142, 116, love which alters when it alteration finds: DR X.4.233; TD LIII.419.

Shelley, The Revolt of Islam I.liv, gestures beamed with mind: MC XLV.350; WB II.i.78. *Epipsychidion,* towards the loadstar of my one desire, etc.: W XXVIII.234; ILH II.2 OMC 88. *"When the lamp is shattered",* bright reason will mock thee, etc.: DR VI.1.117, ILH I.3 OMC 92.

Wordsworth, "To the Cuckoo", wandering voice: DR XII.3.243; PBE XV.175. *Intimations of Immortality",* the glory and the dream: PBE XX.

215, XXXII.345; JO II.i.97. *Sonnet, "O Friend"*, plain living and high thinking: RN III.ii.196; TD XXV.201; Apology, LLE, CP 560.

25. Some attempt must be made to represent numerically the volume of Hardy's literary quotations and the proportion of weak ones. According to my count, following the principles given in my text, but based on the New Wessex notes, with some additions of my own but without an independent re-reading *ad hoc*, there are a total of 699, 355 of them weak. By novels this is, giving totals first, and numbers of weak quotes in brackets: DR 70 (38), UGT 10 (0), PBE 87 (66), FMC 46 (24), HE 42 (20), RN 46 (29), TM 14 (8), L 54 (31), TT 59 (42), MC 51 (19), W 38 (18), TD 79 (20), JO 73 (20) WB 30 (20). I have included as quotations references such as to Candaules (RN I.x.117) where a verbal element is implied although not quoted. All quotations from the Bible are included, and they form a large proportion of the whole, although often they cannot be called literary.

"The Philistines be upon us": FMC IX.111, Judges 16:9. "Nature's holy plan": TD III.51, Wordsworth, "Lines Written in Early Spring". "All's right with the world": TD XXXVII.298, Browning, *Pippa Passes*. "Troubled at his presence": MC XIX.151, Genesis 45:3–4. "Poor wounded name" *Two Gentlemen of Verona* I.ii.115.

26. FMC XVII.150, XX.168, XLIII.320, XLIX.356, LII,382. RN I.iii.48, III.iv.223, IV.ii.273, IV.v.298, I.v.79.

27. DR Introduction 12, 27–9.

28. DR I.3.45, XI.4.227; Introduction 19, 27–8; XII.4.277.

29. DR Introduction 24–5.

30. DR Introduction 14–15; PBE IX.115, XII.154, XIV.167.

31. DR XIX.1.371, XII.5.249, XX.2.397; Pope, *The Dunciad in Four Books* ii.169.

32. WB Introduction and III.2.156.

33. WB III.1.150, III.3.164, III.4.169, 173, III.7.193.

34. WB II.8.114, III.2.158, III.4.171.

35 WB III.5.174, II.8.115, I.4.40.

36. WB I.9.68, III.8.198.

37. Pinion, *Art,* "The Influence of Shelley"; *Life* 37, 42, 53, 117, 128, 131, 324, 135, 136, 189, 150, 239; HE XXVII, *Life* 327, 330, 388, 393, 190, 239; ibid. 6, 37, 78, 106, 111, 123, 162, 114, 122, 255, 265.

38. Bailey, *The Poetry of Thomas Hardy*, p. 250; JO I.i.30, II.vii.144, VI.v.382, VI.viii,407.

39. TD XXI.234; W XVI.144, 147, XVII.153, XIX.172; Perkins, "Hardy and the Poetry of Isolation", ELH 26, 1959.

40. The *Literary Notes* and *The Return of the Native* (references to Entry Nos. in Björk first): 22, I.v.76; 35, I.x.114; 75, I.vii.95; 122, IV.iii.284; 161, IV.iv.292; 197, II.vi.168; 204, II.iv.150; 321–2, I.x.116; 331, IV.vi.308; 415, V.i.330; 443, III.ii 200; 613, IV.iv.290; 880, III.v.227; 885, II.iii.140; 442, III.i.191; 464, III.i.191; 597, III.vii.241; 604, I.ii.38;

611, I.vi.86; 649, III.i.192; A 86, II.vi.166.

41. 904, I.v.76; 919, III.iv.228; 930, 933, I.v.76; 1205, III.iv.224; 1207, I.xiv.136, III.vi.242, V.vii.345; A 73, II.viii.196.

42. 187 n., XXXVI.284; 181, XIV.122; 182, XIX.163; 196, XXIII.187; 198, X.95.

43. Hardy's coarseness: DR VI.1.115ff (Lesbianism); UGT V.i.195 (" 'kissing and coling your to death' "); PBE VII.92 (description of Elfride's kiss), XXII.247 (her diaphanous robe); FMC XII.124 ("alarming exploits of sex"); HE I.34 (" 'catch her alone ... and carry her off to some lonely place' "), I.42 ("a night forage after lovers ... half-an-hour of prime courtship"), IV.64 ("knot themselves like houseflies"), XLI.336 (" 'he has lived strangely' "; TM XXVII.236 (" 'revenge in a better way' ", i.e. rape); TT XV.127 ("pressed his two lips continuously upon hers"); MC XIII.114 (" 'fall in ... cow-barton, and we had to clane her gown wi' grass' "); W XXXIII.272 (" 'he's had you' "); TD X.100 ("faultless rotundities"), XIV.125 and XVI.142 ("Stroking the jar that would no longer yield a stream", "their great bags of milk" – we are meant to think of Tess's breasts), XIX.161 ("offensive smells ... slug-slime"), XXV.198 ("faces court – patched with cow-droppings"), XLIII.331 ("phallic shapes", and Marian's laughter); JO I.ii.36 ("coupled earthworms"), I.vi.58 ("the characteristic part of a barrow pig"), I.vii.69 (" 'I want him to have me' "), V.ii.289 ("the soft parts of her person shook"), V.iii.292 ("The Three Horns", Arabella's husband's pub), VI.341 Epigraph ("the places of her joy she filled with her torn hair"), VI.ix.415–7 (the kind of love-making suggested).

44. 509, XLIX.389; 829, XXIV.189; 812, LIX.449.

45. 342, L I.i.38, TT I.34; A 86, FMC XXIII.190; 545, TT XXXV.244; 906, MC XXV.202; 976, MC XLIV.339; 1108, MC XIV.117; 464, JO V.v.316; JO VI.ix.412; 357, D III.iv.viii. 425.

46. FMC IX.111; LLI/CM 444, Björk, Entry no. 582 n.; Björk xxiv, JO Preface 23, Matthew 26:41; PW 117, Björk, Entry no. 1217 and n.; Björk xxiv, and Entry No. 11, JO II.i.101; Björk Entry nos. 1102 and 1171; Björk, Entry no. 94 n., *Life* 233, PW 107, Carlyle, *Miscellaneous Essays*, London, 1872, I.137–8, MC XVII.143; Stewart, p. 217; Southerington, p. 232; Wright, p. 99.

47. Weber, pp. 90–1 and RES 1941, pp. 193–200; Pinion, *Companion*, p. 154; H. N. Fairchild, "The Immediate Source of *The Dynasts*", PMLA 67, 1952; Wright, pp. 111–13, *Life* 203, 221.

48. Weber, pp. 116–22: the notes *ad loc.* give the references to Weber's other writings about this.

49. Millgate, pp. 171–2: *The Novels of Jane Austen*, ed. R. W. Chapman, 1933, vol. IV, *Emma*, ch. IX, p. 77; Stewart, p. 157; TT V.68.

50. TT XIII.109, *The Winter's Tale* V.ii.125ff. *Julius Caesar* II.ii.30. The New Wessex note refers to the latter passage "for similar Elizabethan superstitions" in a comment on the immediately preceding passage in

Hardy, where Haymoss asks whether the comet means a great tumult or a famine; TT XIII.110, *Much Ado* IV.ii.46; MC XXXIX.303, *Much Ado* III.iii.55; FMC XXII.183, *Twelfth Night* II.iii.170; typescript letter in Dorset County Museum marked "Sept. 17, 1922" quoted by Björk, Entry No. 1297 n.; *Life* 98.

51. Also Chew both compares George Eliot and Hardy in some detail and suggests influence: her tragic conflict is between desire and conscience, his between will and destiny: his outcomes are not determined as hers are by heredity and environment: her rustic comedy is realistic, his not: he may have been influenced, in UGT certainly was, by her success in delineating provincial types.

52. Cox, pp. xliv, 32–3, 360, 27; Rutland, p. 171.

53. Cox, pp. 112, 103; Stewart, pp. 122–4; Howe, pp. 62, 109, 64; Miller, p. 204; L. St J. Butler, "How It Is for Thomas Hardy" in *Thomas Hardy After Fifty Years*, ed. L. St J. Butler, pp. 117–21; R. Morrell, *Thomas Hardy: The Will and The Way*, 1965, p. 170; Webster, pp. 202, 157, 149.

54. Pinion, *Art*, p. 70; Millgate, p. 126. Dutch painting: *Adam Bede* II.xvii, UGT title-page, Stewart, p. 57. Drifting: *Romola* LXI (and surely *The Mill on the Floss* VI.xiii, CHS); DR XII.6.252; TD LV.429; Pinion, *Art*, p. 13 (also W XXIII.194, CHS). Converging streams; *Adam Bede* VI.1 last para.; TD XX.168. Loamshire etc., Miller, p. 81. Novalis: *The Mill on the Floss* VI.vi; MC XVII.143; W. E. Yuill in MRL 57, 1962. Pinion, *Companion*, p. 39 quotes from *The Mill on the Floss*: "Astronomers . . . live up in high towers, and if the woman came there, they might talk and hinder their work." Sword exercise: *Mill on the Floss* II.v; FMC XXVIII.

55. *Adam Bede* II.xvii; UGT II.ii.91; *Scenes of Clerical Life*, "Amos Barton", I.

56. References to *Adam Bede* are given first. Pool suicide: IV.xxxv, RN V.ix. Locket: III.xxii, FMC XLI.301. Hovel: V.xxxvii, W XLI.331. Pallbearers: V.xi, CP 246. Bishop Ken: II.xviii, and see my n. 7 above. Hieroglyphic picture: II.xviii, TM XXV.218. Superstition about death: I.iv, TD XXXIII.255. Greasy pole, etc.: II.xxv, MC XVI.133. Half-wits; VI.liii, UGT II.iii.94–5 *et al.*. Walking with but not touching girl VI.l, TM X.97, XXXVIII.316. Decayed Halls: I. vi, TM VI.74. Unsmiling performances: III.xxv, RN II.vi.163.

57. References to *Adam Bede* are given first. Unvisited by artists: VI.liii, TD II.39 and cf. WB Preface 26. Bent heroes and baskets: V.xlviii, MC XLIII.334. Pointing contrast: I.xv, and see n. 13 above. Peasant depth: I.xvi, Hyde, "Realism".

58. *Life*: Defoe, 61; study of style, 105; Swift 134; lists, 28, 48, 57, 59, 77, 203, 230; knew them well, 28, 330; impressed, 33, 256; a cure for despair, 58; considered good, 40, 51.

CHAPTER 5. The Good

1. For instance, on the novels, Gregor, Mrs Brooks, and Kramer. On the poems: Carpenter, p. 153; F. R. Leavis, *New Bearings in English Poetry*, 1932/1950, p. 59.

2. Gregor, "What Kind", 293, 298, 300; *Web*, 25, 134, 161.

3. Gregor, *Web*, 36, 38, 50, 142, 145; "What Kind", 303.

4. W III.52; *Life* 177; *Web*, 35–9, 178, 144, 168, 143.

5. D. I.vi.iii.118, II.i.i.330, III.vii.vii.505; *Adam Bede*, ch. XXVI, end, "an ingenious web of probabilities".

6. Kramer, 21, 40, 50; and see ch. III. n. 61 above.

7. Bayley, 137, 193, 197, 180, 132, 99, 17, 166, 169, 167, 224.

8. FMC Preface 38; *Life* 104; Brown, p. 36; Merryn Williams, p. 200. Here are some examples of the application of the word poetic to and by Hardy; "His imagination is poetic . . . of a type that more often chooses verse as its mode of expression," Cecil, p. 44; "We begin to appreciate his novels only for the passages where the poet subdues the novelist," Graham Greene, *The Lost Childhood*, 1951, p. 50; "He was . . . a tragic poet . . . who did his work in prose," T. R. Spivey, "Thomas Hardy's Tragic Hero", NCF 9, 1954, p. 181; "Much of Hardy's art is to extract a kind of poetry from such goings on, [such as] his frequent manoeuvring of the action in the interest of some *coup de théâtre* . . .", Stewart, p. 64; "How different is the 'poetry' in the novels from that of [*sic*] our concept of form in them," Bayley, p. 149; "That poetry which, in spite of the sting of poverty, is inseparable from such a condition of life as the countryman's, lies in his absolute dependence on the moods of air, earth and sky," Hardy, quoted by Cecil, p. 65.

9. E.g. "poetic underpattern", "poetic impulse", "poetic emotion", "the weapons of a poet" (pp. 137–8); "poetic style", p. 177; "poetic-dramatic structure", p. 179; "poetic tone", "poetic tension", p. 193; "poetic development", p. 194.

10. Brooks, pp. 137, 151, 157, 158, 233, 199, 219, 284. It may be noted as an example of the doubts raised by this kind of criticism that Mrs Brooks speaks of "organic connection between plot and the poetry of place" in *The Woodlanders*, whereas Gregor (*Web*, p. 142) says "the role of 'place' in *The Native* . . . is . . . occupied by time in *The Woodlanders*".

11. Brooks, pp. 165, 166, 209, 237, 223, 246, 273.

12. Brown, pp. 42, 48; *Life* 99, 98; Virginia Woolf, *A Writer's Dairy*, 1953, p. 92.

13. Brown, p. 142; Alma Priestley, "*The Well-Beloved* and Proust", *Thomas Hardy Society Review*, I. 2. 1976, p. 52; Irving Howe, p. 103; Carpenter, pp. 115–16; Stewart, p. 145; Lionel Johnson, p. 56; Stewart, p. 125; *Life* 179; Stewart, p. 63; TD LVII.436, XXXVI.286. Jude's and Sue's happiness is only mentioned twice, in single sentences, and qualified: "That the twain were happy — between their times of sadness — was indu-

bitable," JO V.v.308; " 'We gave up all ambition, and were never so happy in our lives till his illness came,' " JO V.vii.332.

14. Some narrative poems: At the Railway Station, Upway; At Shag's Heath, The Bride-Night Fire, The Burghers, The Chapel Organist, The Children and Sir Nameless, The Choirmaster's Burial, The Contretemps, The Curate's Kindness, The Dame of Athelhall, The Duel, The Elopement, The Face at the Casement, The Flirt's Tragedy, Her Death and After, In Sherborne Abbey, In the Days of Crinoline, Leipzig, The Lost Pyx, Mad Judy, The Mock Wife, My Cicely, The Newcomer's Wife, The Noble Lady's Tale, The Old Workman, One Who Married above Him, Panthera, The Paphian Ball, The Peasant's Confession, A Poor Man and a Lady, A Practical Woman, The Revisitation, Rose-Ann, San Sebastian, Satires of Circumstance, Seen by the Waits, The Statue of Liberty, A Sunday Morning Tragedy, The Trampwoman's Tragedy, The Turnip-Hoer, The Two Wives, Valenciennes, The Whipper-In, A Woman's Fancy, The Wood Fire. "Hardy's most characteristic type of poem is a narrative with a contemporary plot, a realistic detailed setting, and told in a colloquial and prosaic diction," Cecil, p. 46. *Life* 291.

15. Ch. 3, p. 70 and n. 40, ch. 1, p. 20 and n. 26; Carpenter, 1, 31, 97, 122, 123.

16. W III.46, 51; VII.83; XIII.126, V.71, XXXV.283, XII.116, XVI. 147, XXV.205, XXXVIII.309, XL.325, XLII.341, II.43, XXXVI.293, XXIX.244, IV.55, XXXI.253.

17. Carpenter, pp. 97, 111; JO VI.ii.356; Isaiah, V.35.

18. Brooks, pp. 184, 238, 199, 222, 256–8.

19. Brooks, p. 158; CP 582; Beckman, pp. 87, 73, 72.

20. Cecil, p. 19, Gregor, "What Kind", p. 302; Carpenter, p. 128; Kramer, p. 68; Mrs Brooks, p. 17; *Life* 104, 252; FMC XXXVII.279; TD IV.60; HE XXXI.245; RN V.ii.342; TD XVI.142.

21. Ch. 3, pp. 70–2.

22. "The Withered Arm", WT/GND 56–81; "The Fiddler of the Reels", LLI/CM 123–38; CP 195, 338–57, 319; "Milkmaid", LLI/CM 479, 387; "An Imaginative Woman", LLI/CM 32. On "Poems 1912–13", cf. Quiller-Couch's opinion, quoted by Stewart, p. 230, that Hardy "had constructed 'a pure fairy-tale' out of his long distant courtship".

23. Harold Child, *Thomas Hardy*, 1916, p. 21; Lodge, p. 168; Miller, p. 10; John Holloway, *The Victorian Sage*, 1953, p. 245; Zabel, pp. 72–3.

24. *Life* 104, 150, 301, 105, 153, 228, 247, 147, 114; TD XXXV.274, XXIII.183, XXXI.236, XXXIII.255, L.396; my p. 93; W XXXVII.299 (Melbury); JO I.iv.48 (Jude).

25. Stewart, p. 137.

26. Graham Greene, *The Lost Childhood*, 1951, p. 50; T. S. Eliot, *After Strange Gods*, 1934, p. 54; *Life* 124.

27. Cecil, p. 52; Bayley, p. 19; HE XLIV.356; WB III.8.197.

Appendix: The Dynasts

I make light of the influence of Schopenhauer and Von Hartmann in Chapter 3, but it is crucial in *The Dynasts*. I relegate my discussion of *The Dynasts* because, while it is necessary to make clear my ideas about it, there is little original in them.

It has a certain grandeur because of the grandeur of the events it describes and represents, especially in the panoramic views and the switches to close views. The Dorset scenes are well done but repetitious of the material of the novels, and the exclusion of all except Wessex characters and leading political figures has a grotesque effect. There are some good lyrics, but the blank verse, except for occasional flashes, is bad. The action and meaning, and consequently the people's suffering from their dynasts, is purely military. Being designed for "mental performance . . . not for the stage" only means that it overcomes the time-and-space difficulties of staging: it must still be judged as drama. Hardy's preoccupation with "the point of view", meaning where one is looking at a scene from, and his concern to end with curtain-like mist and darkness, show that he is thinking all the time of a normal stage. The stage-directions and dumb-shows, amounting on the page to about one-fifth of the whole, but effectively — because of the events they describe — to much more, reduce the dramatic element. There are numerous elementary errors in dramaturgy. The largest and most dramatic part of the action is the description or representation of eighteen battles, which is monotonous, as it is in the *Iliad*. The Overworld is not a success. *The Dynasts* is not Hardy's masterpiece nor the climax of his life's work.

The Overworld fails because the Spirits are spectators not actors and because the sense that everything is determined removes interest from the human actors. But also the Spirits are not clearly and consistently dramatic. The Years are "unfeeling, amoral", yet they want to bind Sinister and express pity for the small animals at Waterloo. In their predictions they overlap with the Recording Angels, whose function is to say what has happened or is about to happen. The Pities comment only that this or that is pitiful, which should be left to the action to show. The rumours spread by the Spirit of Rumour are almost always true, but one does not gather from this what would be the characteristic Hardyan idea that ordinary people do get at the truth albeit sometimes in garbled forms, but simply that this is another way of conveying information to the audience. Earth and Sinister are little used, Earth probably because she overlaps with the Pities. The Spirits' speeches take up about another fifth of the whole, which, considering the limitations on what they can talk about, is too much.

These faults are themselves evidence that *The Dynasts* is not Hardy's masterpiece. But it has been held that Hardy prepared for it throughout his life and so it must be[1]. In fact he constantly changed his mind about its form and scope, and wrote it in a hurry. In 1871 "let Europe be the stage and have scenes continually shifting". In 1875, "A Ballad of the Hundred Days. Then another of Moscow. Others of earlier campaigns — forming together an Iliad of Europe from 1789 to 1815". In 1877 "Consider a grand drama, based on the wars with Napoleon, or some campaign." Then there are visits, between 1870 and 1878 to Chelsea pensioners and the battlefield of Waterloo, but these and the literary aims may have been satisfied by *The Trumpet-Major*. After *The Trumpet-Major*, in 1881, comes what Hardy calls his "first written idea of a philosophic scheme . . . as the larger feature of *The Dynasts*": "A homeric Ballad in which Napoleon in a sort of Achilles . . . . Mode for a historical drama. Action mostly automatic. . . . Not the result of what is called motive. . . . Apply an enlargement of these themes to, say, 'The Hundred Days'." Then, in 1886, he thinks of "rendering as visible essences, spectres, etc., the abstract thoughts of the analytic school" and comments in the *Life* that this was carried out in *The Dynasts*: "The human race to be shown as one great network. . . . Abstract realisms to be in the form of Spirits, Spectral figures, etc," and says he was in the British Museum reading room "considering the question of *The Dynasts*". But by 1887 all he has is "another outline scheme for *The Dynasts*, in which Napoleon was represented as haunted by an Evil Genius or Familiar . . . and another . . . in which Napoleon by means of Necromancy becomes possessed of an insight, enabling him to see the thoughts of opposing generals". In 1889 he writes: "For carrying out that idea of Napoleon, the Empress, Pitt, Fox, etc., I feel continually that I require a larger canvas. . . . A spectral tone must be adopted. . . . Royal ghosts. . . . Title: 'A Drama of Kings:.'" In 1892 he had got no further than to "consider methods for the Napoleonic drama. Forces, emotions, tendencies. The characters do not act under the influence of reason." Not until 1896 do we have a brief outline (Hardy says he made "more copious notes . . . elsewhere") which fits the work as completed: "Europe in throes. Three Parts. Five Acts each. *Characters*: Burke, Pitt, Napoleon, George III, Wellington . . . and many others." This agrees with the Preface, written in 1903, saying the work was "outlined . . . about six years back."[2]

It seems probable that Hardy did not begin to write until 1902. Certainly he had not finished, and possibly had not begun, Parts II and III when he published Part I in 1904: there are large differences between the acts and scenes listed in that Part as "Contents of the Second and Third Parts" and Parts II and III as published in 1906 and 1908. In January 1904 he wrote to Gosse: "It is most unlikely that I shall carry the drama any further." The frequent almost-verbatim versification of sources, and the frequent repetition, sometimes verbatim or nearly so, of material from his earlier work, are signs of haste and lack of interest. He spent some time in the British Museum reading room in 1888, 1889 and 1891, but there is not evidence he was there between 1891 and 1898. I believe that *The Dynasts* was the result of a long-standing dream, but that he did little about it until he had rewritten *The Well-Beloved* in book form, and that from then on what Graham Greene has said about him was especially true: he "wrote as he pleased"; and that by this time he was not capable of the extended construction which had always been his weakness in his weaker work, but, as he told Vere Collins in 1922, "I collected a lot of material and then thought it a pity not to make use of it."[3]

Appendix: Notes

1. "A lifetime of preparation preceded the composition. ... *The Dynasts* is Hardy's poetic testament, the work of his ripest years and judgment" (Orel, p. 1).

2. Evelyn Hardy, *Thomas Hardy's Notebooks*, 1955, p. 45. *Life* 106, 114, 148, 183, 203, 221, 247.

3. R. L. Purdy, *Thomas Hardy, a Bibliographical Study*, 1954, pp. 127–8, 131–4; Orel, p. 100; Vere Collins, *Talks with Thomas Hardy at Max Gate*, 1928, p. 83.

Index

Only principal references to Hardy's works are indexed. Poems are not indexed individually and must be sought under *"Poems, Hardy's Collected."*

Addison, 5, 32, 90—1, 95
Aeneid, 122—4, 140, 147
Agricultural Children's Act 1873, 33
Ainsworth, Harrison, 131
Arch, Joseph, 171
Aristotle, 22—3, 58, 87, 131
Arnold, Matthew, 4—6, 49, 69—72, 77, 83—4, 94, 131
Aurelius, Marcus, 70, 188
Austen, Jane, 32, 67, 94, 96—7, 133

Bacon, Francis, 95
Bagehot, 58, 140
Bailey, J.O., 54—5, 59, 64—7, 183
Balzac, 144
Bayley, John, 146—7, 160, 171, 192
Beatty, C.J.P., 122—4
Beckman, R., 153—4
Berkeley, 92
Berle, Lina Wright, 134
Bible, 43, 73—6, 120—1, 186—7, 189
Björk, Lennart, 82—3, 86—7, 128—31
Boswell, James, 96
Briggs, Asa, 49
"Brighton Camp," 120, 188
Brooks, Jean R., 147—50, 173, 193
Brown, Douglas, 28, 30—1, 51, 110, 149, 192
Browning, 120, 188—9
Buchanan, Robert, 132
Bunyan, 188
Burke, Edmund, 5, 49, 91—2, 96
Burney, Charles and Frances, 91
Butler, L.St.J., 136
Byron, 91

Campbell, Thomas, 188
Carlyle, 5, 94, 131, 140
Carpenter, R., 150—2, 192—3
Cecil, Lord David, 27, 110, 160, 192—3
Chalmers, Thomas, 4
Chesterfield, Earl of, 94
Chew, Samuel, 27

Child, Harold, 156
Coleridge, 91
Collins, Vere, 196
Comte, 5—6, 58, 76—83
Conrad, 99
Cox, R.G., 134

Darwin, Charles, 5—6, 53, 58—69, 73, 86—7, 92
Darwin, Erasmus, 58
Davy, Sir Humphry, 50
Defoe, 91
De Laura, D.J., 83—4
Desperate Remedies, 99—100, 122—4
Dickens, 38, 144
Diderot, 40
"Dorsetshire Labourer, The," 28, 39, 133—4, 171
Dryden, 91, 119, 151, 188
Dynasts, The, 50, 54—5, 57, 68—9, 96, 132, 144, 194—7

Eliot, George, 20, 27, 43, 49—51, 91, 94, 112, 134—9, 144, 148—9
Eliot, T.S., 160
Ellis, Havelock, 135
Essays and Reviews, 53, 72—6, 140
Euripides, 151

Fairchild, H.N., 132
Far from the Madding Crowd, 121, 131, 134—5, 159
Farquhar, George, 22
"Fiddler of the Reels, The," 119, 156
Fielding, 87, 91—2, 94—6, 112, 131
Fourier, Charles, 56, 85, 131

Garrick, 91
Gay, 95—6
Gibbon, 91—2, 96
Gittings, Robert, 95, 140
Goethe, 131
Goldberg, M.A., 60, 157

Goldsmith, 96
Goodwin, C.W., 73
Gray, 29, 93, 96
Greene, Graham, 160, 192, 196
Gregor, I., 15, 27, 141—3, 147, 192—3

Haggard, Rider, 28, 34
Haldane, A.R.B., 171
Hand of Ethelberta, The, 74—5, 84—5, 105
Hartmann, Von, 53—8
Hawker, R.S., 188
Hegel, 54, 58
Heilman, R.B., 110, 178
Holloway, John, 156
Horace, 140
Howe, Irving, 135, 192
Hume, 53, 92
Huxley, T.H., 53, 58, 92, 98
Hyde, W.J., 85, 139
Hyman, Virginia, 77—82, 86, 177

Ibsen, 3, 22, 140
Iliad, 140, 194
"Imaginative Woman, An," 156

Johnson, Lionel, 95, 192
Johnson, Samuel, 91—2, 96, 121, 178
Johnson, S.F., 96
Jowett, Benjamin, 47, 73—6, 81—2
Jude the Obscure, 10, 16—19, 39—42, 45—9, 55—6, 66, 69—70, 76—7, 80—2, 85—6, 99, 105—6, 120, 128, 152—3, 159

Kant, 25, 54, 158
Keats, 91, 128, 188
Kettle, Arnold, 37
King, R.W., 118—19
Kramer, Dale, 112, 144—7, 176, 193

Lamarck, 58, 66, 174
Lamb, 91
Laodicean, A, 37, 129, 133
Lawrence, D.H., 22, 49, 83, 105, 119
Leavis, F.R., 110
Leopardi, 54
Lerner, Laurence, 28—30, 171—2
Literary Notes, Hardy's, 77—8, 82—3, 85—7, 128—31
Livingstone, David, 97
Locke, 92
Lodge, David, 62—3, 110, 156, 173—4
Loudon, J.C., 50

Macaulay, Lord, 91
Malthus, 58, 174
Married Women's Property Act 1882, 97
Matrimonial Causes Act 1857, 40
Maugham, Somerset, 110
Maxwell, J.C., 28
Mayor of Casterbridge, The, 12, 22—3, 28—30, 35—6, 41, 44, 99—100, 120, 135, 152—3, 159
Michel, Georges, 4
Mill, J.S., 53, 56, 58, 76—7, 84—6, 92, 140
Miller, J. Hillis, 99, 124—6, 135, 156, 191
Millgate, Michael, 133, 140, 191
Milton, 14, 22, 40, 120, 188
Molière, 91
Morrell, Roy, 136

Newman, J.H., 91, 97, 188

O'Brien, William, 91
Oliphant, Margaret, 39—40
Ovid, 140

Pair of Blue Eyes, A, 36—7, 45
Paris, B.J., 15
Parnell, C.S., 97
Peckham, Morse, 58, 173
Pickering, E.C., 97
Pinion, F.B., 59, 87, 126—8, 132, 172—3, 176, 178, 191
Poems, Hardy's *Collected*, 24—5, 53—4, 57, 63—4, 67—9, 77, 84, 91—2, 101—2, 104, 107, 117—19, 128, 137, 147, 151, 153, 156, 178, 180—7, 193
Pope, Alexander, 94—6, 119, 124
Powell, Professor Baden, 73
Priestley, Alma, 192
Proust, 3

Racine, 96
Return of the Native, The, 4—6, 41, 59—61, 121, 128—9, 152
Reynolds, Joshua, 91
Richardson, Samuel, 91, 94
Richter, J.P., 140
Romains, Jules, 144
"Romantic Adventures of a Milkmaid, The," 119, 156
Ruskin, 5
Rutland, W.R., 55—6, 72—3, 191

Saint-Pierre, Bernardin de, 91

Saint-Simon, 5
Schopenhauer, 6, 53—8, 66, 92, 174
Scott, Sir Walter, 119, 144, 188
Shakespeare, 14, 19, 76, 99, 121,
    133—4, 188—9
Shaw, G.B., 22
Shelley, 91, 124—8, 147, 188
Sheridan, 96
Smith, Adam, 92
Smollet, 91
Snell, Reginald, 180
Southerington, F.R., 59, 86—9, 131,
    172, 176—7
Spencer, Herbert, 33, 58, 92
Spivey, T.R., 192
Steele, 90, 95
Stephen, Leslie, 53, 58, 86—93, 98
Sterne, 91
Stevenson, Lionel, 67—9
Stewart, J.I.M., 131, 133, 135, 159,
    191—3
Swift, 58, 91, 96, 119
Synge, J.M., 22

Tanner, Tony, 178
Tebbutt's comet, 97
Temple, Frederick, 72
Tess of the D'Urbervilles, 5—10, 15—17,
    25, 32—3, 44—6, 55—7, 65—6, 70—2,
    74—7, 80—1, 92—3, 99, 102, 120,
    128—30, 159, 176
Thackeray, 94, 140
Thompson, William, 4

Trollope, Anthony, 140
Trumpet Major, The, 132, 195
Two on a Tower, 79, 97, 133

Under the Greenwood Tree, 34, 136—7

Velasquez, 97
Voltaire, 91—2, 98

Walpole, Horace, 91, 96
Watts, Isaac, 91
Weber, C.J., 131—2
Webster, H.C., 59, 72—3, 86, 136,
    172—4
Weismann, August, 65
Well-Beloved, The, 6, 101, 119, 124—6,
    180
Williams, Merryn, 30—2, 192
Williams, Raymond, 28
Williams, Rowland, 72—3
"Withered Arm, The," 155—6
Woodlanders, The, 9, 20—2, 25, 37,
    40—1, 44, 99, 128, 151—2, 159
Woodward, Sir Llewellyn, 49
Woolf, Virginia, 149
Wordsworth, 5, 91, 120, 140, 188—9
Wright, Edward, 54
Wright, W.F., 131—2

Yuill, W.E., 191

Zabel, Morton D., 110, 156
Zola, 91, 129—30, 144